Hell And High Water

Cecil Healy, Olympic Champion Whose Life Was Cut Short By War

Rochelle Nicholls

16pt

Copyright Page from the Original Book

Copyright © Rochelle Nicholls

First published 2018

Copyright remains the property of the authors and apart from any fair dealing for the purposes of private study, research, criticism or review, as permitted under the Copyright Act, no part may be reproduced by any process without written permission.

All inquiries should be made to the publishers.

Big Sky Publishing Pty Ltd

PO Box 303, Newport, NSW 2106, Australia

Phone: 1300 364 611

Fax: (61 2) 9918 2396

Email: info@bigskypublishing.com.au

Web: www.bigskypublishing.com.au

Cover design and typesetting: Think Productions

Proudly printed and bound in Australia by Ligare Pty Ltd

 A catalogue record for this book is available from the National Library of Australia

For Cataloguing-in-Publication entry see National Library of Australia.

Creator: Rochelle Nicholls

Title: Hell and High Water: Cecil Healy, Olympic champion whose life was cut short by war

TABLE OF CONTENTS

ACKNOWLEDGMENTS & AUTHOR'S NOTE	ii
FOREWORD	vi
PROLOGUE	xi
ONE: CASTLES BUILT ON SAND	1
TWO: THE CELTIC WATER-CHILD	23
THREE: CATERPILLARS, CORN AND THE CRAWL	48
FOUR: SOMETHING SENSATIONAL EVERY SATURDAY	69
FIVE: DROWN MY HEART IN SALT WATER	100
SIX: MORE THAN JUST A 'GAMES'	119
SEVEN: 'A PARTICULARLY RECKLESS FELLOW'	149
EIGHT: LOVE'S GOLDEN SILENCE	186
NINE: THE TRUE VALUE OF SILVER	206
TEN: A FINAL INNOCENT YEAR	246
ELEVEN: WHITE FEATHERS AND OSTRICH PLUMES	277
TWELVE: DIGGERS	301
THIRTEEN: DOWN AND OUT IN ETÁPLES	329
FOURTEEN: THE FOG OF DOUBT	359
FIFTEEN: 'IT HARDLY SEEMS POSSIBLE...'	390
SIXTEEN: LEST WE FORGET	405
EPILOGUE	421
ABOUT THE AUTHOR	431
ENDNOTES	432
BACK COVER MATERIAL	511

For Kristin

ACKNOWLEDGMENTS & AUTHOR'S NOTE

It was while working on my book about Joe Quinn, Australia's first major league baseball player, that I researched other Australian sportsmen of the nineteenth century to compare earnings and accomplishments. I had browsed through boxing, cycling and cricket when a sepia-toned photograph of a dark-eyed young man in lifeguard's kit, as enigmatic as the Mona Lisa, with an irresistible sadness in his eyes caught my attention. As a writer of non-fiction, I receive many letters, emails and tweets with suggestions on what or whom I should write about next. While such suggestions are always welcome, they must, like love, engender a certain 'zing' in the writer's heart before they can realistically be pursued. Biography writing is such a deep commitment, a foray into the life and choices of a real person, that one must be truly beguiled by the subject in order to invest the emotional depth the research deserves. I was mesmerised by the unfathomable sorrow of those eyes. It seemed my subject had come to find me.

An internet search on the young lifeguard, Cecil Healy, presented further arresting facts: his glittering swimming and surf-lifesaving careers, the sacrifice of so much promise for a life in khaki on the Western Front and, ultimately, his tragic death as the only Australian Olympic gold medallist ever to perish on a battlefield. However, beyond Wikipedia and some unpublished treatises by historians in Healy's beachside home of Manly, there was no chronicle of the life of this lost Australian sportsman, and with the centenary of the Great War approaching, his story was in danger of fading into obscurity. Therefore, for the privilege of the authorship of this book, I am deeply indebted to the Healy family, in particular Mike Downman and Vivienne Degenhardt—I am humbled to be trusted with your family's history. This book would not have been possible without your participation and support.

During the two years of research for this book, including consulting over 1,300 historical sources, I was fortunate enough to read many of Cecil Healy's own letters and other correspondence exchanged with family, friends and colleagues. These provided the basis, if not the actual dialogue, for many scenes in this book. For others, some authorial licence has been used to create discourse typical of that which may have occurred. Measurements in this book are provided in imperial units—feet, inches and yards—in accordance with the conventions used in both the British Empire and the sport of swimming prior to World War I.

There are many friends and colleagues to thank for their contributions to this book. I must beg absolution for any omissions—you all know who you are and how much I value your input. Many of the sources in this book were tracked down by my erstwhile research assistant, Vicki Nicholls, who is also my mother, proofreader and dear friend. Many thanks to my editors, Denny Neave at Big Sky, and Tricia Dearborn, who first untied the knots in the story. Duke Kahanamoku's biographer Sandy Hall has been a magnificent supporter of this story and her generosity knew no bounds. To Ray Moran and Ray Peterson of the Manly Life Saving Club, Mark Maddox of North Steyne Surf Life Saving Club, Michael Maher, Scott Calcraft and Denny Froggatt of Manly Surf Club and George and Shelagh Champion: I am indebted to your passion for the Manly surf scene and determination to preserve its history. Thanks to John Macritchie and John Morcombe, both stalwarts of the written word in Manly, and to the many other experts kind enough to share their time and expertise: Bertrand Fareneau, David Wilson, Gary Osmond, John Malone, Graeme Haigh, Jeff Palmer,

Max Rogers, Phillip Morton, Wellett Potter and Ian McCall.

To my dear friends who understand the life and temperament of a writer and have forgiven me all those shindigs I never got to and all the dinner parties I never gave—April Glaser-Hinder, Freda Marnie Nicholls, Joy Coggan, Jenny Glazebrook, Rachel Murray, Gillian Ingall, Vivien Thomson, Alison Foley, Paula Macmillan, Penny Howse and Kellie Holmes—God bless you.

And to my own family—my love.

FOREWORD

By Tracey Holmes, ABC Radio

The concept of Australians being recognized around the world as overachieving underdogs is well known. Our perception of ourselves is in no small part wrapped up in the success of our men and women on international sporting stages. It's a consequence of one of our national pastimes—taking great pride in celebrating our sports stars.

In the twenty-first century though, we are in danger of losing sight of what should qualify an athlete as a 'legend', a 'role model' or a 'superstar'. As sport becomes less about the traditional aims of improving the body, mind and spirit, and more about entertainment in the age of celebrity, our stars are often ranked by superficial measurements—headlines, Facebook followers and fashion choice (or lack of it).

In *Hell and High Water,* Rochelle Nicholls takes us back to a time when our sports men and women were not career athletes but workers who used their spare time trying to make themselves and their communities better; when sport provided a common thread for people to come together and cheer on healthy competition or to raise funds for a friend in need; when the Olympic games had to be cancelled as the world went to war and many of our athletes were sent on an international mission of a very different kind.

That every Australian does not know the story of Cecil Healy—Olympian, surf lifesaver and the only Australian Olympic gold medallist to give his life in war—is an indictment in a sports-mad nation such as this. It's a life that should be celebrated in many forms. Cecil Healy's story is one that should equally capture the minds of everyone, from young children learning of this country's history through to the most hardened aficionados who prefer to measure Australia's history through prisms other than sport.

Hell and High Water is part celebration, part tragedy. Cecil Healy was born a battler and became a leader. One of the greatest moments in Olympic history may never have happened if it wasn't for the good sportsmanship of Cecil Healy that most definitely cost him an individual gold medal in Stockholm 1912. That moment led to a friendship with Hawaiian Duke Kahanamoku that itself spawned the birth of surfboard riding in this country via Healy's other love, the surf-lifesaving movement.

For a man who celebrated so much of his life in the water, Shakespeare could not have dreamt up a crueller end to Healy's life—in charge of a group of men, many whom could not swim, cornered between a river and the enemy.

Australians are familiar with the battle of the Somme. Names like Mont St Quentin and Peronne are wrapped up in any telling of the story of Australia's role in the First World War. Cecil Healy provides a face for the many unrecognized lives that were lost there.

In telling Cecil's story, Rochelle Nicholls transports us to a time and place that seems so foreign and yet provides the very foundations of much that we celebrate and commemorate about ourselves today.

Historically and culturally, this is a most important story, and I thank Rochelle for telling it so that all Australians may become familiar with it.

Tracey Holmes
ABC Radio

'Be faithful to me every summer', says the sea,
'and I will give you the blessing of longevity.'

—Samuel A. Mills, *The Romance of the Breakers* (1906)

'If in some smothering dreams you too could pace
Behind the wagon that we flung him in,
And watch the white eyes writhing in his face,
His hanging face, like a devil's sick of sin;
If you could hear, at every jolt, the blood
Come gurgling form the froth-corrupted lungs,
Obscene as cancer, bitter as cud
Of vile, incurable sores on the innocent tongues-
My friend, you would not tell with such high zest
To children ardent for some desperate glory,
The old lie: Dulce et decorum est
Pro patria mori.'

—Wilfred Owen, *Dulce et Decorum Est* (1917)

Warrant Officer Cecil Healy, the Australian champion swimmer. From a series created for a 1917 recruiting campaign to encourage sportsmen to enlist. [Source: Australian War Memorial: collection ID: P04366.007].

PROLOGUE

'The hero sees values beyond what's possible. That's the nature of a hero. It kills him, of course, ultimately. But it makes the whole struggle of humanity worthwhile.'

—John Gardner, *Grendel*

✳✳✳

4am, 29 August 1918
Salmon Wood, outside Peronne, France

When the surf is deeper than your waist, you stop wading and start swimming. It is the oldest adage in surf bathing. Arm over arm, body against the tug of current and toss of waves. The slap of salt water on face, clean brine in eyes and on skin and tongue.

The first breath hurts; immersion triggers reflex contraction of diaphragm and lungs, the sharp intake of oxygen, before buoyancy takes over and senses align with the sea. Then breathing is simple, feet are flippers and hands are paddles pulling long and hard against giant green ocean.

You can stop any time beyond the breakers, where the sea is now swell after swell and as easy *to ride as a cantering horse. You can tread water and squint back against the glint of sun to where humanity remains, busy as ants, on the white sand, scrunching it between bare toes and squealing at unexpected rushes of foam.*

In 1918, Manly Beach in north Sydney was all green and white and blue—smooth verdant lawns, powdery pale sand, breakers that flung translucent foam into the pristine air. The sea breeze tugged at hats and hair, and the sun was so dazzling it called for smoked glasses. There was ice-cream for the day-trippers, the splendours of vaudeville at the Victoria Hall and window-shopping at Campbell's Emporium on The Corso. Such colour and gaiety stood far from the monochrome moonscape that now surrounded Second Lieutenant Cecil Patrick Healy, 19th Battalion AIF—the pulverised grey hell of France.

Yesterday, under orders from General Monash himself, the 19th had marched along the marshy southern banks of the Somme River, pursuing German troops fleeing east toward the Hindenburg Line. Shattered pine trees—distant cousins, perhaps, of the Norfolk pines that dipped their needles to shade the Manly bathers—stood sentinel over fields churned barren by the blast of bombs and the feet of doomed men and horses. The earth swayed and opened up under the barrage, black soil and rubble raining down on the troops to deaden the wails of the wounded. Ditches thick with grey water sucked and strained at sodden boots, the miasma of death rising to the noses of those who slogged and slipped within, rifles held above eyes streaming in the fug. *So far from his old life beside, and within, Manly's innocent blue sea*[1].

Now, as dawn came, Healy shifted uneasily in his meagre blanket roll. The stony earth was cold and slick with a mossy scum that seeped through his damp uniform and chilled his bones. He could still hear the big guns in the dark, feel the reverberation through those same stones and bones; he was unsure whether it was real or just the battlefield clamour his ears rang with day and night, booming and hissing like an angry ocean. He wanted to roll over and ease the ache where his gas mask lay sharp and ready against his side, but the men packed close around him slept, and he preferred to ache rather than rouse them with his restlessness. Further, Healy preferred being awake to being asleep; sleep was when the dreams came, dreams of rivers choked with green-faced corpses, limbs tangled like seaweed, where the water ran black and sick. In the clear, blameless Manly surf, when the water rose higher than your waist, you duck-dived and began to swim—but not here. In France, you kept your face out of the water and waded on, stepped over half-submerged dead men and watched them sink.

The 'Fighting Nineteenth'—the 19th Infantry Battalion, First Australian Imperial Force—had served in all the major campaigns of the First World War, from Gallipoli to the blood-soaked fields of Flanders. Their distinctive brown-and-green shoulder patches had been on the frontline of the nightmare at Pozieres, at Passchendaele and at Villers-Bretonneux. Second Lieutenant Healy had joined them as an infantry platoon commander on 1 June 1918, finally achieving his cherished transfer to action after two years of chafing behind the lines in the Army Service Corps. Nothing could have been further from the purity of his old blue-water life as an Olympic swimmer and captain of the lifeguards on Manly Beach. The Western Front was an apocalypse of volcanic battles, of men blown to pieces or sent mad by the unceasing noise of bombardment, men with melted faces and blown-off limbs shooting themselves and each other amid the blood and mud and wounded and dying.

As the 19th approached the medieval town of Peronne, the banks of the Somme flattened and widened, exposing Australian backs and necks to German snipers. Peronne itself was formidable, the seventeenth-century ramparts rising sixty feet above the twin rivers, the Somme and the Cologne, which effectively formed a moat around the town. About a mile to the north stood Mont St Quentin. It seemed so inoffensive, just a hump with a few scattered trees, but it commanded Peronne and the land that stretched further east to the German defences on a line between Arras and Soissons. North of the mountain, German machine-gun emplacements crouched on Bouchavesnes Spur. Monash's Australian forces could not take Peronne until they took the mountain and the ridge, both still held by the crack 2nd Prussian Guards.

The 2nd AIF Division, of which the 19th Battalion was a part, was ordered to assault Mont St Quentin. Major-General Rosenthal's plan was to have the 5th Brigade (including Healy's 19th Battalion) cross the Somme on the morning of 29 August 1918, advancing between the villages of Feuilleres and Herbecourt to launch their offensive on the mountain. The Division's advance would cross open farmland dotted with small woods and copses to a bridge where the Canal du Nord met the Somme. When the 19th crossed the river, they would converge with the 17th, 18th and 20th Battalions in a simultaneous strike against the mountain[2].

XVI

This dawn, the cusp of his first foray in command, Healy lay uneasy and wakeful. He was tortured by a desire for clean water—to drink it untainted by gunpowder and gas, to plunge his stubbled face into it and cleanse his gritty, lousy skin, to immerse himself in it, feel the pressure of it against his diaphragm and the wash of it over his body on every stroke—to drag himself through it and become clean.

Another flare of shellfire briefly lit the thicket where the platoon from C Company lay. Cecil Healy felt a stir among the sleeping men, as though they sensed the impending break of day. Carl Bentin was already awake, facing him, the hollows beneath his cheekbones black pits in the silver flash. Just 19 years old but with 18 months of service already behind him, Bentin had been a cook, Healy knew, in Tasmania, before all of this started. The youth had spent months recovering in England after taking gas at Hangard Wood, but here he was again, a teenage veteran, re-equipped with tin hat, gas mask and rifle, a boy soldier ready to march into the black mouths of the Howitzers.

In the dark, Bentin touched a finger to his forehead in a tiny salute and half a grin flickered in his eyes. 'Lef 'tenant, sir', he whispered. The look of trust in the boy's eyes, faithful as a favoured pup, made Healy's cold guts twist.

Reveille.

On his other side, Tommy Cravino stirred beneath his thin overcoat. Tiny Tommy, just 5 feet 1 1/2 inches tall, already twice wounded, a prayer book and rosary in his breast pocket.

Zero hour, 5am, 29 August 1918. Bully beef and cold water. Sky cold and flat, not domed and blue; the world hazy grey, not blue and white. Strange how these details hurt him today, seemed to sting his eyes and ache in his chest.

The order came to move up. It was the same commitment as was needed to enter a big sea—you couldn't call time out if you didn't like how the waves were coming when some poor bloke was out there struggling and getting swept away. *Hesitation could mean death—his and yours.* Now there was nothing but forward movement, a relentless tramp-tramp in no other direction but forward. Rifles and helmets, boots and bullets, men in company, Mont St Quentin a smudged and crouching monster across the river, the red tiled roofs of Peronne huddled at its base.

Open farmland. Men—his men—behind him, waiting for his orders. *His words that might send them to their deaths.*

When you paddle out, everything is both forgotten and remembered, washing the weight of the world from your shoulders, your very heart lifted by the swell.

xviii
The tearing rattle of machine-gun fire.

ONE

CASTLES BUILT ON SAND

'Human nature is like water. It will flow in whatever direction a channel is opened.'

—Kao Tzu, *Religious Dimensions of Confucianism*

***

Human blood contains the same salts as sea water. Some say this explains man's affinity for swimming and the sea.

Prehistoric man swam for recreation, food gathering and survival—primeval depictions of bathing and diving are found all the way from Greece and Persia, across Asia and the Pacific Rim, to North America. While Japanese nobles competed in organised swimming races as early as 36BC, it was not until the nineteenth century that Europeans adopted swimming as a competitive sport, holding the first swimming carnival in Britain in 1837[1]. Australians, with their largely coastal population, swam almost from the time of British colonisation in the late eighteenth century, with the dash across Woolloomooloo Bay by Dunn and Wilson in 1832 widely considered the genesis of competitive swimming Down Under[2].

Swimming for both sport and leisure soon increased in popularity in Australia as a burgeoning population of free men and increased recreation time saw swimming baths constructed along the coast. Swimming and aquatic sports have since become deep-seated within the national character. Australian beaches swarm with bronzed sun-seekers and gliding body-surfers, and the broad, brown rivers resonate with the sounds of splashing and paddling on hot afternoons. Families gather around barbecues on lake shores, watching children take their first strokes in the shallows, and Australian lifesavers perform remarkable feats against the rumbling breakers on the coast, where they drag the drowning from the clutches of the sea through sheer strength and wherewithal. Many of Australia's greatest swimmers speak of feeling most at home when in the water, including triple Olympic champion Shane Gould. 'For me, having harmony with the water is really important', she says. 'In fact, I nearly need it to survive.'[3] It is, therefore, a great irony that Cecil Patrick Healy, among the greatest of Australia's swimmers, was born not aboard a ship or watercraft, not by a rushing river or clear crystalline lake, but amid in a city, during one of the hottest and driest summers on record.

The summer of 1881–82 was a brutal one. Seventeen people died from sunstroke in a single week on the Liverpool Plains in northern New South Wales. Railway workers at Narrabri attempted to strike because of the heat and no rain worth recording fell in the Sydney catchment for months. The countryside was like tinder—sparks from locomotives caused fires to leap up at the least provocation, including at Joadja in the Southern Highlands, where only a lucky change in wind direction prevented a conflagration as a bushfire threatened the local kerosene works. The air over the city of Sydney was stultifying with heat and ash, and carriages kicked up grit that swirled in the hot breeze and stung unguarded eyes. Hollering newsboys, the clank and jostle of trams and the relentless hammering of building and expansion turned the city into a noisy, dirty furnace. Even the great blue expanse of the harbour did little to cool the westerly wind searing in from the inland like the breath of a dragon.

Woodbine Cottage, number 153 on chic Victoria Street in Darlinghurst, had not witnessed the birth of a child for seven years until Cecil Patrick Healy was born there on 28 November

1881, the fourth child of Patrick and Annie Healy. His father was amongst the most respected legal practitioners in the colony, and Woodbine Cottage, a double-storey brick terrace, was one of the best houses in the street, far enough from bustling central Sydney to be exclusive, but near enough for an easy commute by the white-collar professional. Those same Victoria Street terrace houses engendered one of Australia's most bitter legal battles nearly a century later. The disappearance in 1975 of heiress and social activist Juanita Nielsen, who ran a hardline campaign against developers from her home at 202 Victoria Street, remains one of Australia's great unsolved mysteries[4].

In the hot summer of 1881, Patrick Healy, aspirant son of convict parents and now Crown Prosecutor for the district of Sydney, had a heavy schedule of forgers, thieves and embezzlers to pursue. Their offences were often colourful, from the theft of false teeth to pilfering of billiard balls, but despite the many trivial cases he had to attend, Healy's reputation in the New South Wales legal fraternity was that of a giant. 'In drawing up pleas, he has no superior in Australia and in consultations his word (is) law', cried the *Freeman's Journal*[5]. During his years at the Bar, Patrick Healy appeared in landmark trials including the sensational Makin baby-farming case of 1893 and Joachim v. O'Shanassy (1874), now a cornerstone of Australian native title claims[6].

His growing family lived large upon his success and reputation. Cecil Healy's early childhood was spent amid first-rate clothes and toys in the elite suburbs of eastern Sydney. There were parties and fine carriages, inner-city chambers from which his father plied his trade, and then in 1885, a move to a new residence on fashionable Elizabeth Bay Road[7]. Patrick Healy's dynasty seemed assured, with a stepson and five sons of his own, all of whom he provided with every opportunity to thrive and succeed as he had. After Cecil's birth in 1881, Annie had given Patrick two more sons—John in 1884 and Reginald in 1886—to bolster the family line. Following the move in 1885, Healy enrolled his two eldest sons, Harold, aged 13, and Claude, aged 11, as well as the teenage son from Annie's first marriage, James Girard, at the exclusive St. Ignatius College, and took up his own new chambers in the heart of the Sydney CBD. However, beneath this façade of respectability, prosperity and wealth lay a complex family life of secrets and barely suppressed scandal, and by 1887, all was not well at 92 Elizabeth Bay Road.

Despite his privileged standing within Sydney's best circles, Patrick Healy was not untouched by social stigma. Eyebrows had risen when, on 26 December 1868, he had married Annie Louisa Gallott in a ceremony of unseemly haste at St. Mary's Cathedral. Annie Louisa was a widowed single mother, and an immediate source of tattle and speculation for those who had eagerly awaited the eligible young barrister's choice of a suitable mate. Annie's previous marriage—ironically, to another lawyer, Alphonse Bede Girard—had been socially ruinous. She was the eldest daughter of law clerk James Gallott and his socialite wife Caroline Horsey. One of nine children, Annie had been born in Melbourne but raised in Sydney and Maitland, and had married Girard in 1864 at the age of 19[8]. Alphonse had proved far more worldly than his teenage bride. He was the son of a fascinating, adroit Frenchman, Francois Girard, who had fought with Napoleon at Waterloo and then fled to London after the fall of the Emperor. During a British purge of clandestine French revolutionaries, Girard was arrested and transported to Australia[9]. However, he soon gained a pardon and the dapper Frenchman established himself as a fencing *maitre* and dance tutor, earning a fortune in the drawing rooms of Sydney's elite and fathering 12 children in rapid succession. The Girard offspring, all christened with flamboyant French monikers such as Marie Louiseliere, Francis Napoleon and

Jules Pierre Theodore, inherited much of their father's Gallic allure. 'Gentleman Alphonse' was admitted to the Supreme Court as a solicitor in 1862 and married the eligible Annie Louisa two years later. After the birth of their son James Alfred Girard in 1866, he relocated his new family to Grafton on the north coast of New South Wales, where he intended to make a grand fortune in close proximity to the Girard family estate at Walcha.

Annie's plans to enter Grafton society as the esteemed wife of an ambitious young lawyer foundered almost immediately. Within months, there were allegations of serious embezzlement against Girard, from which he fled to Singleton, near Newcastle[10]. There, however, the disgrace only mounted. In 1867, Girard was repeatedly arrested for public drunkenness, on one occasion having been discovered lying incoherent in the mud outside a local hotel. The police prosecutor also claimed he had regularly seen Girard drunk while practising in court. Girard was fined a hefty 20 shillings on each occasion, avoiding jail only by dint of his status as a Supreme Court attorney[11]. In February 1868, the shame of his repeated indiscretions overcame Annie Louisa. Taking two-year-old James with her, she fled back to her own family in Sydney and never saw Girard again. In his typically insouciant manner,

Girard continued to practice in the Singleton police court and, in April 1868, publicly proclaimed his intent to relocate back to bigger and busier Grafton. Just weeks later, the Grafton press announced Girard's 'premature and untimely' death. His intemperate habits had seen him thrown out of his Singleton lodgings and forced into the local Benevolent Asylum—a threadbare institution dedicated to saving the downtrodden—where he had died 'under distressing circumstances' from chronic liver failure. Girard was buried without ceremony in the local Catholic cemetery, and his death went unmourned and almost unremarked[12].

Twenty-four-year-old Annie Louisa squandered no tears on her wastrel husband. Just six months after Girard's demise, she married Patrick Healy in Sydney, the marriage taking place under a 'special licence'[13]. There were many reasons why these expensive special licences were granted, including for couples with family members in failing health or seeking a service outside normal parish hours, or those who suspected a pregnancy. On 7 September 1869, nine months after the ceremony, Annie and Patrick's first child—a girl, Florence Mary—was born. Florence died of diphtheria in 1876, and although by that time Annie had three young sons, the loss of her daughter caused her such grief that it was five years before she was to give birth to another child, Cecil. During her years of sorrow, Annie had found solace in the accumulation of pretty things at her exclusive eastern suburbs home and after Cecil was born, it was she who ensured that her boys, too, wanted for nothing.

However, in 1887, the façade of respectability that Annie and Patrick had so carefully cultivated, with their fine house and air of fashion and exclusivity, gave an ominous creak. Shopkeeper Richard Smith took civil action against Patrick Healy in the Metropolitan Court to recover the amount of £10 7s. 6d. for refreshments and cigars. Despite the temerity of a simple merchant in fronting Healy, that pillar of the colony's legal citadel, judgment fell in favour of Smith[14]. The case rated only a brief mention in *The Sydney Morning Herald* the next day, but Patrick Healy now took far greater care to conceal his dubious financial affairs. His sons remained enrolled at St. Ignatius College, Annie Louisa continued to shop among the George Street boutiques and the family still dined upon comestibles from the finest Sydney provedores and cellars. Annie bore Patrick another son, Eric, in 1888. It was two years later, in September 1890, when Cecil was eight years old, that the thin membrane of pretence truly ruptured.

On Saturday 13 September 1890, a list of bankrupts was published in city and rural newspapers across NSW. Among the miners, tailors, graziers and labourers who had fallen into financial ruin was the name of Patrick Joseph Healy, barrister-at-law. 'The ablest and perhaps best-known Crown Prosecutor in the colony' was publically disgraced, finally exposed as absolutely and utterly penniless[15].

The year 1890 brought decades of prosperity in Australia to a juddering halt as the economic boom that had sustained the nation since the gold rush of the 1850s collapsed as part of the severe worldwide depression. Declining gold production and falling prices for wool (which accounted for 64% of export earnings in 1889) slowed the colonial economy to a wheeze. Banks ran out of money and failed, and half of Australia's 106 million sheep were culled or lost to drought. Residential construction and public works, which had ridden on the back of massive British investment, faltered under demands from British creditors for repayment. Australia's social fabric was rent by maritime and shearers' strikes, as well as unsettling attempts to federate the separate colonies into an independent nation. Discontent, hunger and unemployment were licking like fire at the foundations of the young Australian nation[16].

However, Patrick Healy's financial difficulties—with accumulated debts of more than £720—were largely unrelated to the economic meltdown occurring around him. Instead, years of dishonoured debts and overspending were coming home to roost. His account with the Commercial Banking Company had been overdrawn since 1887, and with the largest Australian bank on the verge of closure, it now called in its outstanding debt of more than £180 as part of its desperate struggle to stay afloat. Healy also owed more than £160 to merchants in Sydney's most exclusive shops, including £75 to Thompson & Giles for luxuries including dresses, ribbons, perfumes and toys. There were debts for hats, debts for dolls and debts for cabdrivers, coffee and claret, all dating back as far as 1886. The boys' school fees at St. Ignatius' College—more than £63—had not been paid since 1887. Perhaps most sorry of all was the unpaid rent for the use of legal chambers, with £65 owed to five legal offices in central Sydney[17]. Patrick Healy's unaffordable high life was unravelling, and the fall would be spectacular.

The report of the assignee, the impressively titled Lancelot Threlkeld Lloyd, revealed the extent of Patrick Healy's attempts to cover up his financial ignominy. In June 1889, finding himself 'pressed for funds', Patrick had sold all of his household furniture and then immediately rented it back, thus hiding the dishonour from his wife and family. A case was also brought against him in the Supreme Court in February 1888 by one Adolphus Rogalsky, suing Healy for 'monies owed' (£33). Despite the threat of legal redress, Healy simply never paid the debt. His sole credit was £50 owed to him by his sister-in-law, Margaret Gertrude Healy, the wife of his late brother Nicholas, for a half-share in a family property that Patrick had sold to her in July 1890. Because the stake had never been paid for, Patrick Healy's sole asset existed only on paper as a debt due to his estate[18].

All of this was, sadly, a familiar tale for Annie Louisa. Her own father, James Gallott, had built a solid reputation as a clerk to leading solicitors in both Sydney and Melbourne, but while both his judicial ability and kindly demeanour were unquestioned, his financial savvy was far more tenuous. Gallott had been declared insolvent twice during Annie Louisa's childhood, first in 1847 and again in 1865[19]. For his daughter, who had perhaps gravitated towards Patrick Healy for his perceived solidity after the waywardness of her French husband, it was a dreadful case of *déjà vu*.

The boys were withdrawn from St. Ignatius College and the Healys left their pretty house on Elizabeth Bay Road for a far humbler rented residence at Roslyn Gardens in inner-city Darlinghurst[20]. Despite its grand designation as 'Thomond Villa', number 22 was a simple single-storey brick house. Its twelve rooms made it one of the largest houses in the street, but it was also one of the most lowly, crouching in the imposing shadow of nearby Roslyn Hall. The area was working-class at best, grubby and noisy at its worst. Perhaps the only consolation for the staunchly Catholic Healy family was the the view of the spires of St. Canice's church, which offered salvation—for free—just up the street.

The legal profession is, however, forgiving of such transgressions by its own. Despite his grievous financial mismanagement, James Gallott had remained working as a legal clerk until his death, aged 72, in 1893. Likewise, within days of his bankruptcy case going public, Patrick Healy was reappointed to the bench of NSW Crown Prosecutors for the summer of 1890. However, his posting was not to the prestigious Supreme Court in Sydney, but to a rural court far from the city, on the plains of the western Riverina at Hay, where he would make his living prosecuting those accused of passing fraudulent cheques and assaulting Chinese market gardeners[21].

***

Patrick and Annie Healy were quick to whisk their son Cecil away from the scandal of rented furniture and vengeful high-street merchants.

In 1891, Australia was still a British colony and, in the grand tradition of the motherland, private grammar schools had sprung up in the highlands above Sydney for the sons and daughters of its elite families, aiming to fill their lungs with crisp country air and their heads with classical literature and languages. While James Girard and Harold and Claude Healy had found clerkships in the city after their ignominious exit from St. Ignatius College, and the younger Healys, John, Reg and two-year-old Eric were too young to understand, impressionable ten-year-old Cecil was of an age to feel the sting of a family fall from grace. Despite his complete lack of capital, Patrick was taking no chances, whisking the boy out of the city almost overnight.

Bong Bong Street, a principal thoroughfare in the town of Bowral, NSW, circa 1890. Bowral was a prosperous town whose bracing climate was favoured by well-to-do families seeking a classical education for their children. [Source: Berrima District Historical & Family History Society].

The Southern Highlands, which was a two-hour train journey from Sydney, may as well have been a world away for the fourth Healy son. In the early 1890s, Bowral was a small but progressive town forming a prosperous triumvirate with nearby Moss Vale and Mittagong beneath the shadow of Mount Gibraltar—'The Gib', to the locals. The area was settled in 1821 as part of Governor Lachlan Macquarie's push for grazing country inland, and by 1890, Bowral boasted kerbing and macadamised footpaths to keep the dust at bay, rustic seats under shady trees, three banks, coffee rooms, a Philharmonic

Society and a School of Arts whose fund-raising raffles were considered incredibly progressive[22]. The region, standing 2,300 feet above sea level, was proclaimed 'the health resort of NSW' and was rich with high-class schools, including Tennyson at Moss Vale, where pupils received tuition in music and painting, and King's for boys in Goulburn, which boasted modern improvements such as ventilated bedrooms instead of stuffy dormitories[23]. It was to Kurkulla at Bowral, a new academy run by Master J. Lee Pulling, that young Cecil Healy was dispatched, far beyond the reach of further social infamy.

James Lee Pulling, master of the Kurkulla boys' school in Bowral. One of the most ambitious educators in the NSW colony, Pulling raised his students on a diet of classics, theatricals and, most significantly for Cecil Healy, sports. [Source: Berrima District Historical & Family History Society; original image appeared in 'The Torch-Bearer', Sydney Grammar School magazine, December 1938].

A man of simple tastes and high ideals, James Lee Pulling was one of the most ambitious academics in the colony. Educated at Corpus Christi College, he was the son of a Cambridge master who had raised his sons on a rich diet of Latin, classics and sports. In 1888, Pulling and his younger brother, William Blomfield Pulling, emigrated to Australia to escape the damp climate that exacerbated William's chronic lung trouble and founded a grammar school at Scone in the Hunter Valley, where William taught until his death in 1894[24]. In 1891, James leased one of the best residences in the Southern Highlands to start his own school, Kurkulla, whose lavish 25 acres of grounds occupied a lofty position on The Gib[25].

One Kurkulla old boy wrote that 'Mr Pulling represents all that is best and soundest in the old-fashioned classical education', praising his 'wide sympathy, sane judgment and kindly tolerance ... which had the whole of a man's life and not merely the passing of examinations, in view.'[26] Pulling was keen on theatricals, and in 1892 his students presented a 'grand melodramatic extravaganza' of 'Beauty and the Beast' at the Bowral School of Arts, followed by a combined Christmas matinee with the nearby girls' school of Miss Swinson—complete with Highland dancing, elastic-band exercises and nine-year-old George

Lord reciting the entire Tennyson ballad 'The Revenge' by rote[27]. However, in true open-air tradition, the Kurkulla boys were also active sportsmen, and it was here that Cecil Healy had his first taste of the concepts that became so fundamental to him later in life—fair play and the purity of amateur athletic ideals. While Pulling was affectionately described by his students as *forma rotunda viri* (the stout man)[28], the master himself played on the Bowral representative tennis team and, writing in the *Australian Journal of Education,* emphatically endorsed the role of games in schools as 'an opportunity to influence the formation of character in boys'[29].

Young Cecil Healy came from a family of keen and competitive sportsmen. His brother Claude was a recognised middle-distance runner and schoolboy sailor. Harold captained the Sydney Amateur Walking Club, was an official with the Amateur Athletic Association and was instrumental in establishing the New South Wales Amateur Sports Club in 1896. Harold also backed a push to form an amateur swimming and lifesaving club in east Sydney in late 1894, a body that amalgamated with the swimming branch of the Darlinghurst Harriers sports club and became known as the East Sydney Amateur Swimming Club, with Harold as its first secretary[30].

Despite the temptations of field sports such as cricket and football played on the lush acreage at Kurkulla, Cecil Healy's upbringing on the shores of Sydney Harbour was a defining factor in his own choice of athletic pursuit. Now 12 years old, he was at home on school vacation in the summer of 1894 when the East Sydney Swimming Club was formed, and joined his brothers Harold and Claude as members for its inaugural season. On the surface, Cecil's affinity with swimming seemed rather futile. Bowral had no aquatic facilities other than the temperamental Wingecarribee River, so there was nowhere for the aspiring young splasher to practise while he was away at school. However, young Cecil swam at East Sydney meets whenever he could, catching trains home for weekend carnivals and dreaming of salt water between times. Even as an adolescent, his love affair with the water assumed adult intensity.

***

There was a brief glimmer of hope for a climb back up the social ladder by the Healy family in 1892 when Patrick Healy returned to working at Sydney's Central Criminal Court. However, for some years Patrick's health had not been robust, and by 1895 his body was failing, although he was still travelling and working, making the long trip back to Hay in April 1895 for the local circuit court. Only in the week preceding his death did he take to his bed. Patrick Healy died on 7 September 1895 at Roslyn Gardens, aged just 52, and his funeral was held at St. Canice's church the following day. His sons Harold and Claude were present, as were his wife, his brother Nicholas's widow Margaret and Annie's brother Walter Gallott. The funeral was also a *Who's Who* of the colony's legal fraternity, with Judge Backhouse and a dozen barristers-at-law in the pews[31]. The Catholic *Freeman's Journal* mourned, 'While he had not the gift of eloquence, [Healy] won his high place at the Bar by his soundness as a lawyer. His knowledge of civil and criminal law was as wide as it was deep.'[32]

Patrick Healy's premature death was attributed to interstitial nephritis and anaemia, both features of chronic kidney failure and often associated with overuse of pain-killers. However, nephritis is also symptomatic of lead poisoning, prostate cancer, Crohn's Disease, Epstein–Barr virus and some forms of leukaemia, any of which could have explained the extended period of ill-health Patrick endured in the years preceding his death[33]. His passing made Annie a widow for the second time, with no source of income and seven boys to support. There was no hope now of an escape from Roslyn Gardens or the dirt and clamour of the inner city. Fifteen-year-old Cecil was brought home from Kurkulla and enrolled at the Jesuit St. Aloysius' College in Darlinghurst—ironically, the same school the raffish and tragic Alphonse Girard had attended.

The demise of Patrick Healy, with all the attendant lifestyle changes it forced upon his family, had perhaps one benefit—it returned Cecil Healy to the sea.

TWO

THE CELTIC WATER-CHILD

*'O Lord, methought what pain it was to drown,
What dreadful noise of waters in my ears,
What sights of ugly death within my eyes.
Methought I saw a thousand fearful wrecks,
A thousand men that fishes gnawed upon,
Wedges of gold, great anchors, heaps of pearl,
Inestimable stones, unvalued jewels,
All scattered in the bottom of the sea.'*

–William Shakespeare, *Richard III* (Act 1, Scene 4, 22–29)

***

The water was deep and clear and green, rippling black tiles visible in the dark depths. He put his feet in: no wavelets lapped against his shins, the surface was as still and perfect as a mirror. Then he drew a breath and pushed forward off the concrete lip, shutting his eyes as water closed over his head. Mindless terror constricted his chest and forced his head above the surface; he gasped for a *second and instinctively trod water, then remembered to open his eyes. Nothing had changed. The yawing space was still silent, the sifted light still silver. The dark, unmoving silhouette of his brother rose above him on the pool deck, nodding approval. He took a deep breath and sank below the surface again, looking back up through the water to the wavering outline of columns and arches, his heart now bursting with unutterable joy....*

There was a Gothic allure, a taste of the drama and theatre that would characterise his future, to the opening act of Cecil Healy's competitive swimming career; a thirteen-year-old boy, a silver cup and a soaring Italianate swimming hall hidden deep beneath the streets of Sydney.

The East Sydney Swimming Club could not have chosen a more spectacular setting for their early exploits. Sydney's earliest swimming clubs used fenced enclosures on the harbour and nearby rivers for their training at Watsons Bay, Balmain and Parramatta, where swimmers were buffeted by waves and tides and threatened by stray sharks. By the mid-1880s, new concrete sea baths at Coogee and Bronte had introduced the shape and structure of the modern Olympic pool, although the lengths and breadths of these early pools varied greatly. In 1885, however, a revolution in bathing—the non-tidal pool—reached Sydney.

At street level, the Grand Natatorium Hotel at 400 Pitt Street, in the heart of the city's banking and finance district, was simply another of Sydney's stately buildings, with its rendered stone façade and Victorian columns. However, the basement of the building housed another world altogether—a great theatre of aquatics, a cavernous underground cathedral of water-sports perfectly concealed below Sydney's hustling, noisy roadways. The self-proclaimed 'grandest swimming baths in the world' included a mezzanine filled with opera chairs and great banks of electric lights, all overlooking a dark sheet of salt water that filled most of the basement floor space like a theatre stage. With the baths replenished daily by water pumped direct from Sydney Harbour, the underground Natatorium was a revolution in aquatic facilities—heated water during winter, conditions unaffected by wind, waves or tide and absolutely, positively no sharks[1].

The East Sydney Swimming Club made their first home at the Natatorium, holding their inaugural meet in December 1894. From the start, the club was a 'crucible for talent' according to historian Mark Maddox, attracting state, national and international race-winners to its stocks in the pool and powerful officials out of it. It was in this atmosphere of splendour, ego and command that the adolescent Cecil Healy, still a Bowral schoolboy, produced an eye-catching performance in his first public appearance as an amateur swimmer. On 23 February 1895, Healy collected a silver cup for victory in a 60-yard handicap race. He was just thirteen years old and seemed primed to ride the tide of success and expectation upon which the new club floated[2].

In 1894, the Grand Natatorium Hotel on Sydney's Pitt Street concealed an aquatic playground in its basement, including a heated salt-water swimming pool. [Source: State Archives NSW: image no.1192].

This early triumph of the fourth Healy son as a sprint swimmer was not unexpected, despite his youth and inexperience. A 1909 report by the NSW Minister of Public Instruction on the health of pupils in the state's schools observed that children from the Southern Highlands were 'not quite so tall, but much heavier—the heaviest children in proportion to their height in the whole State.'[3] The sharp climate, hearty diet and open-air philosophy of Pulling's school in Bowral had markedly influenced Cecil Healy's physical development. Unlike his tall, lean, older brothers, Cecil was a stocky, muscular youth, as suited to the explosive demands of sprint swimming as to the boxing, water polo and rugby union he later excelled at. While it would be a year before Cecil left Bowral for a permanent return to Sydney, East Sydney coach George Farmer encouraged him to attend meets whenever possible in the interim, keen to add the powerful but tractable teenager to the stable of young stars already resident at his club.

When Healy did return to Sydney after his father's death in late 1895, he not only began to swim regularly, but was immediately absorbed into the unprecedented squad of talent that Farmer nurtured at East Sydney. Frederick Claude Vivian 'Freddie' Lane, two years Healy's senior, had joined the club at about the same time and by 1898 was the Australasian 100-yard champion and the 220- and 440-yard champion of NSW. The prodigious Lane, who had won his first race at eight years of age, would become Australia's first Olympic swimming representative and gold medallist, winning the 200-yard freestyle in the moody waters of the Seine at the 1900 Paris Games[4].

There were also the Hellings brothers—Harry, George, Jack and Charles—with Jack a winner at both state and international level. His headstone in Sydney's Waverley Cemetery proclaims him 'the first Australian champion to compete in England'[5]. However, late in 1895, the East Sydney Swimming Club scored its greatest coup, attracting the most famous dynasty in Australian swimming history to the Natatorium. The Cavill family—'Professor' Frederick Cavill, his wife Theophila and their nine offspring—is still 'Swimming's First Family' according to the International Swimming Hall of Fame[6]. A distance swimmer of great repute, Fred Cavill had brought his family to Australia from England in 1879 to mitigate his despair at twice failing to swim the English Channel, falling just 200 yards short at the second attempt. He built swimming baths at Lavender Bay and Farm Cove, where he and Theophila revolutionised the colony's swim training methods and his children stormed the domestic swim scene with their wide-ranging brilliance. The eldest, Ernest, won the NSW 1,000-yard championship at just 15 years of age. Charles was the first man to swim the treacherous Golden Gate strait in San Francisco in 1896, but drowned the following year in California. At the English championships of 1897, the third brother, Percy, became the first Australian to win a race abroad when he won both the 440-yard and five-mile events. He also won eight State and Australian championships between 1895 and 1898. Arthur (known as 'Tums') was NSW 500- and 1,000-yard champion before losing his life attempting to swim Seattle Harbour in 1914. Sydney was a teen prodigy, capturing the 220-yard championship of Australia at age 16, and is also credited with the invention of the butterfly stroke. Fred Cavill's three daughters were also outstanding swimmers. Madeleine was awarded the Royal Shipwreck Relief Society medal for lifesaving in 1908, Alice worked as a swimming instructor in Australia, New Zealand and the USA, and Fredda's son Richard Eve won a gold medal for diving at the 1924 Olympic Games[7].

However, it was the youngest Cavill, Richmond Theophilus, or Dick, as he was known, who arrived at East Sydney in 1895 and outshone all of his older siblings. Born in 1884, Dick Cavill would hold 18 Australian, two English and 22 NSW titles between 1899 and 1904. In England in 1902, he became the first man to swim 100 yards in under a minute, clocking 58 3/5 seconds. He is also credited with developing the independent arm and leg action of the radical new 'crawl' stroke and using it to win his first title, the NSW 100-yard championship of 1899.

Immersed in such a pool of aptitude, it seemed impossible that Cecil Healy could fail to thrive as a swimmer at East Sydney. The move back to the city, although coming as it did in tragic family circumstances, was perfectly timed to capture and nurture Healy's burgeoning talent right at its genesis. He would receive the best instruction in the best facilities and swim alongside some of the most gifted and motivated athletes in the colony. It was the ultimate recipe for success.

Cecil Healy's return to Sydney also brought benefits beyond the pool for the young man. He had always been a rather lonely child, marooned in the middle of his six siblings. The three youngest Healy boys were up to eight years younger than Cecil, while his three older brothers were seven to fifteen years his senior, and following their father's untimely death had gone out to work, finding clerical and banking jobs in the city, which left little time for their schoolboy sibling. It had been Annie's fear for her fourth son, the child she had borne after grieving for years following the death of her daughter, that had seen her send him away to protect him from the family's descent into ignominy. However, for Cecil, the four years of isolation in the Southern Highlands had engendered a sense of rejection and insecurity that would pervade his character and relationships for the rest of his life. As the only child to be sent away, and with little explanation accompanying his abrupt departure, Healy's exile bred in him a deep, unwavering doubt as to his own worth. *Who was he to seek affection or recognition when he would only be pushed away? Was he valued so little that his own mother could choose him, of all her children, for banishment?*

Even as a young teenager, Cecil Healy was already driven by a silent need to earn back the attention of his mother by proving his ability to compete against both his older and taller, and younger and cuter brothers. The division between the boys may have become insurmountable save for the enthusiasm with which Harold entered into the East Sydney venture, drawing Claude and then Cecil along with him. In addition to his administrative duties at East Sydney, 24-year-old Harold was a keen—if blue-collar—participant in the club's handicap races, often swimming off 20 seconds or more for the 100 yards. He was very soon outstripped by Cecil, but this failed to daunt either his enjoyment of the fortnightly stoushes or his new-found affection for his little brother. Despite their nine-year age gap, the pair remained close correspondents throughout their lives, and Harold protected and supported Cecil during his endeavours both in and out of the pool. Claude, too, notwithstanding his preference for middle-distance running, was active at East Sydney as a committeeman, and the shared interest paved the way for a new relationship with his younger sibling. Cecil, however, remained a quiet and rather secretive child, his insecurities evident only in the ferocity with which he threw himself into his training.

While the East Sydney club excelled in its first year, with its swimmers winning three Australasian amateur championships, the balance sheet of the Grand Natatorium Hotel was not nearly so healthy. The astronomical cost of piping salt water almost two miles inland to the pool weighed heavily upon management. Despite pleas to the City of Sydney to mitigate the costs and maintain this 'most useful establishment', the grand bathhouse was doomed[8]. In 1899, the entire hotel was sold to the Salvation Army and its stately halls converted to budget accommodation, with only the skin of its original façade remaining. The luxurious pools that had cured Sydney's rheumatics and nurtured Australia's early swim stars were filled with concrete. The management at East Sydney clearly scented the impending demise of the pretentious establishment at the end of their 1895–96 season, voting unanimously to move the club's headquarters to the Domain Baths run by George Farmer at Woolloomooloo.

***

Young Cecil Healy's immediate and passionate affinity with water was perhaps genetically predetermined, for his lineage was anchored deep in it. His paternal ancestors were Celts from the wildlands of county Clare, a primordial enclave on Ireland's west coast bounded on three sides by water. With the River Shannon and its great estuary to the south, the shimmering expanse of Galway Bay to the north and the Atlantic Ocean hammering at Clare's western edge, Healy's heritage was profoundly linked with primeval worship of water. There were childhood tales of the *madradh uisge*, or sea otter, that giggling, diving denizen of the deep, and the wistful *selkie*, a creature living most of its life as a seal but occasionally shedding its skin to seduce an unwary fisherman in the guise of a beautiful woman. But for all the fables of silver rivers, fairy wells and fountains, Celtic waterways also spawned a narrative of darkness and horror—of the *Augh-iska*, the malevolent spirit pony luring children onto its back to be drowned and devoured, and the *Cata*, Ireland's own river monster, with nails of iron and eyes flashing flame. The Shannon itself was named for Siann, granddaughter of the sea god Lir, who sought knowledge at Connla's Well, despite warnings not to approach it. When the girl caught and ate the Salmon of Wisdom, the well burst, sweeping her away to drown in the sea of her forebears[9].

Perhaps it was this capricious brutality that made water and its resident spirits so beloved by the Irish Celts. In the west of the Gaelic world, isolated outposts such as Clare were 'nearer to the second century than the nineteenth', mused the poet W.B. Yeats[10] and the ancient gifts of foresight and magick were venerated, despite their often malicious and mischievous trappings. The Celts of Clare looked reverently upon the seals and gloomy waterholes, the baleful hags and water horses, for they both harboured the spirits of their forebears and were harbingers of things to come.

Cecil Healy's paternal grandfather, Nicholas Healy, was raised in County Clare with the Shannon at his feet. Both the county and its great river had witnessed struggle and strife since the early Middle Ages. Clare lands were part of the Kingdom of Connacht until the mid-tenth century, when they were violently annexed by nearby Munster, and Vikings also thronged up the Shannon to raid the secluded inland monasteries. During the Confederate Wars of 1641–53, the Irish retreated behind the Shannon and held out for two years against English Parliamentarian forces before a bloody and conclusive defeat, after which Oliver Cromwell proclaimed that the Irish landowners could go to 'Hell or Connacht'—referring to their choice of either death or forced migration across the Shannon[11].

At the turn of the nineteenth century, Irish society was still considerably ill at ease. The Act of Union, passed in 1800, had subjugated Ireland to the parliament at Westminster and the loss of control over their own destiny sat hard with the Celtic people. There was simply not enough land to feed a rapidly increasing population, and competition for acreage drove up rents and ate into the people's already scarce resources. Irish Catholics resented paying tithes[12] to the Protestant church for the occupation of agricultural land, and laboured with no protection for their domestic industries against overwhelming competition from Britain. While most of the

Penal Laws were repealed in the 1780s and 1790s, enabling Catholics to attend schools and vote at elections, they were still debarred from parliament or the higher ranks of the military, and the dark undercurrents of hunger and bitterness rent Ireland into one of the most unstable societies in Europe[13].

From this warlike provenance came Cecil Healy's grandfather, Nicholas Healy, the fighter. Healy was born in County Clare around 1793, with Britain at war with France and competition over land in Ireland inflaming riots between Protestants and Catholics. At a relatively statuesque 5 feet 8 1/2 inches, Healy was the quintessential Catholic Celt, with ruddy outdoorsman's features, dark hair and hazel eyes[14]. He farmed a small plot at Clounkerekan in the north-east of County Clare, as did his friend John McMahon at nearby Kilkeedy. Neither man owned their land, but rented from absentee landlords who could arbitrarily redistribute plots and evict tenants, and by 1818 the pair were, like many subjugated Catholic men at the hands of their oppressors, as dangerous as half-starved dogs. In that harsh winter, the pair were arrested and imprisoned for the crimes of burglary and robbery. While their offences were perhaps understandable, given the desperation and resentment of the occupied Catholic people, the sentences handed down at the Summer Assizes were irrevocable: *life*. They were to be sent to the other side of the world, to Australia, another outpost of the hated English, with no prospect of return[15].

Healy and McMahon were among 28,000 convicts to receive life sentences during the history of transportation to Australia between 1782 and 1842. When transportation sentences were handed down, convicts from Clare were housed in the city gaol at Cork, on the south-eastern Irish coast. In 1818, this fetid prison was in decay and constantly overcrowded, forcing an overflow of detainees onto disused ships in the nearby Cove of Cork. Healy and McMahon awaited their fate in a hulk at the Cove for more than a year. Intended as 'a terror to all evil-doers', conditions on the hulks were so appalling that one-third of all those housed within them died.

Nicholas Healy, John McMahon and 170 other male convicts boarded the convict transport ship *Minerva* at Cork on 26 August 1819. Half-maddened by the stultifying hell of the hulks, they did not go easily. They were brought aboard in irons and inspected by the superintendent, Dr Trevor, and then supplied with blankets and flannel drawers before being marched into the hold under the eye of the ship's master John

Bell and the guardsmen of the 1st Royal Scots regiment. Those brief but precious hours in the fresh air on deck, prodded and peered at as they had been, were too much for some. Stumbling below, encumbered by leg irons and facing another four months in overcrowded darkness, some of the men tried to turn back, perhaps for a last lungful of Irish air or a glimpse of black cliffs and green hills. Dr Trevor described it as a 'mutiny'[16], but go they must, and when the *Minerva* turned her prow south with the men held below at gunpoint, the silver rivers and peat bogs melted away forever.

For the next four months, there was nothing to see but the creaking timbers of the hold and the wild expanses of the Earth's great oceans. At 530 tons, the *Minerva* held sufficient water and rations to make the 13,000-mile journey to Sydney non-stop[17]. Many of the prisoners, unused to a seafaring life, suffered terribly from seasickness, shackled alongside vomiting mess-mates with just eighteen inches of sleeping space per man and thrown about by the violent intercourse of the Atlantic and Indian Oceans at the tip of Africa. However, after three disasters aboard transport ships in 1814, significant improvements in convict transport conditions had been instituted[18]. Warmer clothing, a more plentiful and varied diet and access to fresh air and medical assistance saw a much-diminished mortality rate aboard British convict ships. Just one prisoner died aboard the *Minerva* during its 1819 voyage. Surgeon Superintendent Charles Queade allowed the prisoners up on deck in good weather, so long as they did not interfere with the operations of the ship, and also ordered the removal of their irons a fortnight after leaving Britain, using reinstatement as a punishment to supersede the need for flogging. Some attempt was also made to school the men, with the ship's cargo including 'one hundred spelling books with religious extracts annexed thereto and likewise fifty Testaments'. However, such diversions could not diminish their longing for home. An 1819 parliamentary report by John Thomas Bigge found that while Irish convicts generally arrived in New South Wales in a very healthy state, 'their separation from their native country (was) observed to make a strong impression upon their minds'[19].

Healy and his cohorts were aboard one of 16 prison ships to arrive in Australia in 1819. On 30 December 1819, the *Minerva* convicts were disembarked in Sydney and transported to Parramatta for inspection by the governor and distribution amongst free settlers or to government work gangs. The governor informed them that no reference would be made to their pasts, and that 'their future conduct ... alone [would] entitle them to reward or indulgence'[20]. Nicholas Healy was assigned as a servant to a Sydney gentleman, Mr P. Garrigan. While assigned convicts were supplied with clothing, bedding and medicines, they were forbidden to demand wages, had no set working hours and could not leave their master's property without a pass. Assignment of convicts into the service of private settlers saved the government the cost of their upkeep and (in theory) separated them from mass temptation and vice, thereby restoring a measure of self-respect. However, Healy's 'future conduct' soon expressed itself, and by 1822 he was back in trouble. The details of his crime are unknown, but most secondary offences were trivial—bad language, absconding, or drunkenness. Nevertheless, the convicts were punished severely, often by transportation to faraway settlements at Norfolk Island, Moreton Bay or Van Diemen's Land. Healy was shipped to the port of Newcastle, north of Sydney, in April 1822. Newcastle was the oldest of the secondary penal colonies, having been established in 1804 to confine a group of Irish convicts who had staged an uprising at Castle Hill. Its throng of repeat offenders broke their backs cutting timber, grubbed blindly in rudimentary coalmines and breathed the corrosive by-products of seashells crushed for lime mortar. Outside working hours, the horrors continued. Recalcitrants dragged a log and chain when not at labour, and discipline took the form of inadequate rations, meagre supplies of clothing and the cat-o'-nine-tails.

Nicholas Healy, despite his mistakes and flaws, had a powerful influence over the men around him at Newcastle, and the authorities were quick to harness this before it could be used for ill. On 8 June 1825, he was appointed, by order of the Governor, as a convict police constable. Civilian police were in short supply, and convicts holding Tickets of Leave or with fair behavioural records were often appointed as surrogate officers. Beyond their regular duties, many supplemented their meagre wages (around two shillings per day, or in Healy's case, nothing, as he had no Ticket of Leave) by apprehending absconders, reporting sly grog operations and hunting bushrangers. In 1826, Healy was elevated to the position of overseer of the Prisoners' Barrack, and late in 1827 was recommended for a Ticket of Leave, which was issued on 16 May 1828.

It was almost two years, however, before Nicholas Healy truly escaped Newcastle, when in June 1830 he was transferred to the police outpost at Paterson's Plains, to the west. The area was home to free settlers and a cohort of convicts carving farms from the ancient local forests, and was governed by a small military barracks, a police magistrate, ten constables, two watch-house keepers and a scourge, or flogger. In 1820, the Paterson region had been at the centre of a Royal Commission into the brutal treatment of convicts. Healy was appointed watch-house keeper at Paterson in 1830, but remained in the position for only 18 months. There was a high turnover among the convict constables, who were often dismissed in favour of free men, and in February 1832, Healy was discharged for reasons unspecified.

In that same year, he was granted permission to marry a local girl, Mary Ann Clarke. She was just fifteen years of age, while Healy was almost forty. Mary Ann had her own powerful convict heritage. Both parents had been transported and served terms in the notorious penal colony of Van Diemen's Land (now Tasmania). Her father, dark-featured Irishman Richard Augustus Clarke, was similar in age to Nicholas Healy, and he too was a 'lifer', transported in 1811 for aiding in a burglary committed by his brother John and an accomplice, Patrick Larkin. Both Larkin and John Clarke had been executed for the crime. The teenage Richard had also been sentenced to death, but in September 1809, after six months crammed into Limerick Gaol awaiting his fate, Clarke and a group of fellow death-row inmates had attempted a daring prison break, battering down the walls of their cells and stealing ropes with which to scale the outer walls. The group was apprehended, but their sentences were, surprisingly, commuted to transportation, and Clarke was shipped out on the *Providence* in December 1810[21]. Like Nicholas Healy, Richard Clarke was soon back before the bench, receiving an additional six years in the most dreaded penal colony of all—Van Diemen's Land. Life in that freezing island wilderness, exposed to the worst of iniquity and sin, finally took the fight out of young Richard Clarke. Clarke's record in Van Diemen's Land was spotless, without a single recorded incident of bad behaviour, and in 1818 he was given permission to marry Catherine Pendergast, an Irish maid serving a seven-year sentence for stealing linen[22]. When the two wed in December 1818 in Hobart Town, they already had one child, a daughter, Mary Ann, born the previous year[23].

Despite his exemplary record, the supposedly improving effects of family life and a conditional pardon for good behaviour in January 1820, Richard Clarke risked it all on a get-rich-quick scheme that very same year, trafficking almost 1,000 pounds of stolen mutton in the full knowledge that the sheep carcasses had been obtained illegally. His subsequent conviction and three-year sentence earned his entire family a one-way ticket to another notorious site of secondary punishment, Newcastle[24]. It was to be a further three years before Richard and Catherine were both declared free by virtue of time served. As a free man, Richard Clarke remained in the Paterson area with his family, and by 1830 he had two convicts assigned to him and a 230-acre holding of his own, which he named *Bird Hill*[25].

In 1832, Mary Ann Clarke left the quiet prosperity of *Bird Hill* for life as a convict bride. It would be a further two years until her new husband Nicholas Healy was granted his ticket of leave. Nine months later, in November 1834, their first child, John Joseph, was born, and the following year Healy obtained the conditional pardon that finally granted him full freedom.

Cecil Healy's father, Patrick Joseph Healy, was born in Maitland in 1843, the third child of Nicholas and Mary Ann. Nicholas Healy had opened a general store on the Maitland high street and was anxious to ingratiate himself with the prosperous element of local society. He had three convict labourers, and bought into commercial buildings and rich land near Singleton on the Hunter River. In 1843, the year his son

Patrick was born, he contributed towards the construction of the Hunter Valley's first Catholic cathedral, St. John the Baptists Church in West Maitland, and the following year he ran for a seat on the district council, pledging to 'lighten the burden of taxation, consistent with the public good'[26]. While that bid (and his 1846 candidacy) failed, his disappointment was soon subsumed by a dreadful family tragedy. His eldest child, twelve-year-old John Joseph, drowned in the Hunter River in October 1845. The child had been sent to water a horse and, with summer approaching, entered the water to bathe, whereupon he was seized by cramp and disappeared beneath the surface. While three attending doctors did 'everything that skill and science could accomplish to restore animation', the boy, described by the local pastor as 'a youth of great promise', could not be revived[27].

Nicholas Healy's lasting legacy came in 1851 when he opened the Governor Bourke Inn at West Maitland. The Governor Bourke was one of 24 inns and hotels in the town (with 15 more in East Maitland), and many had colourful monikers such as the Bird in Hand, Red Cow, Seven Stars and Cottage of Content. Healy christened his hotel for the colonial governor Sir Richard Bourke, who, ironically, had actively discouraged the appointment of convict

Ticket-of-Leave holders as police constables. Opening the hotel on 27 May 1851, Healy proclaimed that he offered the 'best selection of spirits, wines, ales, porter and cordials, together with good beds, stabling and paddocks.'[28] His honesty (for an ex-convict) was meritorious. In 1856, he placed a notice in the local newspaper advising that someone had dropped a one-pound note in the bar of the Governor Bourke that, if unclaimed after a month, would be donated to the Maitland Hospital[29].

Nicholas Healy died on 6 January 1861 after a severe and protracted illness, and Mary Ann survived him by more than two decades until her death in 1884. The prosperous and progressive Maitland environment and the stable and ambitious home that Nicholas and Mary Ann provided for their children instilled in their eight offspring an equally ambitious ethos. Two of Nicholas's three sons, Patrick and Nicholas Jr, were university educated and entered the legal profession—perhaps they proved to be the bedrock for the sense of fair play and justice for which Cecil Healy would later be renowned.

However, while Patrick Healy raised his own children in exclusivity, comfort and luxury, the short step away from his father's convict heritage may also have been his downfall. After the drowning death of his older brother, Patrick became the vehicle for the hopes and dreams of Nicholas and Mary Ann Healy, their chance for genuine public elevation, the shaking off of their convict past and acceptance into the best social circles. Young Patrick received every privilege they could afford him: primary education at the Grammar School in Maitland, and in 1860, entry to Sydney University to study alongside future legal giants such as Sir Samuel Griffith, the Chief Justice of Queensland. Patrick gained a B.A. in 1862, winning Dr John Woolley's special prize for logic, and then completed a Master of Arts, encouraged once more by Woolley, who in pressing the university to raise a new generation of responsible gentlemen 'held (Healy) in the highest esteem'[30]. In 1865, Patrick Healy, only one generation removed from shackles and leg-irons, was admitted as a barrister. However, his sudden entry into a world of wealth, privilege and esteem was one that his upbringing, no matter how respectable, had ill-prepared him for, and his new and unaccustomed wealth slipped through his fingers like water. Patrick's death in 1895 left his family with nothing, for in trying to salvage his reputation when his financial ruin was finally exposed, Patrick had sold his only remaining asset—a half share in the Governor Bourke Inn left to him by his mother.

THREE

CATERPILLARS, CORN AND THE CRAWL

'The man, after looking at me for a moment, turned me upside down and emptied my pockets. There was nothing in them but a piece of bread.'

—Charles Dickens, *Great Expectations*

***

The period between 1896 and 1901 was one of muted progress in Cecil Healy's swimming career, a fact that puzzled many pundits given his eye-catching debut in 1895 and his indisputable physical suitability for sprint swimming.

In the five years since his first triumph as a 13-year-old, Healy had consistently placed in heats, but not once did he stand atop the podium. As a result, he was always a fringe selection behind Fred Lane, Dick Cavill and George Read to represent East Sydney at state or national meets. In contrast, Freddie Lane won all but one of the available state freestyle titles in 1898–99 and Dick Cavill shocked the colony with his use of the controversial 'crawl' stroke to win the NSW 100-yard championship of 1899. Swimming commentator 'Natator', perhaps guessing at the Healy family circumstances, defended Cecil's slow progress in *The Referee*: 'If there's one swimmer who has my sympathy, it's Cecil Healy ... Few men have ever prepared themselves under greater difficulties ... I feel sorry that he doesn't meet with greater success.'[1]

The anchor against which Healy's progress strained was the dire social and financial straits thrust upon the family by the passing of his father. Patrick Healy's death snatched away any trace of prestige that his role as legal counsel, however tainted, had retained for his family. The Healys were now barely differentiated from the other working-class families on Roslyn Street in all their tenements and terraces—shabby but clean, respectable but poor, a family to be pitied for their dreadful fall. In the final years of Patrick's life, he had at least brought home enough coins each week to procure meals for nine and afford the boys recreation time to pursue their sporting interests, but now, despite the previous uncertainty as to whether their father would bring home a full purse or a bailiff would demand it at the door and there would only be toast for tea, Patrick's tenuous financial support was gone. Even in the bewildered weeks after Patrick's death, as the disordered tumblers of their lives tried to drop back into place like a badly picked lock, the boys knew there was no question of Annie Healy going out to work. Sewing, taking in washing, scrubbing or—God forbid—factory work: those were for other women of reduced circumstances, not their pretty, high-bred mother. Instead, the older Healy boys—James, Harold, Claude and, as soon as he finished school, Cecil—shouldered the yoke of nine-to-five employment to keep food on their rented dining table and afford Annie perhaps one new dress each season.

In 1899, eighteen-year-old Cecil found a job as a clerk with Richard Hornsby & Sons, the engine and machinery manufacturers founded in Lincolnshire, England, in 1828. From an office on Barrack Street in central Sydney, the firm imported agricultural equipment, tractors and steam engines from a huge plant at Grantham in the UK. Hornsby's were credited with producing the first oil-fired tractor in Britain in 1896, a lumbering 20-horsepower machine with steel wheels powered by their own patented Hornsby-Akroyd Safety Oil Traction Engine[2]. The company would later expand into 'caterpillar' tracked vehicles, the forerunners to some types of modern tank and earthmoving machines. By the turn of the century, the company employed 1,400 workers across the globe and Cecil Healy's days were filled with accounts and ledgers related to belt-driven pumps, shearing machines, corn huskers and scrub cutters. While the Healy boys were tied to their dreary clerical labours, Cecil's swim rivals had little call on their time away from the pool, a fact noted by the sport's commentators. 'What would (Cecil Healy) do had he the spare hours to devote to the game that Lane, Read and Cavill give it?' *The Arrow* wondered[3]. Freddie Lane's father was a successful businessman, and Lane junior's trip to the 1900 Paris Games and several trips to England for the British championships were all funded from the family coffers. To rub further salt into the Healy wounds, Fred Lane had also enjoyed a rich education at St. Ignatius College Riverview, the elite school from which the Healy boys had been withdrawn after their father's fall from grace. *Natator*, too, painted a decadent picture of the lifestyle of Lane and Co., all free to devote themselves full-time to aquatic pursuits: 'The pelts of all were tanned—almost black in some instances, but a bright copper tint in most—through constant exposure to the sun's rays ... When food and sleep do not call for their presence elsewhere, George Farmer's men are either gambolling in the water or stretched out on the handy surrounding platform, whence they may lazily drop in as the inclination seizes them.'[4]

Cecil Healy could do little more than cast longing glances through the fly-specked office windows towards the distant glint of the blue harbour and hotfoot it to the Domain pool the instant the clock struck five to make up the lost miles. Many saw the gap between his circumstances and those of his clubmates and rivals as impossible for young Healy to bridge, but despite a lack of success in the seasons between 1896 and 1901, an impressive fighting spirit characterised Cecil Healy's performances during those years. As his handicap for the 100 yards gradually improved, Healy often gave his clubmates more than 20 seconds start before, like a dog let off a string, flying home to lose by only a touch, never giving up despite giving away what seemed an insurmountable head start. Healy's need to prove himself, born of those old days in the cold Southern Highlands, was stronger than his frustration at his lack of tangible success, and although victory continued to elude him, Healy refused to be disheartened, chipping away at the golden idol that was Dick Cavill, undeterred by the insouciant ease of Freddie Lane's conquests and turning up week after week, losing again and again, but by less and less each time.

It was in 1901, fully six years after his first (and only) race win, that Cecil Healy captured a maiden championship, joining Freddie Lane and three others to win the NSW Flying Squadron title for East Sydney. This event, a five-man relay with each swimmer completing a 100-yard leg, was the most prestigious teams race on the domestic swimming calendar, and Healy's 1901 time was second only to that of Lane.

East Sydney Squadron Team, 1901.

The 1901 East Sydney 5x100-yard Flying Squadron team: (left to right): Reg 'Snowy' Baker, Cecil Healy, Fred Lane, George Reid, J. Meade. [Source: Northern Beaches Council/Manly Library Local Studies Collection. The original image appeared in The Referee newspaper, 20 March 1901, p.4].

An individual championship, however, continued to elude Healy. Finding enough hours in the day for training was not his sole difficulty. Despite his powerful physique and air of substance and competence, Healy's sensitive nature meant he was often assailed by dreadful nerves before a race. Repeated failure to defeat his rivals in competition, despite grand displays at training, had been observed with concern in the press. Despite swimming faster than both Reg 'Snowy' Baker and George Read in the Flying Squadron event, Healy finished fourth behind Lane, Baker and Read in the East Sydney individual 100-yard club championship of 1901. George Farmer had boldly predicted that Lane would become the first man to break the minute for 100 yards at that meet, although *The Referee* opined, 'Lane would have to practice a bit more' to beat the world record of 60 3/4 seconds held by Englishman John Derbyshire. Nevertheless, Lane won the club championship by three yards in 63 1/5 seconds, with Healy fading to finish four yards back.

While the 1901 club championship meet was less than successful for Healy, it did provide an important showcase for the new phenomenon of women's public swimming races. Fifteen-year-old Annette Kellerman easily won the ladies 100-yard race at the East Sydney meet, then further excited the huge crowd with her diving skills, plunging from the top of a platform erected fully 30 feet above the water. Natator accorded her the compliment, 'She possesses nerves of no common order'[5]. Segregated and generally frowned upon, public competition for female swimmers was barely tolerated in 1901. Swimming was a male-dominated pursuit, with women forced to wear full bathing dress and take their aquatic pursuits in sheltered environs far from prying eyes. Although pioneers such as Fanny Durack were receiving some assistance from liberal-minded champions such as Freddie Lane, and women's races were held (albeit behind closed doors) at some clubs, the standard of women's swimming was understandably far behind that of the men. Female performances in the pool were often secondary to the observation of public etiquette: at a ladies-only carnival at Lavender Bay in 1907, some competitors were disqualified for the 'indecency' of their dress after they modelled their costumes upon those of the men.

***

In September 1902, while touring England with Fred Lane, Dick Cavill broke through the golden barrier to become the first man to swim under one minute for the 100 yards, setting an astonishing new world record of 58 3/5 seconds. As early as 1882, Australian swimmers had been breaking world records, with Walter Macindoe taking 30 seconds off the international mark for 1,000 yards that year. By the dawn of the twentieth century, the East Sydney club was at the forefront of Australian swimming, with world records for Percy (half-mile, 1897) and Charles Cavill (quarter-mile, 1896), and by 1902 little brother Dick held every world record from 200 yards to one mile. Freddie Lane was Australia's first Olympic swimming champion at the 1900 Paris Games, winning the 200-yard freestyle, which he only swam because his pet race, the 100 yards, was cancelled. He also took gold in a second event now removed from the Olympic program, the 200-yard obstacle race, in which competitors had to splash under and over a series of rowboats to reach the finish.

East Sydney swimmers, including Healy, were also leaders in stroke development during this most rapid evolutionary phase in the history of swimming. The prevalent early swimming technique was the breaststroke. In the 1870s, Englishman Arthur Trudgen introduced a hybrid technique that combined the breaststroke kick with an overarm stroke, keeping the head out of the water, naming the new style the *trudgen* after himself. Freddie Lane swam a double overarm stroke similar to the trudgen, lying on his left side high in the water, using a small flutter of his legs between narrow kicks. His was considered a good sprint stroke, but too strenuous for longer distances until he won the 1899 NSW mile title using it and the following month set a new Australian 440-yard record. Lane was, however, often in a state of physical collapse after employing his unusual style over such lengthy races.

The revolutionary crawl stroke was not seen in Australia until the late 1890s. Forms of the crawl are evident in early Egyptian hieroglyphs and Roman swimming schools also encouraged a style of overarm propulsion. In 1844, Native Americans were documented using a variety of the crawl during exhibition races in London. However, despite their success, the stroke was dismissed as 'barbaric and splashy' compared with the more genteel breaststroke[6]. The basic crawl technique positioned the swimmer with their chest downwards, unlike the old traditions based on the sidestroke. The head was carried low in the water and the arms were extended forward with a bent elbow so the hand entered the water just beyond the head, pulling powerfully backwards before exiting the water with a fully extended arm. A slight lift of the head was used to breathe and the legs were kept straight, the instep striking the water on each stroke, as distinct from the old trudgen kick where the legs were drawn up and opened on each cycle. The Cavill brothers—Dick being the first to use the style in a race—and Cecil Healy all used variants of this radical new crawl stroke. While controversial, the results became so dominant that the South Australian *Chronicle* proclaimed, 'They crawl to conquer'[7].

While clearly hampered by his clerical commitments, Healy's slow maturation as a swimmer was also the result of continual experimentation and refinement of his crawl stroke, studying Cavill's propulsion technique under the eye of George Farmer. In 1913, Healy recounted to *The Sunday Times*, 'I well remember him hailing me from the platform one morning and saying, "Cec, try Cavill's new splash stroke." I asked him what it was like, and he illustrated it with his arms. I had seen it used once, and then for a matter of a few yards only, but was struck with the idea. I recollect thinking that it was a "funny" way of swimming, and more as a joke than anything else, I used to "splash" my way back to the steps after taking a dive from the board, every now and then receiving some words of encouragement from Farmer to persevere.'[8]

The *Sydney Mail* marvelled that within a couple of weeks of adopting the crawl, men who could do 100 yards in 1 minute 20 seconds had reduced their time to 1 minute 8 seconds.[9] However, the crawl had not convinced everyone. Freddie Lane and George Read continued to develop their own double overarm strokes on independent lines. Natator was bewildered by it: 'How the term "crawl" applies is beyond my comprehension—it is anything but a crawl. "Propeller" would be a better name for it, as both feet are used like so many blades, the forcing of which against the water gives the momentum. It is a very exhausting method of propulsion. Dick Cavill's limit at top speed is 100yds.'[10] The president of the English National Amateur Swimming Association described Cavill's action as 'a lot of spray and a little bit of Cavill. One might be pardoned for mistaking him for a screw propeller that had received a galvanic shock.'[11] However, such was the impact of the crawl that in 1902, the Australian Swimming Association considered reducing the standard times to gain an honour certificate for 100 yards from 67 to 65 seconds as the possibility of more men breaking the one-minute barrier loomed.

***

The 1901–02 Australasian swimming championships were held in Wanganui, New Zealand, in February 1902. Healy was not part of the New South Wales contingent, which consisted of Lane, Cavill and Read, despite having set an Australasian record of 24 2/5 seconds for 45 yards at a club handicap meet on 12 February. He proved it was no flash in the pan a week later in an exhibition race against visiting Queenslander Frank Gailey, who was *en route* to New Zealand, covering the trip in 24 1/5 seconds, more than a second in front of Gailey's 25 2/5 seconds.

Although the 45 yards was not a championship event, Healy's explosive power had pundits watching him with great interest. Prior to the NSW 100-yard championship in March 1902, *The Arrow* predicted that Lane was a 'shot-bird' for the title, but two others were also in contention—Healy, and Bob Craig of the Mort's Dock club. Despite looking 'big and gross' at the start of the season, Craig had beaten Healy in the lead-off leg of the 1902 Flying Squadron championship on 19 March, and excitement about the impending clash was increased by rumours that Lane, who was bound for the British championships the following week, would not start, sending Healy to equal favourite for his first individual honour. True to speculation, Lane did not appear—some reasoned it was a generous move to allow his clubmate to win the title, but as Natator pointed out, 'How [Healy] could have been expected to account for Bob after their race in the first hundred of the Flying Squadron blue riband only a week before needs some explaining.'[12] Lane himself may have been afraid of facing 'the dangerous young boilermaker' Craig after losing to him in the 220-yard championship of 1902. Nonetheless, Lane's absence did little to aid Healy's quest for an individual title. Craig won the hundred by four yards in 62 seconds, primarily through his superior turning ability. Healy flew out to a quick lead, but Craig overhauled him before the second turn and was never headed after that.

Healy took the defeat and his lack of inclusion for the New Zealand and England tours greatly to heart. While he could only watch his rivals stroking up and down as he passed the pool at Woolloomooloo on his daily trudge to the office, hard asphalt beneath his feet, collar and tie tight at his throat, Healy now spied an opportunity to make up lost ground. It was the winter of 1902, when the average Sydney temperature dropped from balmy to nippy and many elite swimmers, thin-skinned and lean, abandoned the water for flannel bags and hot whiskey at their local watering hole. Cecil Healy, however, was not a Kurkulla boy for nothing. Winters on the Southern Highlands saw temperatures hover in single digits for months at a time, snow scudding across the playing fields and frost turning the water in the wash-stands to solid ice. Now, while his rivals toasted their toes and nursed their chilblains, Healy flung himself into winter training, battling through the grey waves thundering over the seawall into the Domain pool, stroking out fierce laps in the half-dark of the short, chilly days. Victories by Lane and Cavill at the English championships added further impetus to Healy's efforts, and he added dumbbells, skipping and sprinting to his already gruelling regime.

Thus, when the 1902–03 season opened on 1 October 1902, *The Sydney Morning Herald* happily reported that Healy had 'already considerably improved in speed', while also taking a shot at Bob Craig, who 'refused to train properly' despite having the potential to hold his own with the Australian champions[13]. While Freddie Lane held every State record from 90 to 220 yards, including the Australasian record of 60 4/5 seconds for the 100 yards, Healy's hard winter training paid off immediately. On 5

November 1902, Healy equalled Lane's record for 90 yards, recording a blistering 53 seconds at a club handicap meet. 'Cecil Healy threatens to make things warm over the sprint distances for Cavill and Lane when they come back', predicted *The Referee*[14].

However, Healy's own coach, George Farmer, had a shock in store for his entire stable of East Sydney stars. In March 1901, a boys' 100-yard race at Bronte featured a teenager recently arrived from the Solomon Islands who, despite his elfin stature, romped away with the race, winning by a dozen yards. The victory came thanks to his use of a never-before-seen variation on Cavill's swimming style that combined a rotating arm stroke with a parallel (scissor) kick of both legs. On the shore, George Farmer, unable to contain his excitement, bellowed, 'Look at that kid crawling!'[15] Farmer was quick to sweep the boy, Alick Wickham, under his wing at East Sydney. Such was Farmer's certainty regarding the lad's potential that by late 1902, *The Arrow* proclaimed, 'George Farmer, finding the 'white trash' among his protégés not quite up to the sprint powers of that youthful South Sea islander, has [thrown] them over and taken up the lad from the coral, coconut and banana-producing clime.'[16]

In 1902, Sydney's swimming elite were upstaged by a teenager from the Solomon Islands, Alick Wickham (right), whose addition to the East Sydney stable forced Cecil Healy (left) into an even more punishing physical regime as he sought an edge over his rivals. [Source: Northern Beaches Council/Manly Library Local Studies Collection: image ID: man01880].

The first really big carnival of the 1902–03 season, on 29 November 1902, included the Eastern Districts 100-yard premiership, with Cavill (now swimming for the Pyrmont club), schoolboy sensation Claude Corbett, Bob Craig and Healy—who had been dead-heating with his clubmates in training—all in the field. However, the big guns were upstaged by Alick Wickham, who Farmer had been keeping under wraps until now. Wickham swam a quick-fire 66 yards in 38 4/5 seconds, defeating every one of his credentialed rivals and prompting Natator to declare, 'Wickham will ... be a champion when he matures a bit more'[17].

Healy was forced to add a new element to his already punishing fitness regime as he sought an edge that would boost him above both his traditional rivals and the upstart Wickham. Healy, Lane and Reg 'Snowy' Baker had been members of the East Sydney water polo team since 1898 under the eagle eye of Harold Healy, and the physicality of that game provided them with significant cardiovascular and muscular conditioning. Now Healy's good friend Baker, who had played amateur rugby union at Warrigals but had moved to Eastern Suburbs for the 1903 season, persuaded Healy to join him there. Healy did so, hoping the combativeness and endurance inherent in rugby would both improve his performances in the pool and overcome the anxiety that still strangled his best competitive efforts. The blond Baker was one of Australia's most versatile sportsmen. He swam and played water polo for East Sydney, represented Australia as a rugby half-back, was a championship club rower and in 1902, won middleweight and heavyweight boxing championships in both NSW and Victoria. Boxing was part of the fitness regime for swimmers at East Sydney, with Lane and Healy both enthusiastic participants, but it was Baker who boxed for Australia in England in 1906 and at the 1908 London Olympics.

The extended and demanding physical regime again paid off for Healy. East Sydney set a new Flying Squadron race record in December 1902, defeating Cavill's Pyrmont squad by 17 yards and lowering their own world record of 5 minutes 22 3/5 seconds by four seconds, earning them the title for a third consecutive year. In 1903, the 100-yard championship of NSW was scheduled to be swum at Goulburn on the southern tablelands on 26 January, the Anniversary Day public holiday[18]. East Sydney's representative trials on 18 January saw Healy defeat Wickham by 1 1/2 yards in a personal best of 61 1/2 seconds[19]. Among the jubilant spectators was the fifth Healy to swim for East Sydney, Cecil's younger brother Reg, who had joined the club late in 1902. Natator praised Healy's victory: 'Apart from the time, the great merit of this achievement is the defeat of the young South Sea Islander, whom we all know is a top-notcher over the distance. With Dick Cavill's hand still not quite right, it seems to me that Cecil must have a chance of annexing the big sprint.'[20]

Cavill, as the commentator had observed, had been injured in a bizarre recreational shooting accident in which a bullet had passed right through his hand, and he seemed in serious doubt for the championship, leaving the way open at last—perhaps—for Healy. However, in a blow to Healy's hopes, not only did Cavill recover in time to smash Fred Lane's world record for 120 yards on 22 January, but an innocuous cut on Healy's own hand turned septic, causing a violent swelling in his entire arm. He was forced to withdraw from the Goulburn championship and, humiliatingly, hand his place to Wickham.

The media mourned his loss, *The Arrow* even writing Wickham off before the race was swum: 'On last Saturday's showing, (Healy) would have done much better than Wickham is likely to do.'[21] However, the machinations did not end there. The day before the race, Wickham came down with such a severe cold that he couldn't make the trip to Goulburn, and it was Healy, poisoned hand or not, who took the train south. As it turned out, none of it mattered much. In front of an overflowing crowd, Cavill won the hundred by two body-lengths from Bob Craig, with a still-feverish Healy half a yard behind in third place. In the miniscule 27-yard pool, Healy had flown out to lead until the 54-yard mark before his weakness on turns allowed Cavill to displace him. The slow winning time of 62 1/5 seconds raised eyebrows among the pundits until it was pointed out that swimming in a freshwater pool, with its much-reduced buoyancy, was a new experience for most of the field.

Despite the result, *The Arrow* was quick to praise Healy's efforts: 'The hundred proved an easy thing for Dick Cavill, but Cecil Healy swam well enough to indicate that, but for his misfortune in the early part of the week, he would have pushed the champion a lot closer.'

FOUR

SOMETHING SENSATIONAL EVERY SATURDAY

'When this yokel comes maundering,
Whetting his hacker,
I shall run before him,
Diffusing the civilest odors
Out of geraniums and unsmelled flowers.
It will check him.'

—Wallace Stevens, *The Plot Against the Giant*

✳✳✳

Small boys came running, dogs barked hysterically and men emerged from sheds and workshops, wiping their hands on oily rags, to see this new marvel.

The children surrounded him as though he were a deity, peering and grabbing and pawing, and Healy had to guide small hands away from hot engine parts before blisters became the order of the day. Mothers scolded and tried to drag the small fry away, but the men lingered, awed, as Healy removed his leather helmet and goggles. When he held out a gloved hand to shake that of the nearest man, there was always a pause before the fellow could tear his fascinated gaze away from the motorcycle to accept his handshake. The bike was an inspired piece of marketing.

It was 1904, and Cecil Healy had been elevated from clerk to salesman at Richard Hornsby & Sons, a position that saw him ranging across the agricultural plains of NSW from the northern rivers to the southern borders, promoting and demonstrating the firm's patented products. Hornsby's had branched out from steam-driven machinery to tractors running on crude oil, and these great workhorses could accomplish everything the steam tractor did without the same demands in terms of fuel and water. The company's stationary combustion engines, the world's first to run on heavy oil, now provided electricity to the Taj Mahal and the Statue of Liberty, and had powered Marconi's first transatlantic radio broadcast in 1901. Now Hornsby-Akroyd engines, which could be towed to virtually any location on a farm or station by a team of horses, were at the forefront of Australian agricultural expansion. Tireless flywheels operated pumps to draw water into previously arid areas. They powered sawmills in timbered country, obviating the need for hauling huge logs through steep terrain and drove huge new electric stands in shearing sheds, bringing the era of hand-shears to a close. Mighty leather belts drove threshers, chaff-cutters and harvesters under the baking Australian summer sun, oblivious to conditions that would have exhausted men and horses hours beforehand.

Hornsby oil engines, such as this model pictured in 1902, were used to pump water for early irrigation schemes on Australian farms. [Source: State Library of NSW: At Work and Play 03910.1E no.1696994].

As a representative of the new petroleum age, Healy was, aptly, given a motorcycle on which to make his journeys. The first cars had only arrived in Australia at the turn of the century and motorised transport was still rare in the cities, while in regional areas it was almost unknown. Healy's machine, with its wide, sweeping handlebars and distinctive *potato-potato* sound, was a show-stopper on the farms. It looked for all the world like a bicycle—it even had pedals with which to crank the engine—but with its thin fuel tank bolted under the crossbar and a small clip-on motor, it could travel at up to 35 miles per hour. The bike ate up the quiet outback gravel roads at ten times the speed of a walking man, and Healy was regularly flagged down by shearers, farmhands and wide-eyed men of the land, all anxious to see this new phenomenon up close.

Healy juggled swim training with a demanding day job that saw him travelling country NSW as a farm machinery salesman. Pictured is an early motorcycle (c.1900) typical of that on which Healy travelled. [Source: State Library of NSW: Family and holiday album 1899–1908/Arthur D. Whitling. IE no.3191604].

Healy loved the long hours on the bike, despite the hard little seat and painful lack of travel in the suspension. Dry, golden-brown Australia rolled past him in an ever-changing panorama. The sky was huge, a flawless blue dome unbroken by city spires. He clattered over silver rivers and their attendant timber bridges, through small towns with wide, dusty streets and timber awnings, occasionally took wrong turns on unmarked gravel roads, but always met some helpful local who would both point the way and detain him for half an hour in sheer fascination at the sight of the stranger and his newfangled machine. The squatters and graziers took to him, for Healy was a young man who listened more than he talked. He was humble in their presence, deferring to their experience of the harsh seasons and unforgiving terrain, but he was also quietly confident in the contribution the marvels pictured in his brochures could make to their productivity. It was a combination that was difficult to resist.

All this time away from the water, roving the back roads of rural Australia, might have been expected to impact negatively upon a swimmer, but for Cecil Healy, the effect was the opposite. In the pool, the year 1904 finally brought the breakthrough Healy had struggled for nine years to achieve.

The year promised to be a torrid one for sprint swimming. 1904 was only one week old when Freddie Lane swam 58 4/5 seconds for the 100 yards in a trial for the East Sydney Flying Squadron team. This extraordinary effort was only 1/5 of a second outside Dick Cavill's 1902 world record and made Lane just the second man in history to break 60 seconds for the hundred.

Fiercely covetous of his place at the head of Australian swimming, Cavill was quick to extract revenge. The Flying Squadron championship on 10 January 1904 saw Lane and Cavill go head-to-head in the final leg. Lane's East Sydney teammates, including Healy, had set him up with a 20-yard lead over his Pyrmont rival, but Cavill rose magnificently to the occasion and closed to within 12 yards, an unofficial clock recording his swim at 56 3/5 seconds, two seconds under his own world record. Meanwhile, in winning the championship, the East Sydney team of Wickham, Healy, Lane and brothers Harold and Snowy Baker set a new world record for the event of 5 minutes 12 2/5 seconds, 5 1/2 seconds better than their record from December 1902.

While his sub-57-second swim was unratified, Cavill made his kingship official just a week later at an invitational 100-yard handicap at Farmer's Baths on 16 January 1904. Hundreds of fans swarmed in and many more clambered onto adjacent hills, fences and other vantage points to see the 50- and 100-yard world record holders Wickham and Cavill in the first heat. Cavill out-dived Wickham, but the pair strained neck and neck for most of the race, approaching the first turn in 23 seconds, almost a second under world record pace. Twenty yards from home, Cavill stretched ahead and was roared home to victory by the overflowing crowd. His time of 58 seconds flat was a new world best, while Wickham had clocked 59 seconds, his own first official swim under the minute barrier, and all of this just in a heat. Cavill airily skipped the final to focus on the state 500-yard championship, which he won easily in a new Australasian record time, while Wickham and Healy lined up side by side for the 100-yard decider. Wickham missed the start horribly and, seeing only Healy's wake before him, didn't over-exert himself. Healy, who, as *The Sunday Times* properly expressed it, 'has had nothing near the good fortune he deserves at the game', won the race in 59 4/5 seconds, becoming the fourth man in history to break 60 seconds and finally winning a 100-yard title in his own right[1]. Australia now boasted the only four swimmers in the world to have broken the minute in the blue-ribbon sprint.

The floodgates of Healy's potential were at last open. Just four weeks later, on 21 February 1904, during a heat of the 150-yard East Sydney Team Relay Race at the Domain, Healy broke his first world record. He covered the first 50 yards in the remarkable time of 25 1/5 seconds, 2/5 of a second faster than Wickham's world record, and stopped the clock more than a second under Fred Lane's world 150-yard record time. Unfortunately, the performance was not ratified, as the event timekeepers were not officially appointed by the NSW Amateur Swimming Association (ASA). Nonetheless, representative invitations began to flow in. When Lane and Cavill received overtures to visit the Western Australian SwimmingAssociation—virtually an international tour—Healy was also included on the guest list, although none of them ended up making the long trip west. A greater honour came on 2 March, however, when Cavill and Healy were nominated for the 1904 Australasian Olympic team. The prohibitive cost of international travel meant the 1904 St. Louis Games were destined to include few, if any, Australian representatives. The Amateur Athletic Union of Australasia had already informed the

Games directors that Australia and New Zealand would not contest the football, cricket, cycling, rowing, baseball, lacrosse, golf or fencing at the Games, but the NSW ASA were willing to send both Cavill and Healy, despite the staggering cost of £120 per man. Once again, however, neither man attended in the end; in fact only four countries—Austria, Germany, Hungary and the USA—sent swimmers to the Games, although the Queensland ASA partly sponsored the attendance of Frank Gailey, whose efforts garnered three silver medals and one bronze medal. However, after becoming a naturalised citizen of the USA in 1906, Gailey remains listed in the official Olympic records as an American.

The long hours spent in the open air on his motorcycle, far from miserly stopwatches and self-imposed pressure to succeed in the pool, seemed to clear Healy's head and allow the fulfilment of his enormous potential. His victories acted as a partial antidote to his crippling pre-race anxiety and, fit and physically mature at 23 years of age, Healy now regarded all rivals as lawful prey, and was party to the greatest 100-yard race in history to that point on 6 March 1904. The NSW 100-yard championship at his home pool in the Domain attracted more than 1,300 spectators, with hundreds more turned away. Cavill, the titleholder, and Wickham, the aspirant, both took a flying start and streaked away down the first 45 yards, but Healy overhauled the pair and touched first at the turn, the great spray and wash of the trio causing waves of excitement among the huge crowd. Only Cavill's superior turning ability saw him draw Healy in and win by 1 1/2 yards, with Healy second and Wickham four feet further back in third place. Cavill's time was 58 1/5 seconds and Healy's 59 seconds in what *The Sunday Times* deemed 'a magnificent struggle'[2]. Healy went under 59 seconds the following week in front of 2,000 spectators, again at the Domain, in an exhibition race against the visiting champion from New Zealand Harry Creaghe, who could only match him for a few strokes. Healy's swim wasn't officially timed, but the media excitedly hailed it as 58 3/5 seconds.

That same meet heralded the advent of another Australian rising star. In the half-mile championship of Australasia, superstar Cavill and Olympian Frank Gailey were joined on the start line by 17-year-old Barney Kieran. The youngster, small, freckled and unassuming, thrashed the incumbent pair by a dozen yards and broke the 880-yard world record with a time of 11 minutes 29 1/4 seconds, in the process also smashing the 400-, 500-, 600- and 800-yard world records. Kieran's coming was described as 'little short of meteoric' by *The Referee*[3]. The boy's upbringing, as the sixth child of an Irish sailor, had been a harsh one. At age 13, he was labelled a delinquent and committed to the nautical reformatory ship *Sobraon,* having 'refused to attend school or obey his mother'[4]. While these training ships were intended to isolate bad boys from society and often taught harsh lessons about discipline away from the prying eyes of authorities, life aboard the *Sobraon* turned Barney Kieran around, for it was here that he learned to swim. Swimming was a necessary skill for life at sea, but Kieran was so enamoured of the water that he swam twice a day for the sheer love of it and soon began to take responsibility for other aspects of his life, working as an apprentice carpenter aboard the ship and earning a reputation for honesty and trustworthiness. In 1904, his first year swimming for the Sobraon Club (under the attentive eye of coach Bob Craig), he finished second to Dick Cavill four times before his record-breaking victory in the half-mile. The following year, he would win six State and six Australasian freestyle titles, equal Freddie Lane's 220-yard freestyle world record and set new world marks for the 200, 300, 400, 500 and 1000 yards and the mile.

Technical difficulties and outright sabotage cost Healy victories in both of the final major meets in the 1903–04 season. The final round of the Australian championships was held on 19 March 1904 at Bondi. One enthusiast assured *The Arrow* that Healy had been swimming 57 seconds for the hundred in training and it was that prospect, in addition to another head-to-head between Cavill and Kieran, which drew 2,000 witnesses to the tidal pool on the famous beach. Cavill, however, did not live up to his billing. Attempting to land an early psychological blow on young Kieran, he had overtaxed himself at a mid-week meet trying for records in the 220 and 440 yards and half-mile, and since then had been unable to sleep or keep food down. Cavill actually withdrew from the meet, leaving Kieran to win the mile and break the world record by 10 seconds. Healy, likewise, was unable to give the crowd what they wanted in the Australasian 100-yard championship. Wickham beat Healy by half a yard with Gailey a body length behind. Healy led at the first turn, but down the final stretch, with no lane ropes to constrain him, Wickham swerved from the shore side of the pool in front of Gailey to get at Healy. Swimmers in 1904 did not benefit from the sterile, controlled environment of modern competitive racing, with enclosed freshwater pools, wave-suppressing lane ropes and physical separation from their opponents. Healy and his rivals, competing in ocean baths with no dividing lanes, had to simultaneously battle the elements, each other and the clock, usually under handicap conditions, which often made for fast, furious and physical racing. Momentarily checked by Wickham's deviation, Healy made a great final effort and his head was level with Wickham's shoulder when they touched, but the victory and the coveted national title went to his clubmate.

The last race of the season was the East Sydney 100-yard club championship on 2 April 1904. 'Nobody can have a chance in this event against Cecil Healy and Alick Wickham', declared Natator, 'and I wouldn't be surprised if the former reversed the result of the Australasian hundred and led the black at the end'[5]. Wickham, however, left Healy standing off the start and although Healy had caught him by the first turn, his technical weakness on the push-off continued to cost him races, notwithstanding his final gallant lunge for the line. Wickham had to equal his personal best and swim 59 seconds flat to win.

***

'It is an axiom that every sport has its day and the day of swimming is evidently with us.'

'A Boom in Swimming', *The Sydney Mail and New South Wales Advertiser* (1898)

The decade 1895–1905 can rightly claim the birth of modern swimming, with three of the greatest 'crawlers' in history now in the water: Cavill, Healy and Wickham.

The advent of Alick Wickham had drawn even greater attention to the use of the crawl stroke to not only swim faster, but also to swim faster over greater distances. Pacific Islanders had a long history of using overarm strokes and a scissor kick to swim—for one cannot catch a wave in the surf using breaststroke—and these movements were known in the indigenous language as *tuppa tup'pala*. Healy acknowledged the leading role Wickham had played in pioneering the crawl in Australia, observing admiringly, '[When] Alick Wickham made his appearance, lo and behold! He was a finished "crawler" ... Who taught him? The Cavills? Certainly not. He could only speak a word or two of English at this time and was exceedingly shy. He was a true son of Nature, and swam one of Nature's strokes, handed down to him from his forefathers, viz. the "crawl".'[6] Wickham, whose great-granddaughter Tracey Wickham won world championships in the 400- and 800-metre freestyle in 1978, introduced a straight-legged six-beat kick to the evolving stroke as voracious eyes turned to use of the crawl to conquer longer distances, theorising that such a kick would aid buoyancy and reduce the fatigue generally associated with use of the stroke.

Now a committed student of the crawl technique, Healy made his own contribution to the speed and efficiency of the stroke. Submerging the face while swimming had been frowned upon since the Middle Ages, when communicable diseases meant people avoided any kind of immersion of the head in public water sources. Strokes such as the breaststroke evolved through the arms reaching forward to brush away anything harmful that might enter a swimmer's mouth. However, the immersion of the face required during the crawl made breathing a continued challenge to a swimmer moving with their head down and arms rapidly rotating. Lifting the head disrupted the stroke, and breathing infrequently, often after eight strokes or more, created oxygen debt and fatigue, which rapidly degraded the stroke quality. The big innovation came from Healy himself, who developed breathing to the side in synchrony with the limb movements. 'I devoted all my energy, thought and perseverance to find out some way to overcome the breathing difficulty; and one day hit on the knack', he explained. 'Until I could breathe regularly, I argued with myself that it (the crawl) was only a freak stroke and unnatural.'[7] To avoid throwing the head back, Healy advocated a rolling movement from the hips that naturally elevated the elbow and allowed space for the head to turn to the side. The concomitant increase in efficiency and conservation of energy meant the crawl suddenly became a viable proposition over much greater distances than the 50 or 100 yards it was previously limited to. Healy claimed he could swim a mile or more by breathing at every stroke in the hollow made by the hand's action in the water. However, he also recognised that his own seemingly radical technique of side breathing was not original; the 'swimming indigenes' of the South Sea islands had been observed to breath unilaterally by turning the head sideways as the arm reached full extension.

The crawl now suited Healy's physical capabilities precisely. The South Australian *Chronicle* enthused, 'Nothing is seen but a huge splash tearing across the bath, much like a wounded alligator or a stricken whale, and the eye can scarcely discern the human element which causes all the commotion. Obviously great strength and muscular development are necessary to keep up so vigorous a stroke for any distance, and all the chief exponents are models of muscular development.'[8] The short, rapid, overarm action of the early crawlers meant the principal impetus came from the upper body, and Healy's was a stocky, powerful frame, broad-shouldered and strong-armed. Dick Cavill had advocated keeping the legs on top of the water, more to prevent the limbs from dragging than to supply motive power, and trained by tying his legs together and practising with the arms only. Healy's style, in contrast, used a well-defined two kicks to each cycle of the arms. 'Cecil Healy preached law and order in the leg kick', asserted legendary Australian swim coach Forbes Carlile. 'He wrote that Cavill's stroke was a 'crude arrangement consisting largely of splash (and) unattractive in every way'. In 1905, Healy regarded the trailing, independent action of the legs 'an old-fashioned method, and his own heavy two-beat kick would become the accepted technique of the Australian Crawl and adopted by future champions including Fanny Durack and Bill Longworth.'[9]

***

Cecil Healy, part salesman, part sportsman, was a most unusual juxtaposition in Australian sport, a serious young man in neat coat and collar who would kneel in the soft, ploughed earth to demonstrate the motive power of the

Hornsby engine before returning to the city to shed his cloak and set a record or two in Sydney's blue water. Despite the ongoing burden of his business responsibilities, Healy charged into the 1904–05 swim season with the same zeal with which he'd finished the previous one.

His technical knowledge of the crawl saw him appointed as an honorary instructor at East Sydney alongside George Farmer. The season was only a month old when, at his home baths, Healy blazed through 100 yards in 58 4/5 seconds, his first official swim under 59 seconds and within 4/5 of a second of Cavill's world record. Starting from scratch, he'd overhauled every one of his rivals but one, giving some as much as 22 seconds start, in what Natator described as a 'hair-raising performance' so early in the year. 'Cec', the commentator was also quick to point out, had already covered himself in glory the week before, swimming 50 yards in 25 seconds dead. 'Truly it looks as if we even now have a man well up to requirements over the shorter distances', he wrote, 'if (as it is rumoured) Dick Cavill would shed the mantle of amateurism this season.'[10]

The aforementioned Cavill had visited Natator over the winter, 'looking round as a ball', to inform him he did not intend to swim that season, but instead to seek employment as a professional coach in New Zealand. Dick's diet largely consisted of ginger beer, ice cream and brandy snaps, and Natator observed wryly, 'He let himself get so very fat during the winter that he doesn't consider there is enough inducement to cause him to enter upon a stiff preparation now.'[11]

Alick Wickham was also off the scene, having returned to the Solomon Islands for family reasons, leaving Healy with an unencumbered charge at the world record. It teetered still more precariously on 14 November 1904, when Healy used a heat swim to thrash out 58 1/5 seconds in a full-frontal assault on Cavill's bastion. This was followed by 25 seconds for the 50 yards in his heat. That event's world record may have been under serious threat had Healy not been interfered with in the final. 'His third successive weekend hair-raiser ... Cecil Healy is swimming splendidly and the sprint championship should be his this season', exulted the papers[12].

The public were now expecting something sensational from Healy every Saturday, and the 100 yards world record may well have been his on 27 November. During a club handicap, he blasted through the first lap in 25 seconds dead and came home in 57 3/5 seconds, and repeated this astonishing effort in the final. However, inexplicably, Healy swam both races in trunks, rather than the neck-to-knee woollen costume required by the ASA for all official events. These suits could weigh as much as nine pounds when wet, and belted trunks were also required to be worn on the outside for modesty purposes. The ASA regulations had been briefly relaxed in 1902, prompting a shocked rebuke from Natator: 'The new rule about wearing trunks inside the costume must be called back: it won't work at all. The old practice (trunks outside) was infinitely more decent.'[13] Thus, the requirement for a woollen suit was reinstated, and as a result, Healy's 1904 watch-breaking performances could not be ratified. While many in the press were critical of his inexplicable decision, Natator wished Healy well: 'He is a good fellow in every way, and nothing but sheer right-down hard practice under circumstances less than favourable has placed him on the swimming pinnacle he now occupies.'[14] *The Arrow* was rather more sniffy, proclaiming that full costume made at least two seconds difference to a swimmer over 100 yards[15].

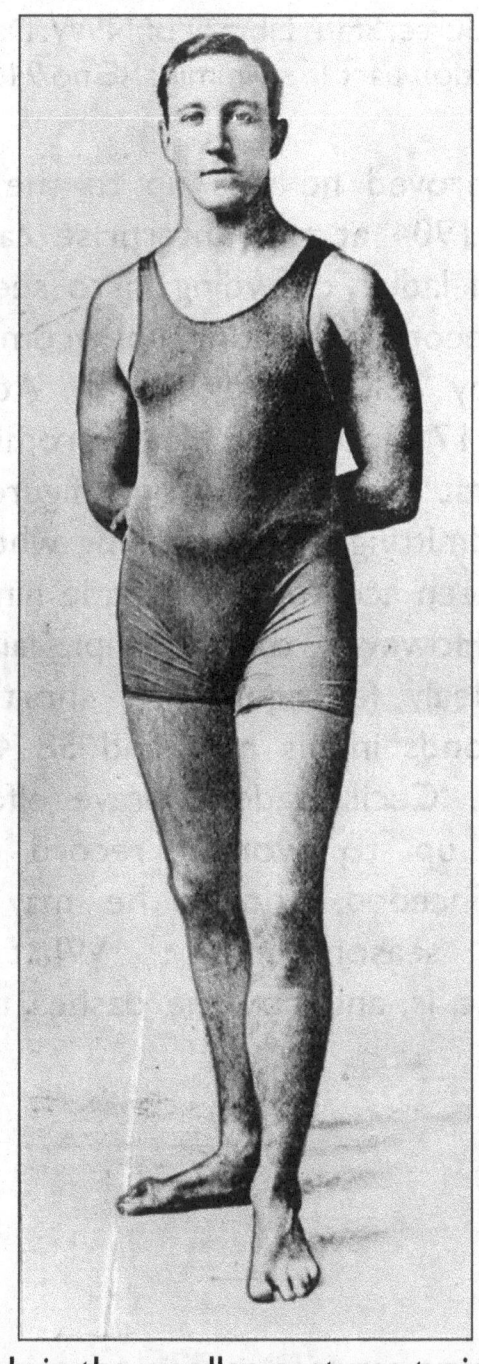

Cecil Healy in the woollen costume typical of male swimmers prior to World War I. A pair of trunks was usually required to be worn over the suit for modesty purposes. [Source: State Library of NSW: Davis Sporting Collection part II: swimming. IE no.946050].

Healy proved he was up to the task on 3 December 1904 at the Enterprise carnival, with hundreds of ladies crowding in to see him swim 58 4/5 seconds, beating newcomer Harold Hardwick by half a body length. At his home carnival on 17 December, Healy promised a 'bold bid to burst up the existing figures for the hundred', admitting that swimming where his best times had been accomplished made him feel more confident. However, the attempt failed. In full costume, Healy fell agonisingly short, swimming 58 1/5 seconds in his heat and 58 4/5 seconds in the final. 'Cecil made a brave effort, but he isn't quite up to world's record mark yet', Natator conceded, 'though he may get there before the season ends ... What a speedy customer he is, and how he dashes through the water!'[16]

ENTERPRISE SWIMMING CLUB.

20th Annual

Championship Carnival

Farmer's Domain Baths.

Saturday, 3rd Dec., 1904, at 3 p.m.

ADMISSION ONE SHILLING.

CECIL HEALY, East Sydney's Crack Sprinter.

PROGRAMME:

CLUB EVENTS:
- 45 Yards Junior Handicap—Trophy.
- 65 Yards General Handicap—two prizes—Entrance Fee, 6d.
- **440 Yards Championship**—Attempt on Club Record.

INTER-CLUB EVENTS:
- **100 YARDS INVITATION HANDICAP**—(best swimmers competing.)
- 50 Yards Inter-Club Handicap—three prizes—Entrance Fee, 1/-
- 65 Yards Handicap for Members of Amateur Athletic Association.
- High Diving Competition—one prize—Entrance Fee, 6d. (one dive from each of three heights on high dive platform).
- Natatorial High Jump Competition—one prize—Entrance Fee, 6d. (Highest Jump or Dive off spring-board over handle the winner). Attempt on Record by an unknown quantity.

DISPLAYS:
- Wrestling on Spring-board by Masters of the Art.
- Shooting the Chute in Fancy Costume—Prize for best costume.
- **Farce**—Neptune preventing sailors crossing the line.

Entries for all Events close with Hon. Secretary at Sports Club, on Saturday, 26th November, 1904, at 9 p.m.

W. R. COATES,
Captain.

F. C. BILZINGER,
Hon. Sec. Sports Club Hunter Street.

Hundreds of spectators, including many ladies, crowded the Domain Baths in December 1904 as Healy made an assault on Dick Cavill's 100-yard world record. [Source:

Northern Beaches Council/Manly Library Local Studies Collection. Series: 2010-03(49), image ID: 1100006570].

Wickham, meanwhile, had returned from the Solomons at the end of December, announcing that he was going to stay in Australia and learn boat-building. He had lived in Sydney since he was a child, he explained, and now could not reconcile himself back to island life. He had also been laid low with fever while in the islands and was still not completely recovered, with the state 100-yard championship just a fortnight away.

Healy (sprints), Kieran (distance) and Wickham (breaststroke) were selected as the NSW representatives for the Australasian championships in Victoria in January 1905. Healy had the edge over the labouring Wickham, besting him in East Sydney's 50-yard handicap in 25 2/5 seconds on 14 January, just 4/5 of a second outside Wickham's world record of 24 3/5 seconds. Two days later, Healy won the NSW 100-yard championship in the tidal pool at Balmain, one of the greatest races ever seen in Australia, with the first five finishers all going under the standard time of 65 seconds. On paper, Healy's winning time of 61 1/10 seconds was astonishingly slow, but there was a significant swell in the pool and a fresh nor'easter whistling into the faces of the swimmers[17].

That summer of 1904–05 saw the seventh and youngest member of the Healy clan join the dynasty at East Sydney. The sixth brother, John Henry, had joined the club in 1903 and established a reputation as a talented high diver, and now 15-year-old Eric Healy, a student at Double Bay Public School, also enlisted with the East Sydneyites. Enthusiastically described in the press as 'one of the most promising young athletes in Sydney', young Healy had the best batting and bowling averages for his school cricket team and had distinguished himself as a rover in the Double Bay schools' Australian Rules football competition. However, true to form, Eric Healy was most at home in the pool. In 1905, he won the East Sydney 150-yard All Schools' Handicap, the Eastern Districts Public Schools' 100-yard championship and was a member of the team that won the 200-yard Team Relay Championship of the Eastern District Schools. With seven brothers on the books—unprecedented in Australian swimming—the East Sydney Club seemed almost top-heavy with overachieving Healys.

In setting a good example for his little brother, Cecil Healy ensured his preparation for the 1905 Australasian championships was immaculate by equalling Dick Cavill's world record for 100 yards at Bondi on 22 January.

Drawn in the fourth heat of the Randwick Plate, a 100-yard handicap for swimmers with a best time of 70 seconds or better, Healy had Barney Kieran right alongside him, and despite missing the turn and then having Kieran cut right across him, Healy flew home through the choppy waves to win by a yard in 58 seconds, equalling Cavill's record after having so often threatened to do so. *The Sunday Times* declared, 'Many a time [Healy's] friends have gone to swimming carnivals to see him accomplish something remarkable, but until Saturday they were disappointed.'[18]

Healy and Kieran then departed on the longest journey that either had ever undertaken, six hundred miles south to the Victorian capital of Melbourne, where the Australasian championships were scheduled for 28 January 1905. Healy now realised that he knew very little about Barney Kieran away from the pool. At 24 years of age, he was far more worldly than his teenage companion, and through both his work and his schooling, had seen much more of Australia than poor ship-bound Barney, who had never set foot outside of Sydney. Taking the boy under his wing during the long three-day journey, Healy pointed out the grandeur of the Southern Highlands and regaled him with tales of steam tractors pulling whole teams of bogged horses out of marshland. Kieran, in turn, spoke of the thing he knew best and missed most: his family. His father, named Patrick just like Healy's father, had been killed in a rail accident when Barney was just five years old, the youngest of six, and he and his siblings had been raised by an unhappy mother and reluctant stepfather. His only brother, who called himself Joe Costa, was also a reform boy, and had risen to renown as a heavyweight prize-fighter, but the only escape from the crowded family cottage for the undersized Barney was truancy, and he roamed the city streets with his mother's frustrated screams of retribution echoing after him. At age 13, Barney had been arrested and sent to the *Sobraon*—one of 5,000 boys sentenced to the training ships on Sydney Harbour between 1867 and 1911[19].

Healy, who had lost his own father as a child and been similarly adrift among a crowd of siblings, was touched by both the boy's humility and his resilience. Just weeks before, the *Evening News* had feted Kieran as the conqueror of Dick Cavill, a champion with a mortgage on every swimming record over 220 yards, but now, as the train rocked slowly on through the dry Victorian countryside, Healy saw not a great adversary, not a kid whose crooked course had just robbed him of a world record, but a lonely and neglected boy who had been locked up as an adult by way of punishment for a child's crime. While Kieran was philosophical about the *Sobraon* and his new career as a ship's carpenter—he was even learning to read—Healy was assailed by an empathy for the young man that he would not have thought possible just days before. His own addled childhood—being shunted from luxury to poverty, hurried away from his brothers and hidden in a highlands school—now seemed positively fortunate. Healy had been protected from much of the family shame and fallout, whereas Barney Kieran had been protected from nothing. The emotional isolation that had kept Healy at arm's length from all but a few—for in their privileged lives, even his good friends Snowy Baker and Fred Lane could never understand Healy's deep internal struggle for acceptance—now gave a little. For the first time in his life, Healy had perhaps found someone on his own wavelength.

***

With both Healy and Kieran qualifying for the national 100-yard final, Melbourne was in a ferment to see what the pair could accomplish, and the race on 28 January 1905 was billed as 'the greatest ever witnessed in Victorian waters'. Hegarty's Baths at St. Kilda, a vast tidal enclosure, seemed perfectly suited to Healy, as the 100-yard race would require no turns. Healy occupied a favoured position on the extreme left of the field, away from the incoming waves, with Kieran near the centre and Alick Wickham and Dan Gailey on the right. Wickham charged off the start like a lit firecracker, drawing a roar from the 2,000 spectators. At 50 yards, Healy and Gailey had joined a titanic three-way struggle for advantage, with Kieran washed back into fourth place. It was only 15 yards from the post when Healy, his huge brown shoulders lifting out of the water like a breaching dolphin, drew away from Wickham and then, remarkably, increased his pace even further to win by three-quarters of a length, equalling his own world record in a time of 58 seconds flat[20]. This was Healy's maiden national championship, and *The Argus* instantly proclaimed him the foremost sprint swimmer in the world. Healy's time was the first sub-60-second swim in Victorian history. In fact, that state had not produced a swimmer capable of beating 70 seconds for the 100 yards until a fortnight before the big race, when 16-year-old Frank Fitts swam 69 4/5 seconds. Young Fitts then took almost five seconds off that time when he went under 65 seconds in the final.

    Kieran, while finishing only fifth in the hundred, placated the fans by using his favoured trudgen stroke to win the half-mile championship by 80 yards. Having learned to swim less than two years before, Kieran had now won the 200-, 220- and 880-yard championships of NSW and the half-mile championship of Australasia. He followed it with an easy win in the national mile championship at Ballarat on 30 January. South Australian Charles Bastard, the only state-paid swimming teacher in the Commonwealth, witnessed the feat and described Kieran as 'a magnificent swimmer, with great vigour and versatility ... [we] do not yet know of what he is capable.' Bastard was far less complimentary of Healy, who in winning a special 100-yard invitation handicap in Ballarat used a crawl that Bastard described as 'grotesque and absolutely devoid of beauty.'[21]

Australian swimmers now held world records for every distance from 50 yards to a mile, and there was talk of sending Kieran and Healy abroad to compete in England at the British championships. By the end of the 1904–05 season, the pair held every Australasian title between them, Healy the 100 yards and Kieran the 220, 440 and 880 yards and the mile. Kieran also held the world records for the 200, 300, 440, 500 and 880 yards, and shared the 220-yard record with Freddie Lane. Kieran did go to England courtesy of a special fund set up to cover the expense of his sojourn, but the fund could not stretch to two, and Healy had to remain at home.

FIVE

DROWN MY HEART IN SALT WATER

*'Why so much grief for me?
No man will hurl me down to Death against my fate.
And fate? No one alive has ever escaped it, neither brave man nor coward,
I tell you—it's born with us the day that we are born.'*

—Homer, *The Iliad* (Book VI, 580–584)

***

It was November 1905 before Barney Kieran returned from England, flushed with triumph after winning all but two of the races he had contested. However, Healy had been busy during Kieran's absence, setting a world record for 60 yards and boxing and working out over winter with his usual vigour. The stage now seemed set for another record-breaking head-to-head between the two at the 1905–06 Australian championships in Brisbane in December.

As Healy and Kieran made another slow train journey together, this time heading north and accompanied by Cecil's brother Reg, they could not have imagined that only one of the pair would return home alive.

***

With Kieran abroad, Healy, Alick Wickham and Snowy Baker had passed the winter of 1905 trying to out-compete each other in the fitness stakes. The trio was tasked with entertaining a group of visiting swimmers from New Zealand in July and did so with a display of trick diving and some lively boxing bouts. While all were accomplished divers, Wickham was the standout. His 1918 record plunge of 205 feet 9 inches (62 metres) from a cliff above Melbourne's Yarra River still stands as a monument to a practice that swimming associations in Australia opposed after 1905: 'In Australia, plunging is discouraged by the association as being a dangerous and foolhardy pastime', the ASA informed the press. 'There is really little skill in it and the chances are that the swimmer, unless he is extremely careful, and an expert, may be drowned.'[1]

Healy's hunger to meet the new season head-on was such that in that same July, when most swimmers were in their winter dormancy, he obliterated the world record for 60 yards at a club social meet, carving almost three seconds off the previous time of 35 1/5 seconds with an unofficial 32 2/5 seconds. His early-season form was so irresistible that by November 1905, the NSW ASA decreed that he and Barney Kieran would represent the state at the Australasian championships in Brisbane. While Healy's selection was uncontested, Mort's Dock club delegate Arthur Griffiths complained that Kieran, who had only just arrived home from England, should be compelled to compete in a selection event, giving swimmers including Bob Craig, Harold Baker and others who had been in hard training a chance to challenge for Kieran's place on the team. As *The Arrow* sarcastically observed, 'Kieran might well say, "Save me from my friends".' While abroad, the teen had set a new world record for 600 yards and won every event he appeared in bar two. His form was indisputable. But despite arriving home in fine fettle, Kieran had made it clear that he needed a rest and did not intend to start in any local races until the national championships in Queensland. The resulting outcry forced him into one reluctant appearance at the Lavender Bay baths in late November, where he easily disposed of his opposition over 250 yards.

Healy ignored these machinations, rattling off a 58 1/2-second performance in a 100-yard exhibition race, and then winning the East Sydney 100-yard championship in 59 2/5 seconds despite missing the start badly. He already had an eye on a greater prize than the defence of his national championship—the 1906 Athens Olympic Games were only four months away, and Freddie Lane remained the only swimmer to have represented Australia in Olympic competition. Here was a chance to join that elite company. Healy won the official NSW national championship selection race from Wickham and schoolboy champion Len Murray, and then, to his delight, his brother Reg won the half-mile after Kieran boycotted the event, guaranteeing both Healy brothers a trip to Queensland. 'The Healy brothers, Cecil and Reg, have established something of a record, in Australia at any rate', reported *The Arrow*. 'They have reason to feel proud of not only representing the state in Brisbane, but by going at the same time. It is a lucky trip for Reg, for if Kieran had competed he would have undoubtedly won. Nevertheless, the East Sydneyite swam remarkably well in the 880-yard test on Monday night last and never gave the popular tip, Bob Craig, a look in.'

Cecil completed his preparations for Brisbane by setting another world record in the Flying Squadron event on 3 December. The East Sydney team of Lane, Healy, Harold 'Son' Baker, Theo

Tartakover and Wickham swam the 500 yards in 5 minutes 4 3/5 seconds, carving two seconds off the record set at Rose Bay the previous February, Healy leading them off with 100 yards in 59 seconds even.

Travelling north in glowing form, Healy gave the fans just what they had paid to see. He swam a new world record of 57 seconds dead in a pre-meet 100-yard handicap race in Brisbane. The time, however, could not be ratified, as ASA rules called for 'a man, when after a record, to be despatched by pistol-shot'[2]. When asked for his feelings on being denied the record, Healy resisted the opportunity to quip on the odd wording of the ASA rule, with all its connotations of execution. Instead, he shrugged off his disappointment, telling the press 'it did not matter' and that he was confident he could reproduce the effort under official conditions. His performance in the national final, however, was somewhat less salubrious—despite the straight course in the Brisbane River, which eminently suited him, Healy's winning time was a sluggish 60 2/5 seconds.

Healy attributed the poor swim to the generous hospitality of his Brisbane hosts. 'We had a good time but there were rather too many entertainments', he told the press. 'They made me real tired.'[3] Among the 'galaxy of good things' to which the visitors were treated was a boating excursion around Moreton Bay. Late in the afternoon, a coastal storm boiled up over the horizon, catching their yacht in an exposed position. Anchors were dropped and the dozen men on board battened down the cabin. 'The elements shrieked overhead in a most appalling manner, as if the forces of the internal regions had been suddenly loosened', Healy remembered. With the wind tearing outside and waves pounding over the open decks, the men crammed into the space below were almost suffocating, the atmosphere 'as unbearable as the Black Hole of Calcutta'. Finally, Healy could stand it no more. He stripped to the skin, thrust his way up onto the deck and plunged over the lee-side of the yacht, where he hung on the hobstays, half-immersed in the pounding waves. Despite the terrible buffeting, it was infinitely preferable to what the men were experiencing inside, and soon Kieran, who was far more experienced at sea, joined him. The daring pair hung from the rails like a couple of shags for almost half an hour, the sea snapping at their legs and wind-driven spray pounding into their faces, before the storm abated as quickly as it had arrived[4].

This escapade notwithstanding, Barney Kieran started the championships determined to silence his critics. After his refusal to compete in the selection trials, his North Sydney club had paid for a private ticket to allow him to compete in Brisbane, provoking further howls of protest that Kieran had not earned his place on the NSW team. Kieran promptly won the 220-yard national championship in a world record time of 2 minutes 28 2/5 seconds. Reg Healy finished second, about 11 yards behind, while Cecil, who had won his heat, finished out of the placings. 'I kept with him (Kieran) for five laps', Healy recollected ruefully, 'but he was too fast, and at the end I was tired out.'[5] Reg then finished third behind Kieran in the 880-yard final and Cecil third behind the champion in the 440 yards. However, Kieran's winning time in that event, 5 minutes 37 1/5 seconds, was a worrying 18 seconds outside his own world record[6]. Both Healys had complained of feeling sluggish in the oppressive Brisbane humidity—now Kieran, with the mile race still to contest, also seemed to be suffering in the heat.

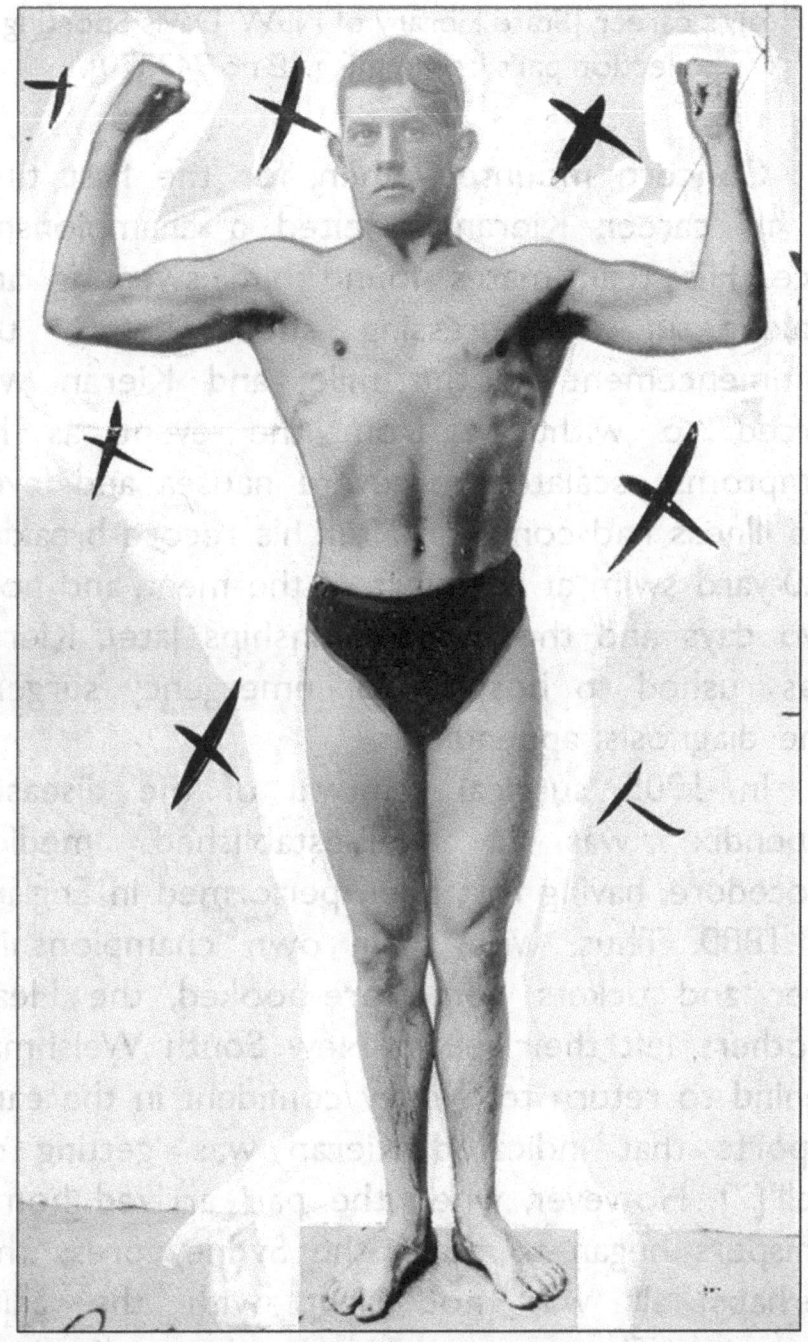

Teenage swim sensation Barney Kieran joined Healy in representing NSW at the Australasian championships of 1905—an event fraught with such tragedy it almost ended

Healy's career. [State Library of NSW: Davis Sporting Collection part I: swimming. IE no.943370].

Concern mounted when, for the first time in his career, Kieran forfeited a championship race. His team-mates found him sweating and shaking in the dressing sheds before the commencement of the mile, and Kieran was forced to withdraw from the event as his symptoms escalated to severe nausea and fever. His illness had come on after his record-breaking 220-yard swim at the start of the meet, and now, two days and three championships later, Kieran was rushed to hospital for emergency surgery. The diagnosis: appendicitis.

In 1905, surgical removal of the diseased appendix was a well-established medical procedure, having first been performed in England in 1880. Thus, with their own championships over and tickets home pre-booked, the Healy brothers left their fellow New South Welshman behind to return to Sydney, confident in the early reports that indicated Kieran was 'getting on well'[7]. However, when the pair arrived home, whispers began to reach the Sydney press that perhaps all was not right with the ailing champion. There were rumours of complications, that the case was rather more serious than first thought, and these proved so persistent that the

North Sydney Club paid for Kieran's mother to travel north to be at her son's bedside. On 20 December, Sydney was abuzz with the rumour that Kieran had died. Many an anxious enquiry was made before a message was eventually received at the offices of *The Arrow* stating that Barney was both alive and kicking. 'Thank Heaven for that!' *The Arrow* spoke on behalf of everyone.

However, two days later, on 22 December 1905, the whirl of rumour, innuendo and unverified tattle came to a dreadful and official conclusion. Sydney's Saturday morning papers delivered the news to many an unsuspecting reader over a plate of bacon, eggs and toast: Barney Kieran was, in fact, dead.

The passing of the young champion, who was just 19 years old, shocked Australian sport as it had never been shocked before. A crowd of more than 3,000 people met the Brisbane train in Sydney when the body of the young swimmer was borne home on Christmas Day. The route to his funeral in North Sydney the next day was lined with silent crowds as some 300 men, vehicles and the Sobraon Band made their sober way past. Cecil, Reg and Harold Healy were all in the procession, alongside many other representatives of the swimming and sporting communities. Expressions of grief poured in from around the world. The London papers mourned, 'One can hardly believe that poor Kieran is dead ... He was resolute to a degree, extremely jealous of his reputation, prudent beyond his years, very patient, and most persevering. He had a kind word for everyone, even for those who sometimes misunderstood him, and was extremely thankful to all those who helped him.'[8] The NSW ASA immediately instituted plans for a perpetual award in Kieran's honour to recognise the champion state at the annual Australasian swimming championships; that award, the Barney Kieran Memorial Shield, continues today.

The *Argus* blamed Kieran's intake of cold foods, coupled with pre-race anxiety, for his death in Brisbane. On the day of the onset of his illness, Kieran was apparently so worried about not breaking the world record for 220 yards that he organised a test swim in the morning against Healy, of whom he was 'very much afraid', claimed the paper. After a great tussle, Kieran was satisfied that he could beat his older rival, which he subsequently did, breaking the world record in the process. But with the race swum in Brisbane's oppressive humidity, Kieran was severely dehydrated afterwards and sated his thirst with cold milk and iced cherries, becoming violently, albeit secretly, ill during the night[9].

Others blamed his demise on his determination never to disappoint the fans who came to see him swim[10]. While touring England, Kieran had concealed a severe attack of influenza in order to appear at every meet he was scheduled for, and his secret suffering drove him almost to the point of physical collapse. Likewise, in Brisbane, Cecil Healy remembered his teammate's desperate desire to keep swimming despite the griping pains in his belly. 'Kieran endured great pain for a couple of days before it was ascertained what he was suffering from', Healy told the *Town and Country Journal*. With his appendicitis undiagnosed until it was too late, Kieran's efforts in swimming race after race at world record pace may well have cost the young man his life.

***

Less than twenty-four hours after poor Barney Kieran was committed to the earth, that dark, heavy element so foreign to him, Sydney's fastest swimmers were summoned back to the water.

Flags flew at half-mast to honour Kieran at the Rose Bay Christmas carnival on 27 December 1905. East Sydney, with a team including Cecil and Reg Healy and Alick Wickham, won the 1,000-yard Flying Teams Handicap Relay (with legs of 400, 300, 200 and 100 yards), Cecil putting in 59 seconds for the hundred. However, as Natator observed, many of the swimmers were simply not prepared for a return to the pool so soon after the shock loss of Barney Kieran. 'Swimmers to a man felt the happening keenly', wrote the commentator, 'and many of them have not yet recovered.'

Cecil Healy's heart was certainly not in it. While Kieran had lain dying in a Brisbane hospital, Healy had returned home, unaware of his friend's true predicament, to continue his conquest of the sprinting scene. He had blasted out 58 2/5 seconds for the hundred in front of a vast crowd, mainly of the fairer sex, at Bondi on 16 December and had won the 200 yards off scratch at the Enterprise carnival four days later. However, this seemingly indifferent continuance of his own affairs in the face of his friend's illness was a public fallacy, and after Kieran's death, Healy was plunged into a sea of guilt that threatened his career.

While Healy had certainly been aware of the agony Kieran endured before his hospitalisation, he could not have guessed at the seriousness of his team-mate's illness. 'It was thought he [just] had colic as he had been drinking a lot of iced milk', Healy said helplessly. He never dreamed that what had seemed to be a mere stomach ache would rip a void through Australian swimming and rob Kieran's friends, fans and the international scene of its brightest prodigy. As he walked in the silent procession to Gore Hill and watched Kieran's casket lowered and the earth piled upon it, Cecil Healy's sombre face gave no indication of the self-recrimination boiling like a hot kettle inside him: *I could have stopped him ... I should have stopped him ... I was the last one with him....* In early January 1906, while the swimming community planned benefit concerts and a memorial fund for the fallen champion, Healy turned his back on them all.

As was his way, Healy's grief was silent, a pain locked bitterly inside him, along with all the other deep doubts and insecurities he shared with no one. Healy withdrew completely, taking no part in the commemorations of Kieran's life and not speaking in the press about his friend or his legacy. Instead, he did the only thing he could—Healy threw himself into a savage training regime, as though seeking to drown the dreadful internal struggle and self-reproach. With his face buried in the salty brine, he did not have to face the questions about Kieran he felt were looming on the lips of every reporter and onlooker, about the teenage boy he should have watched over better while they were so far away from home. The roar of bubbles in his ears, the burning in his lungs, the cramping of his limbs and the near-bursting of his heart were a physical castigation for what Healy felt were all his crimes and shortcomings—for not barring the boy's way to the pool as he staggered again and again, green-faced, to the start line, for not standing between him and the delicious icy temptations of milk and cherries; for not saving Barney Kieran from himself.

The explosive bursts of training for the short sprints were not enough to drown out the persistent inner voice stoking Healy's anger and remorse. His solution was simple, but devastating—Healy abandoned the splash and splendour of the 100-yard dash and, in a move that drew gasps from the pundits, turned to the middle-distance events Kieran himself had so favoured[11]. Cecil Healy had never raced over more than 440 yards during his decade-long swim career. The Athens Olympic Games were almost visible on the horizon, and the press bellowed that Healy, as the 100-yard world record holder, ought to be focussing on bringing home the sprint gold medal. However, Healy ignored the public reaction and reproach. This was the only way he felt he could honour the lost champion and ease the guilt at leaving the dying Kieran that burdened him so desperately. He ploughed on with his own form of self-immolation, deaf to the calls for sense to prevail.

Healy's move was the first real indication of the complexity and turmoil that lay at the heart of Australia's golden sprinter. Beloved for his modesty and upheld for the years of persistence that had driven him past Cavill and Wickham to the top of world swimming, Healy's public persona was one of a tractable, good-natured young man from a much-respected family who had fallen on hard times. He was irresistibly popular with his clubmates, the press and the community for his kindness and humility. However, like his father, Healy had a talent for secrets. He preferred never to speak of the emotions and insecurities that seemed to shame him in their intensity and in the way in which, as now, they would sometimes find release in impetuous, inexplicable actions. His four lonely years at boarding school had driven a wedge between Cecil and his siblings, towards whom he remained guarded about his private affairs. And while he was often eloquent in the press about matters in the pool, he remained close-lipped about his affairs outside it—the longing with which he viewed his rivals and their freedom to lounge around the pool all day and not spatter their fingers with clerical ink and tractor grease, the pre-race anxieties that, even as the world record holder, hounded him before every public appearance. He left the commentators to speculate among themselves about his dramatic switch to middle-distance racing, refusing any word on Barney Kieran or the possible motivation for the move, lest it rip the scab from his grief and release the guilt within.

Cecil now trained solely alongside his brother Reg, who, at 19, was the same age as the tragic Kieran and already touted as his possible successor. On 17 January 1906, Reg won the inaugural three-quarter-mile championship of NSW by 50 yards in a time just three seconds outside Englishman Dave Billington's world record. *The World's News* christened Reg 'the best briny miler in the Commonwealth, with his big heart, staying powers and fast improving form'. The Healy brothers ground out endless laps side by side, stocky, muscular Cecil overcoming the buoyancy advantage of his wiry brother with sheer, gut-wrenching determination. He also started his own racing campaign immediately, winning the 300-yard event at the Drummoyne carnival on 19 January 1906. He surprised everyone present by not only swimming off scratch, but using the crawl the whole way to drive himself to a time of 3 minutes 38 2/5 seconds, the second fastest in history behind Kieran's record of 3 minutes

31 4/5 seconds. The next day, Cecil won the state 220-yard championship in 2 minutes 35 seconds, leading all the way to win by six yards. These two commanding performances drew admiration and wonder from the press. Natator marvelled at the 'staying powers few suspected [Healy] of owning' and *The Arrow* warmly applauded his efforts: 'Looks as if we are going to have a worthy successor to Barney Kieran and Dick Cavill in Cecil Healy ... There wasn't the slightest element of chance in either success—both were clean-cut and decisive, and accomplished in true top-notcher style.'[12]

The true test came on 13 February 1906 in the NSW 500-yard championship. This was the longest distance Healy had yet tackled under race conditions and he did so against his training partner and brother Reg. *The Arrow* predicted excitedly, 'The brothers Healy should prove a hot pair over the distance.' While Reg made the pace, by the 200-yard mark Cecil had drawn alongside and the two brothers had left Bob Craig and Charlie Smith in their wake, the crawl vying against the trudgen for supremacy. In the final lap, when Reg was drawing ahead and many were nodding sagely that the sprinter was flagging as expected, Cecil accelerated from five yards behind his brother, rallying all of his latent powers in a powerful rush for the rope. While the younger Healy did prevail by half a body-length, Natator praised the style and potential of Cecil's performance, 'for he came along and surprised—and is still surprising us.'

Natator was, however, also first to publicly voice the fear Healy's sprinting powers would be affected by his new commitment to distance work, although he hastened to add, 'But I am sure neither he nor his friends regret the fact, for Cec has made it plain and indisputable that he is a swimmer indeed now, and one who might attain as high a plane as any who have gone before him.'[13] This was no doubt a reference to Kieran. Healy had reassured the sceptics with a time of 59 3/5 seconds for 100 yards, even when jostled by an opponent, in the first leg of East Sydney's Flying Squadron victory on 7 February. The triumph was, however, tempered by the news that Frank Fitts, the champion young Victorian sprinter, had undergone surgery that day for suspected appendicitis after also returning sick from Brisbane. It was an eerie repeat of the Kieran case, and Australian swimming held its collective breath as the life of another young champion hung in the balance. Fitts survived, but it was a further reminder of the fragility of young life in pre-penicillin Australia, where even the fit and hearty were fair game.

SIX

MORE THAN JUST A 'GAMES'

'The most important thing in the Olympic Games is not winning but taking part; the essential thing in life is not conquering but fighting well.'

—Baron Pierre de Coubertin

***

1906 was not an Olympic year, according to the four-year cycle upon which the modern Games are scheduled. However, in 1905, the Olympic Congress in Brussels announced the decision to hold the Games in Athens in 1906, both to mark the tenth anniversary of the first modern Olympics and to repair the crumbling reputation of the movement after the inept 1900 and 1904 Games[1]. These Intercalated (interim) Games were scheduled for 22 April to 2 May 1906, and in January there was already talk in Australia of sending the crack Sydney University sprinter Nigel Barker to Athens. Barker, who played rugby union for both NSW and Australia, had won the sprint treble (100, 220 and 440 yards) at the 1904 Australasian athletics championships, setting a new world record for the 440 yards to become Australia's first track world record holder, and seemed a fine choice to bring home a medal.

The 1906 Athens Games were only open to amateur athletes, although international competitors were permitted to accept financial assistance to cover their travelling expenses while abroad. The Greek Olympian Games Committee donated £100 toward the costs of getting Australian competitors to the Games, enabling NSW officials to select Cecil Healy to represent Australia alongside Barker. Thus, Healy became Australia's second ever Olympic swimming representative after Freddie Lane. Swimming Australia has since numbered all of its Games representatives in order of international appearance, and Healy holds the number 2[2]. 'In his particular class [Healy] stands alone', boasted *The Sydney Morning Herald* in announcing Healy's selection, 'and from all points of view he would be a creditable representative and a fit companion for Barker.'[3]

However, there was more to Healy's selection than just prowess in the pool. 'Prominent politicians and other public men are fond of telling [people] that the sending of champion athletes to other countries is the best method of advertising that any country can adopt', mused the *Australian Town and Country Journal*. Early twentieth-century Australian sporting representatives were instruments of shameless propaganda on behalf of the newly independent Australian nation, which had shaken off the apron strings of the British Empire and was now anxious to assert its own unique national character. The Australian cricket team toured England in 1902, as much to boast of Australia's new independence as to bring home the Ashes, and poor Barney Kieran was seen as 'a splendid advertisement' for the burgeoning nation during his own tour of the motherland. Quiet, unassuming and well-educated, Cecil Healy seemed another ideal ambassador for the newly liberated Great South Land.

One man who was definitely *not* going on the boat to Greece was Cecil's older brother Harold. Some sources have recorded Harold as not only accompanying Cecil to the 1906 Games, but participating as an Australian representative in the track hurdles, even suggesting that he won a silver medal[4]. Harold Healy, however, despite some prowess as an amateur race walker, did not participate in the Athens Games. The man who finished second in the 1906 110-metre hurdles event was Alfred Healey, representing

Great Britain. Healey won his heat, and then ran second in the final behind Robert Leavitt of the USA[5]. Harold Healy, of 22 Roslyn Gardens, Darlinghurst, remained at home in Sydney, where he was much occupied with the operations of the East Sydney swim club, in particular its water polo team.

Meanwhile, even the prestige of Cecil's selection to swim the 100 metres for his country in Athens could not distract him from his self-imposed quest to honour Barney Kieran. As a result, Healy also entered the 400 metres and, staggeringly, the 1,500 metres, a distance he had never swum competitively. The NSW ASA then elected to fund him onward to England after the Games to swim every distance from 100 yards to a mile at the English championships in July.

On the day on which the ASA confirmed Healy's selection, 24 February 1906, Cecil faced his brother Reg again in a 300-yard handicap race at Manly's Skinner's Baths, attracting a record local crowd. Reg won the race off an eight-second handicap, with Cecil finishing third off scratch. He then reassured his sprint fans with a time of 1 minute 13 seconds in a special 120-yard handicap, which some claimed was a world record. Dick Cavill had swum faster, setting a world record of 1 minute 12 2/5 seconds at Newcastle in 1903, but there were doubts as to whether that time was official, as it had not been set under race conditions.

Nonetheless, despite the controversy attached to the 'record', this personal best was a fitting sign of form for Healy on the eve of his departure for Athens. However, not even such a triumph could lure him back to pure sprinting. At Watsons Bay on 1 March 1906, just weeks before the Games, Healy led all the way to win his heat of the NSW 880-yard (half-mile) championship by a lap. Reg 'loafed a while' in his, but went on to beat Cecil in the final in 11 minutes 59 4/5 seconds. After 100 yards, Reg had a clear lead, but as they started the seventh hundred, Cecil 'braced himself up' among the choppy waves and pounding rain. It was too late to catch the younger Healy though, as Reg responded to the spurt with purpose to win by 35 yards. The relatively slow winning time (Kieran's world record was 11 minutes 11 3/5 seconds) was blamed on both the weather and depth variations in the Watsons Bay pool, which had one deep and one shallow end. Natator opined the swimmers would have travelled faster in a consistently deep pool. Modern wave dynamics research has shown that Natator's theory was indeed correct: in a shallow swimming pool, a portion of the bow wave generated by the swimmer rebounds from the pool floor and can increase drag through wave turbulence, a phenomenon that does not occur in water deeper than three metres[6].

Natator also noted that Cecil was 'more than ordinarily anxious for some time before the start [of the 880 yards] and consequently did not give himself a fair show'. The scheduling of Healy's trip to Athens, only confirmed in the last few days, had clearly unnerved him, as it now appeared the team would arrive in Greece only days before the Games, leaving little time for training or acclimatisation after the long boat trip. However, the highly strung Healy had plenty of other reasons to be anxious. Already rattled by the death of Barney Kieran, the suddenness of his selection and the prospect of spending the rest of the year in unfamiliar foreign climes[7], Healy's European itinerary was still uncertain, and full funding had not yet been secured for his post-Olympic tour. Of the money gifted to NSW by the Greek organising committee, the ASA proposed to use £50 to cover Healy's trip, supplemented by a surplus £25 from monies raised to send Barker to Athens. However, The Barker Fund committee refused, stating that the money had been raised for the sole purpose of supporting Barker. It was only an appeal to the Consul-General for Greece and a rapid-fire public collection that secured Healy's trip to Europe.

A total of £180 was needed, and with Healy due to leave on the *Mongolia* in five days' time, the fund was still £80 short.

To add to this last-minute chaos, news reached Australia of a new world record for the 100 yards set by American Charles Daniels. His swim of 57 3/5 seconds, a time equalling Healy's swim without the full official costume, took place on 15 January 1906 in wintery New York and was the first time an American had ever held a world swimming record. Miraculously, Daniels repeated the time on the same day after only a short rest[8]. The big American, who was 6 feet 1 inch tall and weighed 11 1/2 stone, now presented a real threat to Healy, who would have eight weeks on board a ship as his far-from-ideal preparation for their showdown.

On 5 March 1906, the night before Healy's departure, the East Sydney club held a 'Cecil-Healy-for-Athens-and-England' fundraiser at the Sports Club on Hunter Street. In front of a packed crowd, club president Dan Levy raised a toast to Healy's health, referring to his 'striking qualities' both as a swimmer and as a man. Mr. Justice Cohen, a colleague of Healy's late father, added a compliment that surely must have touched the young swimmer: 'The mantle of the late, lamented Kieran has fallen on worthy shoulders.' Healy's response was characteristically modest. He said he really thought others, including his brother Reg, had greater claims to being sent, but if it was the wish of the association and subscribers that he should go, it would be ungracious of him to refuse. Still £40 shy of the total required for Healy's fare, the next day the club staged a 'Continental' at Rushcutters Bay where, for sixpence admission, swimmers enjoyed the rare privilege of mixed bathing, augmented by high-diving displays and world record attempts by Wickham and Reg Healy. More than 100 collectors moved throughout the stands shaking tins and appealing for loose change. The Healy family at large had thrown themselves into the fund-raising effort, with a water polo match in February featuring all seven brothers playing against their East Sydney clubmates, surely a record for familial participation. However, as the *Australian Town and Country Journal* noted, 'Cecil Healy ... comes from a family noted for that good spirit which every person who takes part in any sport should possess.'

With his fare finally secured at the eleventh hour, Healy took the express train on 6 March to meet Nigel Barker in Adelaide and catch the P&O mail steamer *RMS Mongolia* to Athens. George Wheatley and George Blake, middle-distance runners from Victoria, were also going, travelling separately on the *RMS Ophir*. More than 100 swimmers assembled at Sydney's Redfern station to farewell Healy, and they gave three ringing cheers as the train pulled away. Healy was similarly feted during his stopover in Melbourne, where he was met by Victorian ASA officials and formally announced as the 'king of sprinters' at the Sports Club. When he left for Adelaide that evening, the train was farewelled with another resounding ovation. Healy, however, had things on his mind beyond the fine wine the Victorians had toasted him with. A letter to East Sydney club official E.S. Marks penned the day the *Mongolia* sailed found Healy 'very glum' at not having had time for a swim while in Melbourne[9].

The Sunday Times in Western Australia also found Healy 'very reticent' and worried about the long sea voyage and lack of training time. As Barker jogged the decks, windmilling his arms and stretching his long springy limbs, Healy could only watch the mocking blue sea slide by from behind the iron railings that would separate him from the water for the next eight weeks. However, as the *Mongolia* ploughed across the Indian Ocean toward the Suez Canal, Healy began to brush aside the persistent spectre of Charles Daniels churning up and down a training pool and carving seconds from the world record. He started working out on deck with dumbbells, and skipping, boxing and running with some of the first-class passengers. His prowess with the gloves soon had a queue of willing opponents lining up to match it with him.

'Soon after I arrived on board I learnt that some of the stewards were in the habit of boxing in the afternoon', Healy wrote home to Harold. 'I sent word round to say that I was anxious to have a spar and no sooner had I done so than I was informed that one had a reputation of being a bit of a pug, and I began to doubt the wisdom of my action. However, I thought that there was no alternative but to see the matter through, and eventually found myself called upon to present myself at the forward part of the ship. When I arrived there, I thought I was in the National Sporting Club—I could see at a glance that word had gone round, for the whole complement of stewards had turned out and, glancing up, I found there was an audience of first-class passengers.' However, the resulting bout with the ship's champion lasted less than a minute. *The Arrow* regretted that there were no boxing competitions on the Olympic Games programme, for 'Cecil Healy might have, in such circumstances, worthily represented Australia "wid de mits" ... Cec "had 'em on" with the crack of the *Mongolia* before the crew and a goodly roll-up of passengers, and Cecil proved himself a veritable Triton opposed to a minnow.'

The seemingly endless sea voyage, with brief glimpses of terra firma in Port Said and Suez, came to a spectacular conclusion in early April. A huge eruption of the Italian volcano Mount Vesuvius had occurred on the morning of 5 April 1906, overwhelming several towns around Naples. Many of the Olympic teams *en route* to Greece via the Mediterranean docked at Naples and witnessed the subsequent destruction first-hand.

***

The 1906 Intercalated Olympic Games were decisive in the future of the newly revived Olympic movement.

The first ancient Games were held in 776BC at Olympia, on the Peloponnesus in modern-day Greece, and the contests were held at regular quadrennial intervals until 393 AD, when they were abolished as a pagan offense by the Roman emperor Theodosius. The 1896 revival of the Olympic Games as an international sporting contest is primarily attributed to the French baron Pierre de Coubertin, and the first modern event in Athens in 1896 was highly successful due to the fervour of the Greek people. However the follow-up in Paris in 1900, held in conjunction with a world's fair, was a disaster.

The events were spread out over a six-month period, ensuring that the press and athletes barely knew the Games were on, and poor attendances saw de Coubertin ousted as chairman of the organising committee. The 1904 edition in St. Louis fared no better. Once again conducted alongside a world's fair and over a six-month period, international representation was minimal, and the event did little to bolster the reputation of the Olympic movement[10].

Anxious to keep the Games in their spiritual home, the Greeks had never supported de Coubertin's idea of perambulating the Games around the world. By way of a compromise, the Baron suggested holding a Pan-Hellenic Games in Athens with a two-year offset between each official Olympic Games. These Intercalated Games were first mooted at the 1905 Olympic Congress in Brussels. While their status as an official Olympic event remains disputed, the 1906 Games were undoubtedly critical to reviving the flagging Olympic movement, and were the most international and best-managed Games to date.

By dint of large donations from the USA, Britain and France, the Greek organising committee rebuilt the marble stadium in Athens for the 1906 Games at a cost of three million francs. The Australian government made no financial contribution, and it was only through the efforts of a few enthusiastic individuals and the generosity of the Greek government that any Australian competitors attended at all. While the schedule included many familiar sports such as cycling, gymnastics, fencing, shooting, tennis, soccer and rowing, the program also featured the ancient events of wrestling, tug-of-war and rope-climbing. In true ancient tradition, there were no masseurs, no new-fangled diets, no chaperones, not even a village to house the teams. Most of the athletes, aside from the British fencing team, who were quartered aboard the luxury yacht *Branwen* in the Bay of Neo Phaliron, were housed in the Zappeion, a communal hall filled with open-topped cubicles in which, 'if someone spoke loudly, snored, or slammed a door, the noise resounded around and around the entire immense area.'[11]

The four Australians escaped the Zappeion by finding rooms in a boarding house run by an English woman, Mrs McTaggart. They were joined there by the Canadian team, including marathoner Billy Sherring, who had arrived aboard a cattle boat and had already been training in Greece for two months. Healy had brought along a leather-bound autograph book, and George Blake and George Wheatley were quick to inscribe themselves as 'Victoria's Main Springs for Athens'. Blake added, 'my mission: the marathon', while

Wheatley wrote that 'the reason why I'm "mission" is to compete in the 400, 800, & 1500 "meet us"'. The little book proved a veritable 'Who's Who' of 1906 Olympians. Healy was very popular, and the pages quickly filled with compliments. American triple jumper Thomas Cronan wished 'the Olympic champion' luck, and US runner Francis Connolly expressed the hope that 'some day will find you in Boston, "the Athens of America", where it will be a pleasure to me to show you around.' There were signatures from New Yorker Martin Sheridan, who won gold in the shot-put and discus, and silver in the standing high jump, standing long jump and stone throw, and the rebel Peter O'Connor, winner of the triple jump, who defiantly signed himself 'Irish athlete'. In protest at being forced to compete under the British Union Jack, O'Connor had scaled the flagpole of the main stadium and hoisted his own Irish flag. The little book also contained a hilarious hand-drawn cartoon of a steward being ordered to 'give the boys all the oranges they want', underscored by the signatures of Wheatley, Barker, Connolly, Cronan and Healy.

Cecil Healy's autograph book from the 1906 Athens Olympic Games included the monikers of Australian track representatives George Blake and George Wheatley and a whimsical cartoon perhaps depicting some of the deprivations endured by the team. [Source: Vivienne Degenhardt/Mike Downman].

The conditions for the athletes in Greece were far from the privileged luxury enjoyed by modern Olympians; in fact they were often downright hazardous. There were few opportunities for the swimmers to train in a designated pool, and Healy, with only days before the Games began, was forced to take radical action. Blake recalled that 'Poor Cecil had a heartbreaking job. He and I used to walk five miles to Phalerum each day and hire a boat. We would row half a mile or so out into the

Mediterranean and Cecil would dive overboard. He would race to the shore and back. With snow on the surrounding mountains, Cecil would leave the water almost frozen.' Blake would then run back to Athens for his own training, and would be lucky to get a bath afterwards, as water was strictly rationed. The night before the marathon, Blake and the other competitors were put up in a farmhouse near the start-line, with some having to sleep on the floor. It was cold and infested with vermin, and Blake didn't sleep at all, which probably contributed to his finishing out of the medals. Wheatley also found the going difficult, as he had endured a bad attack of sunstroke on the trip over, and his training had been so affected that his Australian team-mates often gave him false times during his runs to cheer him up[12].

However, the greatest danger came on an Athens evening just prior to the opening ceremony, when the Australian team were sightseeing around Syntagma Square. Local elections had brought a restive air to the Greek capital, and without warning, a shot was fired at the window of the cafe the Australians were seated in. Blake wrote home, 'Suddenly there was a stampede and soldiers appeared firing shots. Men and women went down, and right by us a woman and her child fell with blood streaming from wounds. The crowd surged to escape the shots. We led the crowd, and although I was a distance runner I was a sprinter that night. We ran miles through the streets and got quite lost. Barker dived into a billiards saloon and hid under a table.' Three people were killed and 57 injured as soldiers with bayonets charged the crowd. Canadian Elwood Hughes, who was with the party, said, 'If I hear any more guns popping, I will do the mile in 4:30.'

It was a distinct relief for all when the Games proper began on 22 April. More than 60,000 spectators crowded the Panathenaic Stadium to watch the athletes march past in rows of four during the opening ceremony, each team preceded by a flag bearer, under the gaze of royals including King Georgios and his sister Queen Alexandra of Britain, King Edward VII, the Prince of Wales and Princess Mary[13]. The Australian media had had the laurel wreath as good as placed upon Healy's head from the moment of his selection, so the headline in the papers of 26 April 1906 was a dreadful blow to the high national hopes: *'Healy defeated'*[14].

The first heat of the 100 metres—the metric hundred, or 109.363 yards—on the afternoon of Wednesday 25 April saw Cecil Healy and Charles Daniels meet head-to-head for the first time. During 1905, the 18-year-old Daniels had won every American championship bar the quarter-mile, and broken most of the American records. He was a fine all-round athlete, with successes in rowing, running, high jump and the shot-put, and he had also made his own significant addition to the technique of the crawl. Daniels reasoned that if he could use his arms independently to his legs, he ought to gain in speed through maintaining continuous momentum during each stroke. He devoted three months to learning to stroke with his arms after the leg stroke was finished, and then promptly carved more than 11 seconds off his 100-yard time. John Derbyshire, the Englishman with a best time of 59 4/5 seconds, was also in the Olympic field. Daniels won the first heat, with Healy second and Derbyshire third. All qualified for the final, to be held two hours later, along with the powerful Hungarian Zoltan de Halmay, who had won the last English championship in 59 seconds flat. For the first time, the crawl was truly on show at Olympic level. There was Healy, with his powerful overarm, scissor kick and side breathing and Daniels, with a peculiar combination of scissor and crawl leg movements: he would give a great scissor kick with every other arm stroke, slapping it down with a great splash as Kieran had, and would wriggle his feet rapidly up and down between times[15].

The formidable field of opponents proved too much for the underdone Healy, and de Halmay and Daniels, who had finished first and second, respectively, at the 1904 Games, dominated the race, with the 1904 result reversed and Daniels taking gold with the Hungarian second. Healy battled on to finish third, but he never blamed his late arrival in Athens and long shipboard confinement for the result. Instead, he explained, he was literally lassoed by the starter. Two posts had been driven into the bottom of the pool and a rope stretched between them from behind which the competitors would all start while in the water. Each competitor was supposed to have one hand resting on the rope, but was permitted to lean forward as much as possible before the start. When the pistol was fired, someone yanked on the rope and Healy was caught up in it, losing two yards on his rivals. This, he said, most probably accounted for his defeat.

The first medal of Healy's Olympic career was a bittersweet one. He would not be leaving Athens empty-handed, but he certainly was not bringing home a medal of the colour he most desired. The loss, even though it was to the world record holder in Daniels, was a serious disappointment for Australian sports fans, who had freely expressed their faith in Healy as peerless over a short distance. There was much condemnation of both Healy, in particular for his recent commitment to longer distances, and the Australian officials for the team's belated departure for Athens. The *Freeman's Journal* hoped that in the 400 metres and mile, 'Australia's representative will have struck his proper form', but Healy could do no better than sixth in the 400 metres and did not finish the mile[16].

***

Healy used the weeks between his disappointing result in Athens and his rematch with Daniels, de Halmay and Derbyshire in the 100-yard championship of England in July to good effect. It was June before he was called upon to race again, and so here at last was time to regroup and train in the fashion of Lane and Cavill, free for the first time from the demands of his day job at home. There was plenty to train for, with the 100-, 220-, 440-, 500- and 880-yard and mile championships all on Healy's program in England. By the time he re-entered the competitive arena, Healy had regained the fitness (and some of the confidence) he had lost during the Athens debacle. He burst to notice in Britain on 8 June, winning the 120-yard event at Watford Baths and easily defeating Faircloth, the southern England champion. Five days later,

Healy equalled the British record for 100 yards at West Ham, swimming 59 seconds to equal de Halmay's 1905 record.

Charles Daniels had suffered no post-Olympic letdown, and set a new world record for 120 yards in Bath on 5 July. In an ominous warning to the Australian in the lead-up to the English championships, Daniels swam 72 seconds dead to beat Healy by a yard and break Cavill's record of 72 1/2 seconds. Just a week later, Daniels and Healy came face to face again in the unofficial championship of the world, the English titles, at Nottingham. With de Halmay and Derbyshire also in the field, it was almost a replica of the Athens final. The pool was a short one, necessitating two turns during the race and sending a shudder of apprehension through the Healy camp. Well-known Sydney timekeeper W.T. Kerr was in Nottingham to watch the race, and said Healy was 'unlucky in the start', which he disapprovingly reflected was a shout of 'Go' instead of a pistol shot. Healy was the last of the five men to get away, and had his usual difficulty in the turns, but he gave Daniels a grand race, clawing back through the straights everything he lost at the ends. The American was a yard and a half ahead going into the last lap, but Healy made it 'a hummer', Kerr said, calling on all of his brilliant finishing powers. Only

Daniels' superior height and reach proved the difference at the finish, where the pair were only separated by the judges: Daniels was ruled to have out-touched Healy to win in 58 3/5 seconds. Derbyshire was some distance away in third and de Halmay was, according to Kerr, 'completely broken up'[17].

While Sydney's *Sunday Times* mourned that 'The Australian invariably loses much more than such an excellent swimmer should in the kick off', Kerr declared, 'It was the opinion of a good many that Cecil Healy should have won in two more strokes.' *The Referee*, too, was stout in its defence of Healy, calling the race 'Cecil's greatest'. 'We Australians had to console ourselves with the knowledge that kicking-off was not swimming', the paper concluded. Healy himself graciously described Daniels as the finest bath swimmer he had seen, owing to his remarkable turning ability, to which Natator agreed gloomily, 'This is just what the Australian top-notcher is not.'

In August 1906, Healy made his first visit to France, accompanied by William Henry, secretary of the British Royal Life Saving Society. Writing home, Cecil said admiringly, 'Immediately on arrival in Paris, a visit was made to the baths, where a number of swimming enthusiasts met us. Each visitor swam one length, 80 metres, and when I finished they gave me much applause; the crawl evidently pleased them, and the next day they were all trying their hands at it, and wherever I went in they watched my movements intently.'[18]

The 1906 European swimming season was revolutionary. The English and Europeans had rarely seen anything like Daniels or Healy, neither their speed nor their technique, and Healy generously taught the crawl stroke to swimmers from many other nations, who often immediately profited: Meyboom of Belgium, Andersen of Sweden, Scotland's Haynes and Germany's Kurt Bretting all won championship races soon after receiving Healy's tuition.

Healy had plenty of credibility to back up his pedagogical work. After his demonstration swim in Paris, it was up the Seine to Charenton for the 'Championship of the World', a 100-metre scratch race on 5 August, where he faced the French, Italian and Belgian champions. The lake course included turns at a rope stretched across the water, conditions not conducive to fast times, but Healy smashed his competition to set a new open-water world record for the 100 metres of 68 seconds, more than five seconds faster than the winning time in Athens. Two days later, Healy set another open-water world record, this time for 200 metres in a handicap race on the same course. The event had a staggering 64 competitors and Healy swam off scratch, finishing in a time of 2 minutes 21 seconds. When the record was announced, Healy received a huge ovation and was mobbed by crowds of admirers. Healy later rated that performance as the best of his career.

In Germany, Healy and Henry were guests of the Hamburg ASA, and were accommodated in a small guesthouse with a group of international competitors. 'Among the swimmers staying in the house were Bruckner, the Hungarian representative, and one of the German swimmers from Stettin', Healy wrote home. 'They both stood over 6 feet tall and could not speak a word of English, nor I one of German. Yet despite this disadvantage, we became great friends, and would spend hours together with only a little French pocket dictionary between us as a means of conveying our thoughts.' The German Swimming Association carnival in Hamburg on 13 August was one of the biggest in European history, with 39 events and 412 entries, and Healy praised the military-style efficiency of the operation: 'Proceedings were started punctually to time, and the organisation and management generally were excellent ... There [was] quite an army of officials and a timekeeper for every competitor. The time of every man who finished was taken and entered in a book prepared for that purpose. It was like an accountant's office.'[19]

Healy's time for the open 100 metres was 1 minute 11 3/5 seconds, beating de Halmay's German record by 2 1/5 seconds and pleasing the mighty crowd immensely. The relatively slow time came from having to start without a dive, and no push-offs were allowed at the turn of the 100-metre course, with ladders placed across both ends of the baths to prevent it. Ten minutes later, Healy kept the crowd in raptures by starting in the 500 metres, but he only secured fourth place, saving his best efforts for the *Kaizerpreis*, the Kaiser's Cup, an invitational 100-metre scratch race. Healy swam almost four seconds faster than his open 100-metre effort to win in 1 minute 7 seconds, equalling the 1897 world record of Englishman J.H. Tyers. So much did he revel in the straight course, without any of those troublesome turns, that Healy also smashed the previous European record of 1 minute 13 2/5 seconds set earlier in the year by de Halmay, and the performance left fans wondering what might have been, considering that 1 minute 13 seconds had won in Athens. In typically modest fashion, Healy described the swim as 'Not too bad.' The day's racing concluded with a grand prize-giving banquet and a ball that lasted all night.

Healy's follow-up tour of the United Kingdom washed away the last bitter aftertaste of his experience in Athens. He won invitational races in Edinburgh (defeating Yuille, the Scottish champion, over 50 and 100 yards), Dublin (setting new Irish records for the 100 and 220 yards) and Sunderland, where he captured the 220-yard championship of England. That race, however, was a farce. His old English rival John Derbyshire simply didn't turn up, meaning Healy had to swim the course alone. He then spent more than a month racing back on the Continent, including in Brussels, where he won the 100 and 200 metres in record times, and Rotterdam, defeating the Dutch champion over 100 metres. Questioned as to why his performances on the Continent were generally better than those in England, Healy's response was simple: most courses in Europe were in open water, without the dreaded turns.

Healy's long year away ended as the European winter closed in during November 1906. At his final appearance in England, at the Ravensbourne gala of 4 November, he made a huge effort to break Daniels' 150-yard world record of 1 minute 36 seconds. At the 100-yard mark he appeared to be on track, but over the last 50 yards he swam erratically and tired visibly to finish in 1 minute 37 2/5 seconds. 'It was a fine performance and evoked great applause', the London papers reported generously. Before he sailed home on 9 November, Healy was the guest of honour at a banquet of the Ravensbourne Swim Club and Royal Life Saving Association at Frascati's Restaurant in London[20]. Many of those present signed Healy's autograph book lavishly as 'one of the best of Australian friends and "companions in arms"' and 'one of the best boys I know'.

William Henry of the Life Saving Society, Healy's travelling companion and chaperone through his long tour, also signed the book, and Healy later wrote gratefully of the kindness extended to him by Henry and his wife. Through Henry's organising ability and benevolence, Healy had competed at every major meet in Britain and on the Continent, and at their 12 October general meeting, the East Sydney club proposed a hearty vote of thanks to Henry for services rendered to Healy. Henry was duly elected the first life member of the club and Healy, in his absence, re-elected captain and honorary swimming instructor.

Healy arrived home on 20 December 1906, just in time for Christmas, aboard the *RMS China*. Natator reported that 'The traveller never looked better, and reported himself in capital health.' Many friends and prominent athletes were on the wharf to welcome the champion home, and East Sydney hosted a welcome-home dinner for their club captain at the ABC Rooms in Pitt Street. A reception was also held by the NSW ASA, at which Chairman James Taylor paid tribute to Healy's qualities as a man and his powers as a swimmer[21].

***

As though anxious to prove he was still a contender after his long absence, Healy threw himself straight back into the domestic swim scene upon his return to Australia. Just two days after stepping onto the dock, he appeared at the Vaucluse–East Sydney combined swimming carnival, dashing off 100 yards in 60 seconds as though starved of contact with water by his long sea voyage. At the same meet, Reg won the state 440-yard championship (an easy victory by nine yards) and Cecil combined with Wickham, Tartakover, Son Baker and Fred Lane for the Flying Squadron Championship. The team failed by just 1/5 of a second to lower their record of 5 minutes 4 seconds, but Healy did well to swim his leg in 61 seconds.

Healy's nine-month absence from Sydney, in particular from the questions he dreaded and the seemingly inescapable reminders of Barney Kieran, had gone some way to easing the tumult he had experienced in the wake of Kieran's death. He showed no sign of returning to his pre-Olympic middle-distance training regime, but raced in sprints at every opportunity, near and far. He and Reg even took the train west to the country towns of Bathurst and Dubbo to appear at their local carnivals. Cecil took 4 3/5 seconds off the Bathurst baths record for 100 yards on New Year's Day 1907, giving Reg 11 seconds start and winning by a touch in 60 3/5 seconds. The trip to Dubbo for the Australia Day carnival on 26 January 1907 was no doubt an eye-opener for Cecil after the greenery and prettiness of Europe, for Australia was in drought and ravaged by the nation's worst ever rabbit plague. Advertisements in country newspapers called for 'Good careful practical rabbiters in gangs of not less than five. Bonus up to £2 per 1,000. No "yahoos" need apply.' In a single week during 1907, 18 tons of rabbit skins were garnered in New South Wales alone[22]. Ironically, the Dubbo swim meet was washed out by torrential rain after Healy's appearance in the special 100-yard handicap[23].

The one trip Healy did not make was to the Australasian championships in February 1907, which were held in Christchurch, New Zealand. In his absence, his national 100-yard title fell to his East Sydney clubmate Harold 'Son' Baker. Reg Healy's dominance of domestic middle-distance events had secured him a berth on the New Zealand tour, and while he came home *sans* a title, he did meet his future wife, Christine 'Dudu' Henrys, while abroad, and would return to New Zealand in the winter of 1907 to settle with his new bride. Meanwhile, Cecil set a new Australian record for 100 yards of 57 4/5 seconds at his home club carnival at Rushcutters Bay on 16 March 1907, just 1/5 of a second outside the world record, despite battling waves and pouring rain. He even returned for a second attempt on the record, paced by Wickham, whom he had easily defeated in his first swim. This second effort yielded a time of 58 seconds flat.

As the season drew to a close, on 16 April 1907 it all came together. At his home pool, Healy reclaimed the 100-yard world record from Charles Daniels, avenging all his disappointment from Athens, and perhaps finally purging the chaos and turbulence of that preparation. The record was lowered to 57 seconds flat, a full 3/5 of a second better than Daniels' New York effort.

SEVEN

'A PARTICULARLY RECKLESS FELLOW'

*'The life savers represent the very highest class.
They are the Samurais, the oligarchs, the elite.
They strut the beaches with superiority that is insolent,
yet, at the same time, tolerant of the
shortcomings of the lesser breeds—
a gladiator caste, envied by all men, adored by all women.'*

—Egbert T. Russell, *Lone Hand* (1910)

***

He struck out hard for the buoy, green breakers rising in front of him like translucent foam-flecked mountains, salt water pouring over his pumping brown arms and shoulders. As he lifted his head to sight the bobbing red marker and the position of his rivals, another wave rose before him and Healy instinctively lifted his stroke and kicked hard to ascend it.

However, a strange heaviness was upon him, and he barely made it to the crest before the wave surged over him, splashing hard into his face and pushing him roughly back in the direction of the beach. Momentarily stunned, Healy gasped and coughed and tried to resume his stroke, but the same encumbrance was now hauling him both backwards and downwards. He couldn't get his legs up to kick properly, and his chest and arms were barely breaking the surface. It was like swimming while tethered to a grand piano—his usual powerful crawl could now barely haul him up the face of the next wave, and as he struggled over it, he was again dragged shoreward, back into the trough.

Healy turned, using a kind of one-armed backstroke to stay afloat, and then he saw it. The thin, corded rope attaching his belt to the reel back on the sand usually floated on the surface behind him, light and buoyant. Now, a great black mass of seaweed rode the swell between him and the shore, submerging the rope, entangling it in slippery, waving tendrils. The ocean was dark blue out here, a deep channel running with a current as powerful as a team of horses. And now the inexorable swaying drift of the heavy weed and its swamping grip on the rope was going to drag him right to the bottom.

All thoughts of the other competitors and the race were now gone. Healy trod water, hauling up on the line with all his strength to try and break *the grip of the weed, but with nothing to leverage his feet against, his efforts were in vain, and as another wave rolled over him, he could now barely get his face to the surface to breathe. The sinking, entangled rope would drown him, drain the oxygen from his lungs, leave him as another blue-faced corpse upon which fishes would feed ... Struggling to free himself from the belt, he went down again, saw rippling refracted sunlight through the clear swell above him, fought with ever-numbing fingers against the stiff buckles, and still the weed-tangled line pulled him under, under....*

Until the twentieth century, many, in fact most, Australians feared and distrusted the seas that surrounded their island continent. For pool swimmers, there was little attraction in the rough-and-tumble ocean, where unseen rips, unpredictable currents, rollicking waves and marine predators all conspired to impede a jolly good time. Bathing during daylight hours was largely forbidden anyway, and beaches were primarily a place to stroll, to be seen by the right people and to enjoy the sight of the waves, all from a safe, dry distance[1]. However, for Cecil Healy in 1907, the open ocean was a new playground of extraordinary fascination.

While in London in the company of William Henry, Healy had written home praising the work of the Royal Life Saving Society and regretting his own lack of training in rescue and resuscitation methods. He had even competed in, albeit somewhat unconventionally, the British King's Cup lifesaving challenge and despite the brevity of his introduction to the sport, his love affair with the surf was instantaneous, the allure of its challenges and dangers absolute. For the first time in Cecil Healy's life, an interest outside the swimming bath commanded his precious spare time and attention. Upon his return from the Athens Games, Healy made a beeline for the Sydney surf, in particular the surf at Manly on the city's north shore.

As Federation began the shaping of a new Australian identity, the archetype of the white bushman pastoralist was fading as coastal dwellers, particularly those around Sydney, discovered the surf as a new place for recreation and sport. Australian culture now boldly embraced a new class of surf bathers and sun-seekers, of men rushing eagerly into the breakers, the women remaining near the fringe with children and wavelets around their feet, of basking in the sun like seals and lounging in deckchairs with hats over their eyes and newspapers ruffling in the breeze. This cultural shift also engendered a new form of Australian icon: the surf lifesaver[2].

At the turn of the twentieth century, sea-bathing became both popular and legal on Sydney's beaches, with Manly's Ocean Beach the centre of a new age of beach culture. [Source: Northern Beaches Council/Manly Library Local Studies Collection: Series: 2016-05(50), image ID: 1100010043].

The twentieth-century obsession with sun and surf was not unconditionally reciprocated by the ocean, and many unwary lives were sacrificed to the sea in the early days of the bathing craze. In 1903, 273 people drowned in Australia and by 1910 that number had risen to 547, with drowning the leading cause of 'death by violence' in the Commonwealth, exceeding deaths from falls, burns and injuries inflicted by animals[3]. While Edward 'Happy' Eyre was employed as a professional lifesaver in 1904, the escalating rate of public drownings on Sydney's north shore prompted the formation of the Manly Surf Club on 7 August 1907 under the presidency of Frank Donovan. The aims of the club included prevention of drowning by public education, ensuring the effective rescue of persons in distress and the resuscitation of the 'apparently drowned'[4].

The Manly Surf Club rescue and resuscitation team, including Cecil Healy (front, right), were renowned both as powerful swimmers and for their community spirit and devotion to duty. [Source: Northern Beaches Council/Manly Library Local Studies Collection: Series: 2004-08-26(2), image ID: 1100000655].

These chivalrous ideals naturally attracted many leading sportsmen to the ranks of Sydney's new lifesaving community. As early as 1893, Manly Council had requested that lifebuoys and lines be procured to combat the dreadful toll of drowning—17 souls had perished at North Steyne alone by 1902—but such tools were only of use if able and well-trained men were available to use them. *Lone Hand* magazine gushed in 1915 that 'Probably no place in the world (certainly no place in Australia) shows such a remarkable collection of athletes as are to be found on any of the Sydney beaches any Saturday or Sunday.' First-grade footballers, Australian champions in boxing and wrestling and elite swimmers were all among those signing up to safeguard Sydney's beaches. And on the north shore, Cecil Healy was among them, joining the ranks of lifesavers in their characteristic pose—feet apart, one hand shading the eyes—who formed a symbolic part of the emerging Sydney beach scene.

Twenty-six-year-old Healy joined the Manly Surf Club in November 1907, just four months after its inception. His membership was a real coup given the extent of both his athletic abilities and international observations of lifesaving methods and techniques. The club was the first to be formed on Sydney's northern beaches, but by the end of 1911 there were a further eleven clubs strung like pearls along the city's lengthy coastal fringe. The village of Manly was a new and vibrant centre of the new age of beach culture: no matter whether one had plenty of money or little, the cool surf could be enjoyed for nothing, and day-trippers flocked across the Harbour to sticky their fingers with ice-cream and immerse their bodies in the briny wash. However, such unrestrained indulgence began to raise the moral hackles of the local powerbrokers, and the Manly Council acted in October 1902 to rein in both unrestricted (often naked) marine frolicking and the high casualty rate among unwary bathers, announcing a by-law that forbade surf bathing between 9am and 8pm under pain of a £1 fine[5].

It took the unlikely figure of *Manly and North Sydney News* editor William Gocher—thin, middle-aged and hardly the white knight one imagined at the front of a crusade—to launch a challenge. Gocher indulged in insouciant midday swims at Manly on three consecutive Sundays, clad only in an ill-fitting and inappropriate costume. The police, as guardians of public morality, declined to detain him, being more concerned with people actually drowning than with the rompings of a skinny correspondent in the shallows, but within a year the Manly Council had yielded to public calls for daytime bathing, provided that a modest neck-to-knee costume was worn. Gocher's historic efforts passed into folklore as an indirect genesis for the surf lifesaving movement in Manly, and he was later elected vice-president of the Manly Surf Lifesaving Club in tribute[6].

The Manly Surf Club rescue and resuscitation team of 1907, the first of its kind in Sydney, included some of the world's strongest swimmers, including aquatic royalty in the form of Healy, Alick Wickham and Gus Tartakover, alongside local notables Arthur Relph and Bill Kellam. However, there was much more to lifesaving than brute strength against the sea. As Ray Moran, historian at the Manly Life Saving Club, explained, 'Just being a good swimmer is not enough. Surf lifesaving needs a certain temperament of person—public spirited, willing to do their duty and protect the public, and with a real focus on teamwork.' Surf historian Mark Maddox agreed. 'Surf lifesaving in the early twentieth century was at its most elemental. There were no digital weather reports, live radars, or Twitter feeds of shark sightings. Lifesavers needed empathy with the environment—they relied absolutely on their eyes, their senses and their experience to interpret the surf and the weather. And that environment changed every day; lifesaving was, and is, incredibly dynamic and challenging.'[7]

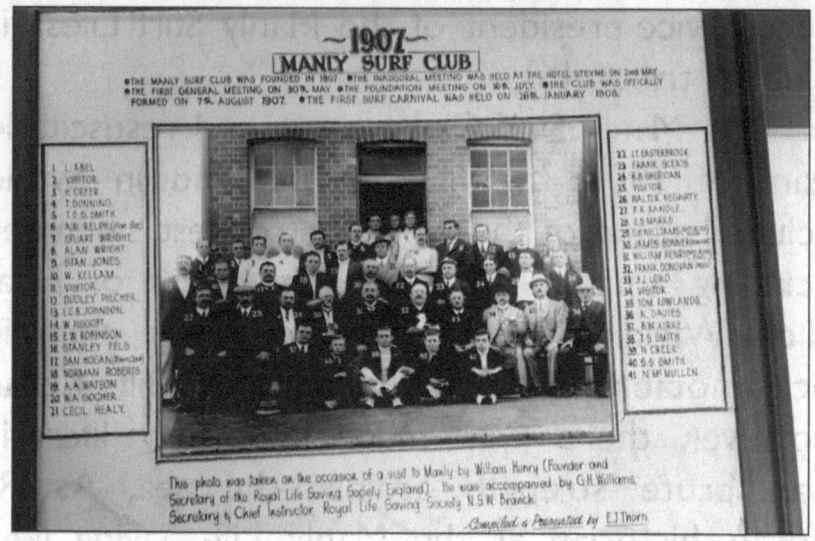

Cecil Healy (21, second row) joined the Manly Surf Club in its inaugural year of 1907, alongside local luminaries of the surf including Bill Kellam (10) and Arthur Relph (6). This photograph depicts supporters of the club during a 1907 visit from Healy's old friend William Henry (31), secretary of the Royal Life Saving Society England. [Source: Manly Surf Club].

Cecil Healy pictured with an early surf rescue reel. Also shown (foreground) is the belt worn by a rescue swimmer with its cork inserts for buoyancy. [Source: Northern Beaches Council/Manly Library Local Studies Collection: Series: 2007-07(60), image ID: 1100003964].

Mike Downman, a former Manly lifesaver and great-nephew of Cecil Healy, is one who knows first-hand the risks of an unpredictable ocean. 'In the days before inflatable boats, lifesavers had to know the ocean. Rescues were made in teams running a line off a reel, and swimmers had to combat waves, tides, rips and weed that could sink a rope and drown the beltman.'[8] As a beltman or rescue swimmer, Healy himself almost suffered this very fate; in 1922, lifesaver Arthur Holmes witnessed several narrow escapes by beltmen whose lines were fouled by seaweed and recalled, 'At Collaroy many years ago, Cecil Healy nearly met an untimely end this way.'

Healy, along with the club's other powerful recruits, was part of Manly's revolutionary approach to rescue and surf safety. Rescue equipment evolved to include cork belts, lifelines and reels (which were a great improvement on the old method of coiling lines on the sand) and the club adopted a new rescue method that had been unwittingly pioneered by Healy himself while in England in 1906. Competing in the King's Cup lifesaving competition, Healy had not been conversant with traditional lifesaving techniques and, although leading in the swim to reach the rescue patient, he had been disqualified for attempting to bring the man ashore in an unorthodox manner. The style he instinctively used now became standard rescue practice at Manly, with one arm placed around the patient's chest, leaving the other arm and both legs free to swim.

Public demonstrations of rescue techniques attracted new members, young and old, to the burgeoning lifesaving movement on Sydney beaches prior to World War I. [Source: Northern Beaches Council/Manly Library Local Studies Collection: Series: 2004-10-15(8), image ID: 1100000727].

The club constructed a lookout platform on the beach, and a lifesaving class with 40 students commenced in November 1907 under the instruction of George Williams of the Royal Life Saving Society. To pass, each man had to acquire knowledge of rescue and resuscitation methods, swim 400 yards in eight minutes or better and show competence in the water with clothes and boots on. Furthermore, club members had to drill for two months to gain the bronze medallion and proficiency certificate of the Surf Life Saving

Association of Australia and attend beach patrol on weekends and holidays in rotation. Even the club's executive was required to gain proficiency certificates.

Mobile lookout towers, such as this one constructed by the Manly Surf Lifesaving Club in 1914, gave lifesaving crews an elevated view of bathers, sea conditions and hazards such as sharks and rips. [Source: Northern Beaches Council/Manly Library Local Studies Collection: image number: 002/002041; original image appeared in Town and Country Journal, 18 February 1914].

Healy was an enthusiastic supporter of surf bathing in its embryonic days in Australia, and backed the campaign of William Gocher for the right to bathe at any hour of the day. In 1907, he also spoke out vehemently against proposed changes to 'acceptable bathing dress' that would force men to add a modesty skirt over their bathers. 'The King and Queen of England attended swim meets at the Bath Club where the (old) costume was worn', he protested. 'The idea of skirts is perfectly ridiculous: why, they will be ordering us to wear stays next!' When the idea of segregating the sexes on the beaches was suggested by the Manly Council, Healy responded, 'Do the municipalities propose to organise a body of women lifesavers? Are women in difficulties in the water to be left to their fate and men prevented from going to their assistance because the ordinance says they must confine themselves to a certain part of the beach?' A proposal to restrict bathing to half an hour at a time really raised his ire. 'How are we to maintain our supremacy in the swimming world if long-distance champions are confined to half an hour's swim? Counting the time taken up in disrobing, it would take men of greater prowess than the great Kieran himself to cover [a mile] in regulation time. A suspicious person might be justified in wondering whether—judging by the fact that certain municipalities own swimming baths adjacent to the beaches, which have been poorly patronised since surf bathing became a craze—there was not method in the present madness.'[9]

Within a year, Healy had become a leader at Manly Surf Club, vocal out of the water and powerful in it. He performed with distinction in many surf carnivals, and in October 1908, the club's founding captain, Melnotte Roberts, handed the reins to Healy, who would retain the captaincy until September 1913. Arthur Relph was a great friend of Healy's, and he, too, took an active leadership role with the club. 'No one man can run a club effectively', Relph declared. 'It has to be a team effort and Cecil Healy certainly [has] the necessary attributes of leadership.'

***

The surf was viewed by some as the *bete noir* of the swimmer anxious to maintain pace in the pool, a place of exhaustion that compromised the stroke and exposed the competitor to all manner of potential hazards, not the least of which was death by drowning. However, Cecil Healy's new preoccupation with the surf had not impacted on either his desire or his performance in the swimming baths; in fact, the addition of surf swimming to his already gruelling physical preparation only enhanced his power and stamina. The big sprinters all started the 1907–08 swimming season in ferocious form. Fellow surf devotee Alick Wickham went within 1/5 of a second of his 50-yard world record in his first appearance after a winter in the surf in October 1907, while Manly youngster Len Murray also swam 24 3/5 seconds for the fifty in the first event of the season. Healy himself started the season with a sub-57-second hundred in the East Sydney 100-yard handicap in October, an eye-popping effort indeed, but Charles Daniels would raise the bar for the hundred during season 1907–08, setting an astounding new world mark of 55 2/5 seconds in his favoured setting of a short pool, which aided his artistry in turning. Natator publicly expressed doubts about Healy's ability to break the 56-second barrier, but Healy shrugged off such reservations with continued excellence in sprints and an occasional dabble in middle-distance racing. On 14 December 1907, Healy won the 500-yard championship of NSW by 20 yards, his time of 6 minutes 23 1/5 seconds besting brother Reg's winning effort of the previous season by more than ten seconds.

After missing most of the 1906–07 domestic meets while in Europe, Healy set his sights on winning everything possible on his return. Naturally, he wished to stamp his authority on his pet 100-yard event and reclaim his national title from Son Baker. The East Sydney 100-yard championship on 28 December 1907 featured the three fastest sprinters in the world in Healy, Baker and Alick Wickham. The trio went neck and neck for the first three-quarters of the race, before Healy's superior strength, honed in the Manly surf, saw him stretch to win by three yards in 57 3/5 seconds from Wickham, who himself had put four emphatic yards on the reigning national champion Baker.

On 4 January 1908, Healy erased his rivals in the 440-yard state championship at Manly, this time using the trudgen to leave his brother Reg and rising star Harold Hardwick far in his wake. Two weeks later, on 18 January, at the Mosman Swimming Club carnival, Healy won the NSW 300-yard championship, and then, stunningly, smashed Barney Kieran's old world record for 200 yards just six days later, lowering the record from 2 minutes 13 4/5 seconds to 2 minutes 11 1/5 seconds in a handicap race against his brother. Natator conceded, 'There is nothing like perseverance and there are no half measures about popular "Cec" when he lays himself out for anything'[10].

The ASA penchant for sharing around the hosting rights for national championships saw the 1907–08 title series move to Perth. Healy, with his East Sydney clubmates Dickman and Garland, made the long trip west by sea, but this voyage had no negative impact on Healy's performances.

He easily won both the 100- and 220-yard titles, the 100 by a dozen yards in a time of 57 1/5 seconds, a time not bettered in Australia until 1927.

Healy's dominance was now approaching the echelons of his old rivals Cavill and Kieran. With nobody in his own stable at East Sydney able to match him and East Sydney arguably the most powerful club in the nation, it seemed Healy would have to look overseas again for the competition necessary to push him under 56 seconds. However, the Perth championship series had a surprise in store in the form of a stocky schoolboy who had won the 220- and 440-yard championships of Victoria before his fifteenth birthday in 1906. In Perth, at his first national appearance, young Frank Beaurepaire annexed both the 880-yard and mile titles with ease. Healy, who had intended to return home after the sprint events, could not resist this new challenge, and extended his stay by a week to square up to Beaurepaire in the quarter-mile (440-yard) championship. The redoubtable Beaurepaire mocked that 'if Healy does win, it will be the hardest race he ever swam', before beating the veteran squarely for the title. However, despite the defeat, Perth's *Sunday Times* gushed, 'Cecil Healy is (still) the Adonis of the natatorial world.'

The upstart Beaurepaire was completely unabashed. A month later, on 10 March 1908, he covered 220 yards in 2 minutes 34 1/5 seconds at his home pool in Melbourne, breaking Healy's record by 1/5 of a second. The papers were already calling Beaurepaire 'a worthy successor to poor Barney Kieran', and he was quickly booked to represent Australia at the 1908 Olympic Games in London.

Audacious Victorian teen Frank Beaurepaire shocked Healy with victory in the 440-yard Australasian championship of

1908. [Source: State Library of NSW: Davis Sporting Collection part II: swimming. IE no.946050].

These Games, initially scheduled for Rome, were moved to England after the carnage caused by the Mount Vesuvius eruptions of 1906. On paper, Healy was the obvious candidate to attend his second Olympic Games, but with limited funds available from the NSW ASA, was now expected to raise his own fare, which proved impossible. The VSA paid Beaurepaire's travel costs, as did the QSA for Frank Springfield, while Healy's old East Sydney clubmate Theo Tartakover, who was already in London, also attended, representing NSW. Overall, the Australasian team fared very poorly in London, failing to win a single gold medal compared with Britain's tally of 30 and America's of nine. Beaurepaire and Tartakover did not progress past the semi-finals of the 100 metres and Springfield was swum out in the heats of the 1500 metres. Beaurepaire, Tartakover, Springfield and Snowy Baker could finish no better than fourth in the 4x200-metre relay.

While he made no public comment about Daniels' superhuman 55 2/5 seconds over the hundred yards, both the loss of his world record and the public doubt over his ability to regain it rankled quietly with Healy. He started the 1908–09 season in what was becoming his trademark fashion, like a scalded cat, setting a new world mark of 63 1/5 seconds for 110 yards in christening the new municipal baths at the Domain on 17 October 1908. However, he reserved his most commanding statement for the East Sydney 100-yard handicap on 14 November. Off scratch, Healy powered to a time of 55 seconds flat for the 100 yards, 2/5 of a second better than Daniels' record. Unfortunately the record could not be ratified, as appropriate timing provisions were not in place. 'Cecil Healy is still our champion sprinter, and no one can touch him over the hundred-yard course', boasted the *Catholic Press*. 'It will be a pity if he does not meet Daniels again before he loses his form. As a rule, swimmers go off quickly, and Cecil has a decided tendency to put on beef. Although Daniels beat him by a touch in England, he is confident he would reverse matters if they raced again, especially over a course without a turn.'[11] However, the Australian public were robbed of the chance to see the world's best go head-to-head when Daniels declined to visit Australia in 1909 after failing to appear in both 1906 and 1907. The following year, Daniels married American heiress Florence Goodyear Wagner and retired from competitive swimming to a life of luxury.

The redesigned Domain Baths, pictured here in 1908, featured a two-storey stand with dressing sheds on the lower level and a large-capacity spectator stand above. The pool suited Healy entirely—at 110 yards long, there was no need for turns during the short sprints, one of Healy's particular weaknesses. [Source: City of Sydney Archives, image no: 094174].

The new Domain baths would play host to the Australasian hundred-yard, half-mile and mile championships in January 1909, with the *Catholic Press* predicting that 'Cecil Healy should keep the sprinting honours, but we cannot see a New South Welshman who is at all likely to beat Beaurepaire over the distances.' While the new pool, at 110 yards long, suited Healy entirely with its lack of turns for the sprints, the architects had obviously not foreseen the massive public interest in the Healy–Beaurepaire rivalry. On 15 January 1909, more than 7,000 spectators tried to cram into the venue through the single entrance, with police summoned to control the dreadful scrimmage. The 100-yard field saw the fastest sprinters in the Commonwealth engaged, including Healy, Hardwick and Wickham. By halfway, Healy was 1 1/2 yards in front, even crossing in front of his rivals with 25 yards to go to finish three yards clear in 58 1/2 seconds, thereby defending the title he won in Perth and capturing the crown for a fourth time[12]. However, Beaurepaire was equally impressive, defeating a tiring Healy over 220 yards, winning the half-mile by 40 yards and the mile 'with ridiculous ease'. He wasn't Healy's only young rival, either, with Harold Hardwick equalling Healy's official Australasian 100-yard record of 57 seconds late in 1909. Hardwick was 20 years old and had been a brilliant schoolboy swimmer, winning his school 100-yard championship in 1906 in 62 4/5 seconds. However, at the NSW championships on 15 January 1910, Healy won the 220 yards by three yards, dashing past Hardwick in the stretch after the youngster had outstripped him in the turn. Despite the foul weather, the time of 2 minutes 29 4/5 seconds was just 1 2/5 seconds outside Kieran's 1905 world record.

Both Healy and Hardwick made the trip to Melbourne for the 1910 Australasian championships on 2 February, where 4,000 people (half of whom were women) jammed into the St. Kilda baths for the first day, crowding the stands, the roof and even the springboards and the steps leading down to the sea. Beaurepaire and Healy were the star attractions, Beaurepaire as a distance champion and Healy unbeaten in the national 100-yard championship since 1904. There were seven starters in the hundred, including Hardwick and, startlingly, Beaurepaire. A heavy swell was rolling diagonally across the St. Kilda course, but Healy was ideally positioned on the north side and won by over a length after leading all the way. Hardwick finished third and Beaurepaire a creditable fourth. Healy's dominance continued throughout the remainder of 1910, and he set a new Australasian record for 100 metres on 26 November and another for 150 yards at Rushcutter's Bay in December.

Healy was truly one of the 'big men' of Australian sport, enthused *The Catholic Press*: 'Swimmers in the front rank have always been on the big side ... Some of our leading natatorial artists, such as Ernest Cavill and W.F. Corbett, have been men of stature, and one of the latest,

Cecil Healy, though not tall, has a frame of Sandow-like proportions, and indeed, owes much of his speed to the high training his muscular system receives from constantly dumb-belling.' However, Healy was no muscle-bound thrasher. *The Referee* wrote admiringly, 'From the time he enters the water until he grasps the rope, [Healy] is the centre of a disturbance, the visual signs of which are swirling water, flashes of brown arms and rapid headway. In the middle of all this, however, is a beautifully adjusted human machine impelled by a perfect combination of physical and mental effort. Healy in the water seemingly goes by clockwork. Everything is rhythmical, and one almost feels the nervous energy that carries him over rather than through the water and then culminates in the irresistible dash at the end that is the climax of his effort.'[13]

***

Cecil Healy and fellow members of the Manly Surf Club with belt and reel. By 1910, the club was renowned for innovation in training and rescue technologies, and for the audacity of its rescues. [Source: Northern Beaches Council/Manly Library Local Studies Collection: Series: 2004-10-15(8), image ID: 1100000720].

Cecil Healy in the uniform of the Manly Surf Club. Healy developed a reputation for both fearlessness and recklessness in the surf, his underlying self-doubt often driving him to acts of daring few would attempt. [Source:

State Library of NSW, Davis Sporting Collection part II: swimming. IE no.943370].

By 1910, the Manly Surf Club, with their new technologies and training systems, had reeled off a string of daring rescues upon which the club's reputation for audacity was growing, and the adrenaline of combat against an often-savage sea further fed that element of Cecil Healy's character that he so fiercely concealed beneath a warm and generous persona. The anxiety accompanying his early efforts to beat the big men of world swimming had, over the years, morphed into a silent but desperate need to prove himself—to prove that he was good enough to win, that he was brave enough to accept a challenge, that he was worthy of both self-respect and the respect of others. When he joined the surf lifesaving movement in 1907, his record in the pool was so impressive there could be no public question as to his achievements, but the inner monologue demanding that he assure both himself and the public he was the fastest and the boldest now manifested itself as outbreaks of daring that often drove him into serious danger.

The *Catholic Press* publicly chided Healy for being a 'particularly reckless fellow, who seems to delight in tossing the dice with the old chap who carries the scythe.'[14] In October 1910, the NSW Surf-bathing Association, of which Healy was now vice-president, staged a carnival to honour the visit of Healy's old friend William Henry from the Royal Lifesaving Society in London. Foul weather forced the cancellation of most events, but Healy and Henry still gave an exhibition of surf swimming in the crashing waves. With the sea running mountainously high and the water a maelstrom so that the strongest swimmers feared to venture in, the pair would swim two or three hundred yards out to sea and coolly ride in on foam-crested walls of water.

Reports of sharks in conflict with humans at Manly came as early as 1890, with fisherman warning bathers of the presence of the carnivorous fish around boats and piers. A fatal attack on a swimmer in Sydney Harbour in 1895 prompted calls for fenced enclosures to protect bathers in the open sea[15]. Healy, however, was undeterred by such dangers. 'I would not mind trying my hand [wrestling a shark]', he told his brother Harold, 'provided my adversary was given a little dental treatment beforehand.'[16] Despite that quip, Healy was among a group of surf swimmers who believed that sharks would not attack humans close to the shore, and in 1910, he undertook to prove the theory with a swim from the North Steyne dressing sheds to Fairy

Bower—in short, the entire length of Manly Beach, a feat never previously documented. This followed a savage attack on a group of fishermen at North Head in 1909, a fatal mauling at Newcastle just a fortnight before Healy's swim and sightings of large sharks feeding on salmon at Manly all summer. Healy was accompanied by a surf boat from which swimmers regularly leapt into the water to escort him, but his pace beat them all off, and he even sprinted the last 50 yards in to shore. Healy's passage was, reported the *Telegraph,* 'uninterrupted', and he emerged from the surf exclaiming, 'There you are! I've proved it!' The swim did not exactly have the desired effect, however, with some claiming Healy had set a bad example to others not as lucky as himself[17].

In 1910, a surf carnival to honour the visit of British lifesaver William Henry was cancelled due to rough conditions, but Henry and Healy repaid the crowds with a demonstration of surf swimming described as 'thrilling'. [Source: National Library of Australia; original image appeared in the Sydney Mail and NSW Advertiser, 26 October 1910, page 32].

Regardless of the genesis of his bravado, Healy's boldness and courage in the surf saved many lives. Sunday 29 January 1911 was everything a Manly summer day ought to be—a blue, clear, brilliant sky and beaches packed with bathers dabbling and diving in the foamy breakers. However, on the beach, Healy was brooding and bruised. Just days earlier, unheralded Manly swimmer Tod Solomons had burst through the pack to snatch the national 100-yard championship from him at his home pool in the Domain, with its beautiful straight course. Healy was racked with introspection. *What should he have done better? Had he missed something in his preparation or race plan?* The dark hurricane of recrimination eventually burst like a boil in the only means of expression Healy knew; pushing himself to the very edge, drowning his doubts in risk and physical pain.

He was out in the surf assisting a rescue of four adults and a child in difficulty when a further dreadful cry for help was heard. Two more victims—Mr P.A. Hannelly, aged 26, and W.B. Bradley, a 13-year-old lad from the country—had been swept out to sea and were already far beyond the line of the breakers. Leaving his clubmates to help the group of five stumble back to shore, Healy struck out toward the rapidly disappearing pair, scything through the water like a torpedo. He was immediately grabbed around the neck by the struggling, terrified pair, and had to push Hannelly away, urging him to float on his back while Healy supported him and tried to hold up the half-drowned teenager, waving desperately to the lifeguards on the beach to run out a line.

A frantic crowd had now gathered on the shore, pointing and crying and, as the lifelines were run out, eagerly trying to help haul them back in. The result was a near-catastrophe. Three times, the lines snapped under the strain, and by the time fellow lifeguard Jack Reynolds finally reached Healy, Bradley was unconscious. Reynolds took charge of the boy, leaving Healy to support the limp and exhausted Hannelly for more than 20 minutes until further help arrived and the pair were towed to shore, where Bradley had been resuscitated after strenuous efforts. Healy was visibly exhausted by the strain of supporting the drowning Hannelly; it was the nearest brush with death of his career. The effort earned him a silver medal from the Royal Humane Society and the Manly Surf Club's gold medal for meritorious rescue, and the father of another youth he later rescued also insisted on presenting him with an expensive watch and chain[18].

***

Despite the Manly Surf Club leading the efforts to improve lifesaving techniques, obtain suitable lifesaving equipment and improve bathing conditions for swimmers, their relationship with the Manly Council was often tense. In 1909, the club had leased a large brick hall opposite the beach as a clubhouse, installing electric lighting, toilets and showers, and a gym equipped with punching bags and dumbbells. A petition they submitted to the Manly Council for their own permanent facility was provisionally approved on 15 March 1910, but a cohort of aldermen, fearing the club would take control of the beach away from the Council, rose in protest against the plan and the final move was stalled[19].

Strangely, the Council was far more receptive to the ambitions of the North Steyne Surf Bather's and Life Saving Club, formed just up the beach from Manly in December 1907, and they were granted consent to build a beachfront clubhouse without argument or condition. However, the true schism arose in September 1911 when Manly instructor Bill Kellam secretly proposed to the Manly Council that a new club be formed purely for the purpose of lifeguarding, with all surf swimmers and social members excluded. Reassured that their power would not be usurped, the Council instantly carried the attendant resolution and, to rub sea-salt into the wound, gave the new organisation consent for a clubhouse on the beach. The response from the Manly Surf Club was as cold as the winter wind. In a letter forwarded to Council on 19 September, the club withdrew from any future rescue activities at Manly, a move made with regret after years of faithful service and considerable expense. Secretary Watson concluded, 'Our members are at a loss to understand what has induced your Council to depart from its promise and show such scant consideration to a body of men who have done so much to promote the best interests of surf bathing.'

Meanwhile, the new club—known as the Manly Surf Lifesaving Club—formed its committee, with Bill Kellam as secretary and Mayor Quirk in the chair assuring the 50 members they 'would receive every assistance from the Manly Council', which was met with applause. The fallout of that move was serious unrest in the Manly Surf Club ranks, with some committeemen unhappy at the withdrawal of the club from lifeguarding activities. When Council offered the club another opportunity for a clubhouse in return for Sunday and holiday patrols, club captain Healy adamantly refused, instead calling for a strike in protest. Some members did leave to fulfil their lifesaving ambitions with the new club, but Healy was not among them. At the club's general meeting on 13 October 1911, he expressed frustration that Kellam, a valued and seemingly dedicated club man, had not consulted the committee before approaching the council. However, President Frank Donovan laid the blame for the split squarely upon the council's attempts to restrict the number of surf bathers at the beach, this despite a public report from the Surf Bathing Association congratulating the Manly Surf Club on its lifesaving proficiency. However, the rift was irreparable, and more than a century on, the Manly Surf Club and the Manly Surf Lifesaving Club remain distinct and disconnected entities[20].

EIGHT

LOVE'S GOLDEN SILENCE

'Set me as a seal upon thine heart,
As a seal upon thine arm,
For love is as strong as death—
Many waters cannot quench love,
Nor can the floods drown it.'

—Solomon's Song, *The Holy Bible* (chapter 8, verses 6–7)

***

'Manly is real', wrote Cecil Healy.

'Campers may become enraptured with Freshwater, Bondi may have its devotees, Coogee its habitués, and Cronulla its enthusiasts. But none of them enslave the mind, memory, and heart, or worm themselves into the affections like Manly does those who learn to know her. It has an indefinable something, a personality that makes one forgetful of its blemishes, and like it for its very faults. Admittedly it has, as it were, been badly brought up, its education has been woefully neglected. Still, its natural charm rises superior to every militating circumstance. Always it is Manly.'[1]

Cecil Healy was in love. Weekends spent immersed in the blue breakers and dusted with the white sand of its beaches started a lifelong love affair for Cecil Healy with the Manly peninsula in northern Sydney. Even after all his travels throughout Europe, from the wild, grey strangeness of the North Sea to the glittering temptations of the Mediterranean, Healy's affection for the soft and rhythmic energy of the Manly surf remained unsurpassed and unwavering throughout his life. 'Even in its angriest mood, the Mediterranean tosses no surf upon its shores', he wrote wistfully, 'only big cumbersome waves that lash themselves into a fury on the pebbly beaches and rocky coastline. The sound they produce is a revengeful, vindictive roar, not like the purr of the Pacific's surge, which is as music to the ear of the surfer. One misses the breakers with their snow-white crests that illumine the face of the water as with a smile, revealing a row of glittering teeth.'

The easy seaside charm of Manly's northern beaches attracted Healy to move from central Sydney across the harbour to the pretty village in 1909. [Source: Northern Beaches Council/Manly Library Local Studies Collection: Series: 2004-10-15(8), image ID: 1100000721].

Manly's famous commercial strip The Corso, pictured in 1912. The opportunity to bathe, eat ice-cream and promenade along the seashore attracted crowds of day-trippers to the village and the surf lifesaving movement grew alongside. [Source: Northern Beaches Council/Manly Library Local Studies Collection: Series: 2005-07-26(5), image ID: 1100002208].

Such was his affection for the northern beaches that in 1909, Healy left the family home in Darlinghurst for a new life in Manly, boarding at a large house on the hill overlooking the wharf and cove. This now meant a long daily commute across the harbour to reach Hornsby's offices in the city, but for Healy, the ferry ride was another opportunity to commune with the sea, and he would have sacrificed much more than an extra hour of sleep for a chance to live on his beloved northern peninsula. His choice of new residence was rather a grand one. The steep streets around Addison Road above the main Manly shopping and entertainment district were home to many affluent and influential Manly residents, with grand Victorian mansions such as *Hawthorn*, *Kulnura* and *Uyeno* occupied by bank managers, investors, architects and wealthy merchants. Healy's new home at *Karoon*, on the corner of Darley and Addison Road, had been home to surveyor Adam Maitland and his wife Victoria since 1900. The big house also rang with the energy of six children, all daughters[2].

Addison Road flows across the hill parallel to the famous Corso, in the heart of Manly's commercial district. The two are connected by Darley Road, and in 1909 there were many middle-class boarding houses and guesthouses in the area, close as it was to the shops, quay and beaches. Healy may have sought accommodation in the area through friends; the mother of his Manly Surf Club teammate Gus Tartakover owned a boarding house, *Kyverdale*, in Addison Road, one of at least six in that street. However, it was to the Maitland home he went, a house, he soon discovered, that was full of beautiful, intelligent, sporty women. 'A man feels he's a man when his skin is a real good brown', wrote local poet Samuel Mills in 1906. 'In fact, the man who has been browned in the breakers has a fatal tendency to fall in love on the slightest excuse or provocation.'[3] And it was Adam Maitland's fourth daughter Muriel who became the first woman ever to turn Healy's head and heart away from his beloved sea and create an unimaginably tragic complication in his life.

During the early twentieth century, there was a powerful feminine influence in Addison Road, with at least 12 households headed by women, many of these boarding houses such as *Karoon*. Victoria Maitland's husband Adam, a licensed surveyor since 1875, was often absent, working in the NSW outback as District Surveyor at Forbes and with the Closer Settlement Advisory Board at Condobolin. His children had been born and raised on the central plains, but Maitland was of good stock, more than just your average rough-hewn bushman in dirty flannels and a battered felt hat. Born in 1851, he had come to Australia from Essex in England as a teenager with his parents and sister. His father, Ernest Leslie Maitland, was a civil engineer and his sister, Jeanette Jessie, married prominent Sydney lawyer and politician Sir Albert Gould[4].

Maitland's wife, Victoria Maria Elizabeth Jones, was made of far plainer and sterner stuff. Born in 1859 at Cadow Station, a 31,000-acre spread located 35 miles from Forbes, her mother Elizabeth and two of her siblings had died of typhus when she was three and Victoria had been raised by her Protestant father, Edward Jones, and his new wife, Georgina Breathour, the Irish-born governess from neighbouring Bundaburrah Station. Jones never smoked, drank, or swore, and was reported to milk 100 cows a day at Cadow. He was a silent man who sought no public positions and filled none. Victoria had never left Cadow before marrying Adam Maitland in 1879, and her first three children, Edith Clare, Kate Clara and Edith Elsie, were all born at nearby Forbes. In 1885, the family moved to Condobolin, where Adam worked as a mining surveyor and their other five children were all born, including her only son, Ernest, and daughters Muriel, Vera, Ethel Una and Olive[5].

Perhaps persuaded by his wealthy and high-ranking sister, Lady Gould, herself in a position of great social influence as the wife of a Sydney senator, Maitland brought his family to the city at the turn of the century. His eldest child, Edith Clare, and his son Ernest had died as infants, but his two eldest surviving daughters, Kate (known as Clari) and Elsie, were now in their late teens and ready to make an entrance into good society. The younger girls were enrolled at Manly College under the eagle eye of principal Miss Hayes-Williams, and the country lasses immediately proved themselves clever and able. In 1901, both Muriel (aged 14) and Vera (12) received prizes for composition, geography and history, with Vera obtaining additional honours in English, arithmetic and poetry. Little Olive, who was just eight years old, was commended for her sewing and brushwork.

Adam returned to work on the scrubby western plains, leaving his wife to both raise a large cohort of daughters and keep up the big house at *Karoon*, which she did by taking in boarders. However, Victoria Maitland was no downtrodden fishwife. Her daughters were well schooled, and Victoria herself was a successful social hostess. She was a member of the 'Manly Matrons' committee, whose 1910 ball, complete with flags, palm trees and pink-shaded lights, was voted 'Best of the Season' and proved a worthy showcase for her daughters Muriel, Una and Vera. The girls, often in concert with the Tartakover sisters, attended dances at the tennis club and the town hall, and were the embodiment of the 'Gibson Girl', the modern woman portrayed by American artist Charles Dana Gibson in the early twentieth century as competitive, sporty, emancipated and beautiful.

The athletic interests of the Maitland sisters were of the genteel variety still favoured in high society prior to World War I. Drawing-room games such as table tennis were in vogue among the middle and upper classes, and prior to the Great War, Sydney was replete with table tennis clubs and ping-pong societies. The Maitland girls were all skilled players, and their mother hosted a tournament at *Karoon* in April 1902, with Clari, Muriel and two young gentlemen representing the Federal club in a match against North Sydney, with Federal winning by 80 games to 42. The event was a precursor to the 1902 Ladies Ping-pong Championship of NSW, held at the YMCA in Pitt Street to accommodate the large crowds of spectators. The tournament garnered 64 entries, including both married and single girls, with Clari, Muriel and Elsie Maitland all in the field. Muriel and Elsie were declared 'the most dashing players, their driving being very good', and Clari played using a custom long-handled vellum racket that ensured the balls came noiselessly off the bat. Muriel finished runner-up in the tournament, and *The Newsletter* gushed, 'Some splendid play was witnessed, the dashing style of Miss Muriel Maitland being much applauded.'[6]

Thus, into this hothouse of blooming feminine achievement and modern, slimline figures came the 28-year-old bachelor Healy, one of Sydney's most eligible young gentlemen. Despite his native shyness, Healy was a sought-after social guest and, with a reputation for honesty and spotless living, a most adequate member of Sydney's Edwardian middle class, hence it was something of a surprise that, given his immense public profile and clean-cut nature, he had not yet married. The median age of Sydney bridegrooms in 1911 was 24 years and Healy's associates Arthur Relph (married in 1890), Dick Cavill (1903), Fred Lane (1908) and Snowy Baker (1909) were all family men. However, a certain cult of bachelorhood had developed in Australia in the late nineteenth and early twentieth centuries, with a distinct shift to later marriage as British migrants brought with them the ethic of a 'proper time to marry' that had developed among the English middle and upper classes during the 1850s and 60s. The Australian

Department of Demography also speculated that the sizeable proportion of Australian men of Irish extraction, such as the Healys, were notoriously diffident toward marriage. The 1890s Depression, more severe even than that of the 1930s, saw a further trend in the postponement of marriage, exacerbated by a further economic recession in 1902–04. At the turn of the twentieth century, Australian males still heavily outnumbered females, and in 1911, only 42% of men aged 25–30 in NSW were married[7].

Healy, however, had no shortage of female admirers. Many surf rescues conspicuously involved a female 'victim', and the *Sydney Mail* speculated slyly that 'the old-style faint is quite superseded by distress in the breakers when the desired man is about.' One scorching weekend in January 1911, crowds poured like flies into the breakers at Manly and many bathers were getting into trouble. Miss Irene King and her friend Miss Gillespie were caught in a deep channel that had formed at South Steyne, and Healy came to the rescue of the 'fair Irene', who had been under twice and promptly grabbed Healy about the neck. She was a big, strong maiden, and witnesses said the struggle Healy had with the drowning girl was an 'exceedingly fine performance' in terms of both propriety and surf rescue technique.

By 1909, Cecil Healy (left) was a sought-after member of Sydney's middle-class social circles. [Source: State Library of NSW, Album 101: Photographs of the Allen family, March 1902–February 1907. IE no.710102].

Going solo ... Despite no shortage of female admirers, questions remained as to why Healy remained unmarried as his public profile and social reputation grew. [Source: State Library of NSW, Album 101: Photographs of the Allen family, March 1902-February 1907. IE no.730153].

When Cecil Healy and Muriel Maitland met in 1909, she had already been 'out' for three years, her entrance into society having occurred in June 1906 at the Manly Cottage Hospital Ball, a veritable fairyland of ferns and flowers for more than 400 guests. There was something about the 22-year-old, even amongst such a large family of vigorous and clever sisters, that caught at Healy in a way his shy and reticent nature had always resisted. Perhaps, for all her city education and her fine pin-tucked blouses and silk gloves, a little of the backblocks in which she had been raised remained—a little dash, a little open-air wildness. However, Muriel's was also a devoted nature, her mind quick and intelligent, and her competitive streak was one Healy would surely have identified with.

Those pre-war years were a gay time in the Maitland household, a joyous whirl of the north shore's well-to-do, athletic and educated. Elsie married into the prominent local Moore family in 1910. Her husband Alan was the son of a wealthy ironmonger, and the family, which included several prominent aldermen, lived just around the corner in Darley Road. Una later wed one of Australia's richest men, felt manufacturer Henri Van de Velde, who was also a fanatical sportsman and boxer, while Vera enjoyed the same passion for golf as her lover Harold (Bill) Targett, a veteran of the Boer War. Targett was a respected Sydney sportswriter, a great raconteur with whom Healy would have had much in common, given his long relationship with the press and willingness to comment on most matters sporting.

Pre-war Manly was also a wonderland of romance for young lovers, as there were plenty of streets to wander amid gracious homes with handsome porticos, shaded by spreading Port Jackson figs. At the northern end of Addison Road lay the great white crescent of beach backed by a low stone wall, green walks and asphalt paths beneath the Norfolk Island pines. Here, Samuel Mills observed, 'He and she sit placid and composed, both silent, for an hour together; he evidently sure he cannot get away, and she evidently sure it is no use for him to try. It is only vitalised temperaments that come to conclusions like those. I have never seen anything so expressive of victory and calm as that of a woman who sits in the sunshine on the beach at Manly with her lover.'

However, there was very little promenading or shy handholding for Cecil Healy. His relationship with Muriel was both complicated and, in truly Healy fashion, secretive. She was feisty and enthusiastic, but Healy maintained a physical and emotional distance that both propriety and Healy's own doubts and insecurities demanded. Despite women regularly casting themselves into his path on the beaches, Healy's knowledge of the fairer sex was extremely limited. He had been raised in an almost exclusively male household, educated at boys' colleges and his swim training was confined to a segregated male environment. Even if he had had the natural insouciance of a Dick Cavill or Snowy Baker, nothing could have prepared an already reticent young man for life in a household of pretty, eligible and vigorous women.

It would be understandable if Healy was cautious about entering into a relationship in a house where not only Muriel's mother but her five sisters resided, all curious, all knowing, or worse, all disapproving, and any chance of a relationship was further stymied by factors of a social and spiritual nature. The Maitland family were Anglicans and Healy was a Catholic, a virtually insurmountable barrier to any pre-war relationship. Adam Maitland may have approved of Healy as a man; Maitland himself was an imposing figure, well over six feet in height, his bronzed form topped by a luxuriant mane of white hair, and he was a good man, known in both the country and the city as sober and true. He was a man of the land, which Healy had grown to love and respect on his travels to agricultural areas with Hornsby's. Further, Maitland's true passion was surfing, an enthusiasm he indulged until his death at 86 years of age in 1936[8]. This was almost certainly another point of commonality between himself and the youthful enigma who lived beneath his roof, the young man who had earned every available accolade as a swimmer and lifesaver, and yet was so modest about himself, who was so publicly beloved and yet so privately restrained. However, while Adam Maitland was convinced of the power of surf and sun to relieve human physical ills—for they had apparently cured his own mid-life infirmity—this Victorian belief in the vitality gained from nature came with an inextricable link to morality. Vigour must be pure, unsullied, untainted by lustfulness or, God forbid, Papacy. And so while personal regard may have been high, the religious and moral barrier between Healy and Adam Maitland's daughter was not to be overcome.

***

The summer of 1911 saw huge public interest in the continued rivalry between long-distance champion Frank Beaurepaire and sprint hero Healy in the lead-up to the national swimming championships at the Domain in January. Healy won the 100-yard NSW selection trial, touching out fellow Manly sprinters Tod Solomons and Harold Hardwick. However, those who dared dismiss Healy as good for little beyond the sprint distances were silenced when he set a record in the same week using the crawl stroke over three-quarters of a mile (1,320 yards) to win the President's Cup handicap, giving his rivals up to 4 1/2 minutes head start and taking 16 seconds off Beaurepaire's 1909 Australian record[9]. *The Sydney Morning Herald* praised Healy's resourcefulness and determination over the years when he had consistently been beaten by Lane and Cavill and had been heavily criticised for the perceived inelegance of his crawl: 'For a long time looked upon as simply a sprinter, by grim doggedness and perseverance, Cecil has gradually lengthened the distance, until his recent remarkable doings have caused many to prophesy that at the coming meeting he will turn the tables on his great antagonist.'[10] Not only had Healy persisted with the crawl over short distances, he had continued to adapt his stroke for longer swims, experimenting with a greater longitudinal roll of the body and altering his arm action to enable rotation of his head to the side to breathe more regularly. Beaurepaire, on the other hand, continued to use his own version of the trudgen with the addition of small leg flutters to maintain momentum between strokes.

The headlines preceding the Australian championships in January 1911 trumpeted, 'Healy and Beaurepaire: who will win?' The *Sydney Sportsman* warned that 'Healy was the champion when Beaurepaire was in the paddling pool, and he is not only still on top, but, as his hair recedes from his forehead, his powers in the water become greater.' However, Beaurepaire was said to be in the 'best of nick', and there were some who still expressed fears that the strenuous combination of surf and pool swimming would weary Healy and blunt his sprinting powers, which as it turned out, proved to be the case.

Healy lost his 100-yard title, not to the pundit's choice in Beaurepaire, but to the unheralded Tod Solomons, while nineteen-year-old newcomer Bill Longworth won the three-quarter mile in a world record of 17 minutes 42 seconds, with Healy second and Beaurepaire third. The latter pair were so busy watching one another and swimming so close together that their arms kept colliding that they let Longworth get away from them. A week later, on 17 January, Healy and Beaurepaire faced

Longworth again over 440 yards, the crush of people trying to enter the Domain so great that the entrance gates were carried away and the streets were choked with taxis and buses. This time, Longworth was beaten by Harold Hardwick, with Healy six yards away in third place, Beaurepaire having pulled out halfway through the race citing illness.

While the rivalry was not as fierce or public as that with Beaurepaire, Healy recognised that Harold Hardwick was an equally dangerous opponent on his day. However, the next battle between these two in February 1911 was not in the pool. On 30 January, five people had died and a dozen others had been fortunate to escape with their lives after a vicious undertow swept them out to sea at Coogee Beach. Only the quick action of lifesavers Son Baker and Jim Clarken had prevented further casualties. Baker, with no lifeline and at one time having three women hanging off him, rescued five people in a heroic display of endurance and skill. A carnival was arranged to celebrate these achievements, with the feature entertainment being boxing matches between some of the nation's greatest sportsmen, including a bout between Healy and Hardwick, which was described as 'most lively'[11].

Such frivolities aside, the thirty-year-old Healy now faced unremitting challenges in the pool from young tyros Hardwick and Longworth. On 26 February 1911, Longworth broke Healy's world record for 100 metres (110 yards), taking 3/5 of a second off the old mark of 1 minute 5 seconds in an interclub 110-yard handicap. The 1911 NSW state championships at the Domain on 4 March had Healy and Longworth drawn side by side in a field of six. Stroke for flying stroke, the pair were level after 50 yards, although by the 70-yard mark, in defiance of the bellowing home crowd, Longworth was drawing away. However, Healy gallantly went after his Rose Bay rival, his shoulders lifting out of the water in his traditional flying finish, and the two men appeared to touch simultaneously. There was a roar of approval from the packed stands when the judges gave the race to Healy after what was universally acknowledged in the press as one of the bravest races he had ever swum. The pair reappeared that afternoon to contest the NSW 880-yard (half-mile) title. Again, the powerful youngster bolted off the start, even turning back cheekily at the 50-yard mark to see where the elder statesman was. Healy chased doggedly, but even his renowned finishing powers were unable to peg back Longworth's early advantage and he finished some 50 yards behind his younger rival. A further defeat by Longworth over 220 yards on 13 March prompted speculation that Healy might retire[12],[13].

NINE

THE TRUE VALUE OF SILVER

*'The tumult and the shouting dies;
The Captains and the Kings depart:
Still stands Thine ancient sacrifice,
An humble and a contrite heart.'*

—Rudyard Kipling, *Recessional*

***

**1 June 1912
Stockholm Harbor, Sweden**

As the little group stood at the rail, the Scandinavian cold stung their faces, and their noses and fingertips tingled. Feet were stamped and hands tucked into pockets and armpits as *R.M.S. Osterley* nosed among islands dark with pine trees, neat yachts bobbing at small docks and fishermen in little blue boats waving as they steamed by. Then someone pointed, and the men leaned across the cold rail, staring through the silver haze for a first glimpse of the white city of Stockholm.

The Australian Olympic movement, depressed at its lack of success in the 1906 Athens and 1908 London Games, was completely motivated for the Stockholm Games of 1912. Lessons had been learned in the wake of Healy's failure in Athens in 1906, when the young swimmer was shipped out at the last moment and left with no time to acclimatise or train upon his arrival. In January 1912, a full six months before the Stockholm Games, the Australian state swimming associations were already fundraising to send their men to Sweden early. By 1 February, a squad had been chosen and in April the team were *en route* to Stockholm, arriving a full six weeks before the opening ceremony. It appeared to be the perfect preparation, and the *Daily News* trumpeted, 'Australia should have very little difficulty in winning all the freestyle events.'

After its lack of success in the 1906 and 1908 Olympic Games, Australasia sent its strongest team to the Games of 1912, with 24 men and two women competing in athletics, rowing and swimming. Cecil Healy (back row, fifth from left) wears the team boater and blazer with the Australasian coat of arms. [Source: State Library of New South Wales, IE no.3242569].

At 30 years of age, Healy had finally eschewed the longer distances he had swum since Barney Kieran's death in 1905, confining himself to the 100 yards and 220 yards at the NSW State swimming championships—that state's Olympic selection trial—in January 1912. He was the defending champion and joint record holder for the 100 yards and had won the national 100-yard title five times, racing undefeated over that distance for six years until his shock defeat by Tod Solomons in 1911. Now, Healy had Solomons, Hardwick (who shared the 100-yard record), his long-time rival Alick Wickham and Billy Longworth, the national 100-metre record holder, to beat, and with limited places on the Games team up for grabs, everything was at stake.

The press christened the race 'the finest contest ever seen in Sydney'. Healy flew off the start and set a terrific pace, the great men thundering down the Domain pool with heads down, churning the water to foam like human torpedoes. Wickham led slightly at the halfway mark but no one let up, and by the 80-yard mark, Longworth and Hardwick were abreast in the lead. To the packed stands, it seemed the old champions of the last decade, Healy and Wickham, were destined to miss the Stockholm boat when Longworth forged ahead to touch out Hardwick for the win, but a late-diving Healy grabbed third place from Wickham, securing an Olympic berth by the length of his fingers. Longworth's time of 56 4/5 seconds was an Australian record for the 100 yards and a world record for the straight course[1].

Teenager Billy Longworth was the undisputed star of the NSW selection trials, winning all five freestyle events from the 100 yards to the mile.

He was dubbed 'the season's brightest star', 'our natatorial planet of greatest magnitude' and 'William the Conqueror' by an adoring media pack. In the 220 yards, he had put half a body-length on Healy by the 50-yard mark, and although the old man 'clapped pressure and steam on' and his many admirers bellowed his name and caused him to respond with every sinew, the young fighter from Rose Bay carried too many guns and won by three yards in a new Australian record of 2 minutes 27 2/5 seconds, taking a full second off Barney Kieran's 1905 mark. Only Dick Cavill had ever won five titles at a NSW championship, in 1903–04, and probably without such brilliant opposition. Such was the public clamour to witness the selection battle that the gate for the three NSW championship meets took £170 for the Olympic effort.

Losing both of his pet events to his younger rival prompted Healy to heap more ginger into his training. At the interclub 110-yard (100-metre) handicap of 11 January 1912, Healy cut a swathe through Longworth's record over the Olympic distance, taking a second off the old mark with a 1 minute 4-second heat swim. While the record was not ratified, as the time wasn't recorded under official conditions, the performance showed that Healy was still very much a member of the power generation of New South Wales swimming. When the Sydney contingent of the Olympic swimming team was announced on 1 February, Longworth, of the schoolboy's face and strong man's physique, was immediately selected, alongside the gigantic Harold Hardwick, the reigning 220-, 440- and 880-yard champion of Australia. Healy was nominated in his proper place as their aging but 'bronzed and pleasant-looking' monarch—four times state and five times Australian champion, and now also reserve manager for the swim team[2]. E.G. Findlay from Western Australia was originally selected as the fourth member of the team, but lack of finance saw his entry withdrawn and his place taken by little Leslie Boardman, who had finished fourth in the 220 yards at the NSW championships. The *Daily News* described the quartet as the 'thin bronzed line of muscular Australia'. Hardwick, Boardman and Healy were also team-mates at the Manly Surf Club, and Australia seemed set to unleash a new generation of swimmer-surfers upon the world[3].

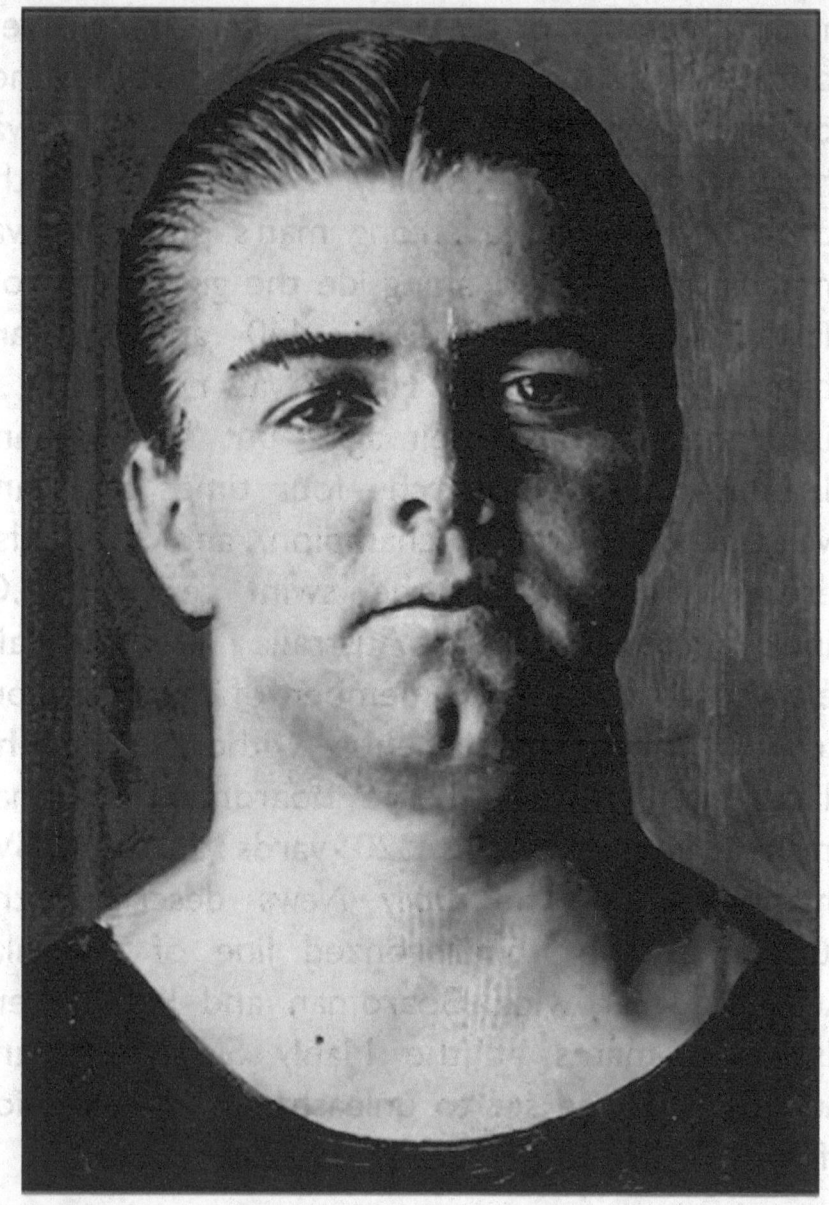

Bill Longworth dominated the 1912 Australasian Olympic swimming trials, forcing Healy, 10 years his senior, to produce extraordinary efforts to both qualify and protect his reputation as the monarch of Australian swimming. [Source: State Library of NSW, Davis Sporting Collection part II: swimming. IE no.946050].

Joining Healy, Longworth and Leslie Boardman on the 1912 Olympic swim team was giant Harold Hardwick, holder of national titles from 220 to 880 yards. [Source: State Library of NSW, Davis Sporting Collection part II: swimming. IE no.946050].

Joining them on this first combined Australia–New Zealand Olympic team was veteran middle-distance swimmer Malcolm Champion, the pride of New Zealand, who first represented the Kiwi nation in 1901 and still held national records over many distances. Notably absent from the squad was Frank Beaurepaire. After accepting a job as a swimming instructor in a Victorian school, Beaurepaire had been blacklisted from the sport as a professional. Clause B of the International Swimming Federation's definition of an amateur, adopted for the Olympic Games, stated that 'An amateur is one who has never taught, pursued, or assisted in the practice of swimming, or any other athletic exercise, as a means of pecuniary gain'. Beaurepaire's employment was deemed a breach of these fiscal restrictions and Australia's greatest middle-distance talent was forced to watch from the docks as his rivals donned their dark-green blazers and sailed without him.

Notable inclusions in the 1912 Australasian Olympic swim team were Misses Fanny Durack and Wilhelmina (Mina) Wylie. The Stockholm Games were the first of the modern Olympic era to offer events for female swimmers. While the *Daily News* called the addition of women to the team 'a wise step', particularly the inclusion of Durack, who held multiple records for swimming, springboard and fancy diving events, the wider reaction was rather less sanguine. The NSW Ladies Amateur Swimming Association sternly objected to women swimming in front of a mixed audience, the president proclaiming that 'A girl in the habit of exposing herself at public carnivals [is] likely to have her modesty hopelessly blighted.'[4] Such were the public strictures imposed on female swimmers in Australia, including segregated changing, bathing and carnivals, that at Melbourne's Brighton Baths, the only brass band permitted to play at a schoolgirl competition in the early 1900s was one with all blind players. Unmoved by the possible stain upon their reputations, Durack, the daughter of an Irish publican, and her friend Mina Wylie, whose father ran the famous Coogee baths in Sydney, even accepted the humiliation of having to pay their own way to attend the Games. A public subscription, which included donations from Billy Longworth's father and prominent businessmen Sam and Anthony Hordern, was insufficient to fund both girls, however, so Wylie had to delay her departure for Sweden in order to raise the balance of her fare.

The 1912 Games witnessed the debut of women in Olympic swimming competition. Public swimming was still segregated in Australia, with women bathing, changing and competing out of sight of men. [Source: State Library of NSW, Davis Sporting Collection part II: swimming. IE no.946050].

Australia's female swimming competitors at the 1912 Olympic Games were forced to pay their own fares to attend the Games. A public subscription subsidised travel for Fanny Durack, but Mina Wylie (pictured) was forced to delay her departure for Sweden in order to raise funds for her fare. [Source: State Library of NSW. Mina Wylie, her family, swimming colleagues and friends—travelling, holidays and swimming competitions from ca. 1883–1930s. IE no.1136298].

The team members were repeatedly feted before their departure, but none of the dinners, speeches, or toasts meant as much to Healy as that given by the Anti-Lunch Brigade. The Brigade was a growing movement of athletic and professional Sydney men who had adopted Healy's regime of exercising during the corporate lunch hour, a hitherto unknown notion within the Australian working class. From the outset of his swimming career, Healy had juggled training with his school and business responsibilities, and the idle lunch period seemed perfect for some precious extra exercise. Healy told Perth's *Daily News* that 'I got the idea in Fremantle while swimming in the championships here some years ago. When I was training in the Fremantle baths I noticed that several fellows used to come down and have a swim, afterwards taking their lunches in the baths. On arriving back in Sydney I mentioned this fact to several of my friends, and we started the same scheme.'[5] Such was the popularity of the concept that the new 'cult' at the Domain attracted such luminaries as international rugby forward Blair Swannell, barrister Charles Helsham and Major Philip Chambers.

However the difference between Healy's regimen and that in the west was that Healy strictly eschewed any midday meal, taking only a glass of hot milk and a biscuit following his swim. He believed that most people both ate too much and too often. 'Why should we gorge when we are only eating because it is a custom?' he told the *Daily News*. 'Why do we have three meals a day? It is only custom that makes us eat the three. You are stoking more coals than the old boiler can hold.'[6] So for the 'high priest' Healy and his 80 followers, there were no more counter lunches, ham sandwiches, sardines on toast, sausage rolls, chipped potatoes or salads, just a dip in the briny and a frugal snack afterwards. The health benefits of that hour of swimming and diving—one devotee claimed it had added 15 years to his life—went beyond the physical. Learning to resist the tantalising, demoralising odours of the city restaurants engendered a new mental strength in the Brigade members. Now they only glanced through the windows of the eating houses at the pinched and dyspeptic faces within, and then turned nobly in the direction of the baths and their hour of happy self-denial. Healy attributed his own longevity in sport to the way he looked after his diet and the vigorous self-discipline this created. While he was at the Games, Healy intended to convert as many people to the anti-lunch crusade as he could.

On 4 April 1912, on the eve of the team's departure for Stockholm, Healy and Boardman were entertained by the lunch-hour bathers and presented with a series of framed photos of themselves in competition. While the Brigade seemed confident of certain victory for its boys, Healy was careful to inform the group that he 'had a wholesome respect for the world, which was a very large place.' Healy was feted by the East Sydney Club the following night, and the Manly Surf Club the night after, whence he received both a purse of sovereigns and, the greatest honour of all, the club's first ever badge of honour. J.P. Wright, in making the presentation, said they were all proud to know Healy[7].

On 10 April, the New South Wales Olympic contingent departed aboard the Orient liner *R.M.S. Osterley*, replete with funds, time and every attention to their comfort, in stark contrast to Healy's trip to Athens in 1906. With the group were swim manager A.C.W. Hill of the NSW ASA (another member of the Anti-Lunch movement) and team director Vicary Horniman. Hill's position was an honorary one, meaning he had to pay his own way to Stockholm. Upon his return in October, Hill was forced to resign as secretary of the NSW ASA in order to resurrect his business and finances, which the expense of the trip had left in tatters.

Following hearty welcomes and sightseeing trips for the team in Hobart, Adelaide and Fremantle, the *Osterley* ploughed across the Indian Ocean for the first stopover on foreign soil for many of those aboard in the exotic port of Colombo, Ceylon (now Sri Lanka). For much of the crossing, the team had slept on the open decks to combat the hot and muggy conditions in their staterooms. Healy and several others formed a sports and amusements committee to overcome the monotony of ship life, with deck billiards, quoits, euchre and an amateur theatrical production to mark the crossing of the equator in which Boardman was a huge success in the role of a lady. The swimmers kept fit with boxing sessions on deck led by Hardwick, who had recently won the Commonwealth heavyweight championship. Healy, in his role as team patriarch, was doing more work than the others, adding skipping and extra physical exercises to his daily routine[8].

The swimmers had their first splash in three weeks during the Colombo stopover, dipping eagerly into a hotel pool while the rowers and runners were out seeing the sights. Healy also tried his luck with the local waves, but while he was in the water, he noticed a young local armed with a large knife running up the beach and beating his breast. Emerging from the surf, the puzzled Healy learned that the young man had been supposedly protecting him from sharks, and he was assailed with loud demands for remuneration. Healy duly gave the young man a coin, not because he had survived his swim in the ocean with all limbs intact, but purely for the originality of the young man's 'baksheesh extracting business'[9].

From Colombo, the *Osterley* passed through the Gulf of Aden, Suez and Naples, arriving at the French Mediterranean port of Toulon in late May. Here, the swimming team split up. The men continued on overland through Germany and Denmark to Sweden, but Fanny Durack stayed on board. She was meeting Mina Wylie in London, where the pair would train until just prior to the commencement of Olympic competition in July.

The Stockholm Games were eccentric by today's standards, but are widely regarded as the greatest example of the event's cultural endeavours. In addition to a plethora of athletic contests, the Stockholm program also featured an art competition that invited athletes to express themselves through short stories, painting, architecture, music or poetry[10]. The Games were wholeheartedly embraced by European sports fans, despite the earlier Olympic debacles. By mid-June, three-quarters of the tickets to events in the main stadium had been sold and the organising committee were decidedly uneasy that demand might far outstrip supply.

Also decidedly uneasy was the Australian men's swimming team. A new swim centre had been built at Djurgårdsbrunnsviken, an inlet not far from the Stockholm city centre, with the 100-metre course bounded by a steamboat pier and rows of pontoons. While the straight course favoured the Australian swimmers, the water temperature of only 60°F (15°C) did not. Healy wrote home that 'The course is still very cold. We all get in a swim every day, and Hardwick and myself have done a few "quarters". Boardman cannot stand the cold water for more than a lap, and Longworth has not yet gone four.' The weather was chilly and damp, and as the Games approached, the team was barred from practicing on the official course and confined to small indoor pools and hot showers, which Hill reported made them tired and lethargic. Healy and Longworth both complained of the wearying effect of so many turns, and Longworth, struggling with the unfamiliar lack of buoyancy of the freshwater baths, became increasingly anxious about not striking form[11].

In typical fashion, Healy steeled himself against the odds. In addition to a morning swim indoors, he took a dip alone in all weathers in the open water of the harbour each afternoon, despite the freezing conditions. Hill reported that 'One day he could hardly speak on coming out: his tongue was nearly frozen.' The others were eventually induced to join him, but only for a good cause. One rare fine Sunday, Healy, Longworth and Boardman went to the shore for a sunbake, but then had to go into the water in order to satisfy some Swedish girls who wanted to see the Australians swim. Boardman was taken aback by both the liberalism of the local girls and Swedish attitudes toward women: 'I was greatly surprised to learn while in Sweden that all the massaging there is done by ladies', he told the *Saturday Referee*. 'At first we found this decidedly embarrassing.'[12]

By July, the tension and weather were taking a toll on the Australians in the form of both boredom and ill-health. A frustrated Healy wrote, 'Things are very slow here just now, and we are beginning to feel the strain of waiting for the games ... We undoubtedly made a mistake in coming here so early.'[13] Meanwhile, sickness had assailed almost every team member. Healy had concealed the fact he had been almost deaf for weeks with an inner-ear problem that had started back in Sydney. Hardwick and Longworth also had ear problems that required specialist treatment, while Boardman was complaining of sore eyes.

It was a relief to finally start racing on the evening of Saturday 6 July 1912. Healy faced two Americans in his heat of the 100-metre freestyle, finishing second behind Perry McGillivray in 1 minute 5 1/5 seconds with Ken Huszagh third. McGillivray's winning time of 1 minute 4 3/5 seconds was fast, and that heat was shaping up to be the quickest of the night, with the other heat winners Kurt Bretting and Walther Ramme of Germany, Les Boardman and Harold Hardwick all at least a second slower[14]. However, heat four blew them all out of the water. American sprinter Duke Kahanamoku exploded down the course in a world record time of 1 minute 2 3/5 seconds, more than two seconds faster than McGillivray and taking 1/5 of a second off Charles Daniels' old mark. The wiry Hawaiian, whose exceptionally large hands and feet evoked memories of Daniels himself, was a mysterious figure in Stockholm. Until a month or two prior to the Games, he had not figured in America's Olympic plans, and would not have been sent to Sweden had he not journeyed thousands of miles from his island home to offer his services. However, earlier in the year, Kahanamoku had been credited with a 55 1/4-second effort over 100 yards, which, despite not being ratified, had certainly caught Healy's attention. Before leaving Australia, Healy had told the papers, 'The Yankees are likely to spring a surprise on us, you know. There is said to be a native of Honolulu who is credited with having done some marvellous times. If he is entered, he is likely to give us all a shock.'[15]

Healy described the standard of swimming as 'greatly advanced from that I witnessed at Athens six years ago'. Longworth, in particular, greatly admired the speed and technique developed by Kahanamoku: 'He puts one in mind of a highly powered motor boat, his feet churning the water in much the same manner as rapidly revolving propellers ... While his arm action is about the same as ours, his footwork is much faster: he gives fully six kicks for every stroke.' Healy later realised this crawl technique was perfectly suited to the conditions in Sweden. With the motor-power derived from the ankles alone, and not from the hip and knee joints, the body remained flatter on the surface and required less effort to stay afloat in the less buoyant semi-fresh water.

Kahanamoku kept the world's best at bay through the second round the following afternoon, leaving the Germans Ramme and Ritter in his wake with another quick time of 1 minute 3 4/5 seconds. Longworth and Hardwick were both beaten by Bretting in their race, and Ken Huszagh won the third race in 1 minute 4 1/5 seconds after a titanic struggle with McGillivray and Healy, the trio separated by only 3/5 of a second. Despite his minor placing, Healy scraped into the semi-finals as the best of the third-placed men, while Boardman finished fourth and was eliminated.

Healy's mental and physical powers—honed by years of racing and endurance training and the self-imposed daily immersion in the freezing Stockholm waters—came to the fore when the semi-finals were swum just hours later. He backed up easily to earn a place in the final with a straightforward win over Ramme and Longworth, despite the pedestrian time of 1 minute 5 3/5 seconds. That race, while vaulting Healy into the Olympic final, also, sadly, marked the final appearance by the much-heralded Billy Longworth at the Games. Longworth had been thrashed by 80 yards by Canadian George Hodgson in his heat of the 1,500 metres, left in the wake of 'the flying man-fish from Honolulu' in the 100 metres, and had now been well beaten by his own team-mate in a race he had made his own back in Australia. However, what the Australian media had dismissed as 'ear trouble and indifferent form' was now revealed to be far more serious. Longworth's 'bad ear' was actually an abscess of the skull, a suppurating lesion that lay within millimetres of his brain and required emergency surgery immediately after the race. The doctors stated that had the operation been delayed, even by a few hours, the result may have been fatal[16]. However, the greatest drama was still to come.

While the packed stands at Djurgårdsbrunnsviken whispered and speculated about Longworth's wavering exit from the Games, the field was announced for the second semi-final. German Kurt Bretting emerged from the dressing-rooms and stood, a solitary and clearly bewildered figure, on the otherwise empty pool deck. The whispers from the seats rose to a buzz, and then to baffled shouting like stormy surf upon a beach. Spectators were on their feet, pointing and exclaiming, while officials scuttled around and threw up befuddled hands. Bretting still stood alone at the poolside, shrugging and holding out his hands in confusion. Four of the five men scheduled to swim alongside him were missing, including the new darling of Stockholm, Duke Kahanamoku.

The *Sydney Sportsman* shrugged off the absence of Italian Mario Massa and the three Americans, McGillivray, Huszagh and Kahanamoku, as them 'probably having a good time inside the cafes', but in Stockholm, the uproar was tremendous. A search of the swimming complex failed to unearth the absent competitors, and officials had no choice but to disqualify the absent swimmers and allow Bretting to swim alone, under which extraordinary circumstances he produced a creditable 1 minute 4 3/5 seconds.

Longworth's illness and the shock disappearance of all three Americans now catapulted Healy into pole position for the gold medal. Kahanamoku, even if he were even found, would be sitting in the stands while Healy had only to beat the Germans, about whose previous times he had serious doubts, for at home they were permitted to touch in the shallow end of the baths, stand up, take one or two paces, and then plunge in again, a practice Healy described as 'farcical and ridiculous'.

However, this seemingly assured path to Olympic glory held no allure for Healy. American team officials had finally surfaced, loudly defending the absence of their swimmers from the semi-final. The trio had been resting at their hotel, mistakenly believing their performances in the second round had granted them automatic progression to the final. An international jury was hastily convened to thrash out this unprecedented complication, and the American protest that the program that had been handed to them was misleading was eventually dismissed. It seemed that the final would proceed *sans* USA.

It was at this moment, had he known it, that Healy's path to Olympic heroism was laid open. When news of the elimination of his American rivals reached the Australian camp, he was surrounded by excited team-mates and officials, all babbling about his own strengthened chances for gold. However, after one great rush of exhilaration and realisation, when he could almost feel the thrilling weight of the medal about his neck, Healy shook them off. The adrenaline was fading as quickly as it had risen. *This wasn't right.* What a hollow victory it would be, beating only half of the world's great contenders. If he were to win—and Healy wanted the winner's laurel with the desperation that had driven him into the icy waters of Stockholm's harbour day after freezing day—how could he stand on the podium and see Duke Kahanamoku in the crowd, knowing the best had been in the bleachers and not alongside him in the contest?

The stands at Djurgårdsbrunnsviken witnessed one of the most iconic moments in Olympic history in 1912 when sprint favourite Cecil Healy protested on behalf of his disqualified American rivals. [Source: Library of Congress, George Grantham Bain Collection, image no. LC-DIG-ggbain-09464].

Healy sought out the Australian team management and insisted upon an appeal on behalf of the eliminated swimmers. His petition was greeted with stares of disbelief, even an attempt to sit him down for a cup of tea and a good dose of valerian. This was *gold* for Australia. The rules were clear, and the Americans had broken them. How could he consider taking their side? However, Healy was as unmoved as a mountain. He wanted the second semi-final re-swum with the Americans and Massa in the field, declaring that it would be unsportsmanlike to bar their entry, despite knowing full well that the best effort he had ever produced over 100 yards was a full two seconds slower than that of the flying Hawaiian[17]. His intensity was irresistible, his conviction unwavering. The stares became shrugs, hats were reluctantly donned and the wording of the petition muttered over and reluctantly agreed upon.

Healy saw the officials out the door and on their way back to the pool deck, and then promptly presented himself at the German team hotel. He had a rather uneasy relationship with the German swimmers, feeling they were 'too aggressive in demeanour, although admirable in their enthusiasm, patriotism, and ambition'[18]. However, today he mustered his halting schoolboy German to request that their team, who also had representatives in the 100-metre final, submit a similar petition to his own. The reaction was one of indignation and anger—Bretting could lose his place in the final! As it stood, he and Walther Ramme were almost guaranteed medals and glory for German swimming—the Americans and the Italian were out! Healy waited for the furore, little of which he understood but the tone of which was clear, to die down. He then suggested that the petition should exempt Bretting from the re-swim, and appealed to the German sense of honour in not excluding the best swimmers from what ought to be a contest of the very best. It was the mention of honour that did it. The German team management agreed to meet the Australian officials and submit a joint appeal for the reinstatement of Mario Massa and the three Americans. Healy went away satisfied, even though he could feel the penetrating stares right between his shoulderblades as he departed.

Healy's extraordinary petition was, surprisingly, upheld. The jury declared that the three Americans and Massa would start in an extraordinary semi-final from which all those with a better time than the person finishing third in the first semi-final would progress to the final. The special semi-final took place the following day, 9 July, and the enthralled spectators witnessed another Kahanamoku world record of 1 minute 2 2/5 seconds, with Ken Huszagh second, equalling the time of the third placegetter from the first semi-final. McGillivray finished outside the qualifying time and Mario Massa retired halfway through the race.[19]

On the morning of the final on 10 July, the Swedish newspaper *Dagens Nyheter* applauded both the Australian and German swim teams: 'Not only Stockholm, but the whole world of sport will ring with applause for your sporting action in permitting the semi-final of the 100 metres to be re-swum. You as much as anybody realise the prowess of the swimmers you have voluntarily admitted to the final contest. You will have done more than win an Olympic event; you will have shown an unsurpassable example of sportsmanship for other Olympiads to emulate.'[20]

And so the greatest crawlers of the Games, Kahanamoku, Huszagh, Bretting, Ramme and Healy (who was now facing three men who had all posted faster times), assembled on the pool deck. Nerves frayed by the tension of the last three days, Bretting made a false start, setting the other four on edge and causing several to topple into the water simply to gain a moment to regroup. However, when the pistol finally exploded for a clean start, they all hit the water together and the splashing and foaming was tremendous, heads down, arms ploughing through the chill darkness, feet frothing and white water spraying behind. At the 50-metre mark, Kahanamoku had edged in front, with Huszagh and the two Germans side by side and Healy a couple of metres behind. With 20 metres to go, Healy was still at the back, and with ten metres left, he was still last. There were ten strokes to swim, and the gold medal seemed to have grown wings and flown away.

However, now Healy came with a tremendous finishing spurt. His shoulders rose out of the water like a titan's and his arms travelled faster than any of the others, his powerful legs scything the water aside and propelling him like an outboard engine. In five strokes, he had pulled past Bretting, and then Ramme and Huszagh. There were two metres left to swim. Lungs bursting and arms on fire, Healy squeezed one last ounce of effort for one last desperate lunge at the line ... but he only reached Duke Kahanamoku's feet. The Hawaiian had won, in 1 minute 3 2/5 seconds[21].

For a minor medallist, Healy took the Swedish crowd by storm. He found himself hoisted shoulder-high by a rush of Olympic officials and all the Australians present, the crowd stamping and applauding in what Healy later modestly described as 'a very flattering reception', while his brother Harold called it 'one of the greatest tributes ever accorded him by followers of swimming.'[22] Sydney's *Lone Hand* magazine went so far as to christen Healy 'the white champion swimmer of the world', but the loss inspired nothing but respect and admiration between the Australian and his conqueror. During the medal ceremony, Duke Kahanamoku reached for Healy's hand and lifted it higher than his own in a victory salute on the dais, calling the Australian 'the true Olympic champion'[23].

Prior to the 1912 Olympic Games, Healy had heard tell of a 'native of Honolulu' credited with exceptional sprinting speed. Duke Kahanamoku left all in his wake over the

100-metre course, despite the freezing Swedish waters. [Source: Library of Congress, George Grantham Bain Collection, image no. LC-DIG-ggbain-10653].

Healy described the experience of the final to *The Sunday Times* as 'one I am not likely to forget.' Some speculated that had the race gone any further, the result may have been different, for at the end, Kahanamoku was exhausted and had not one stroke left in him. Healy himself had had an inkling the Hawaiian might misjudge the race. A Mr Darnell of London had offered Kahanamoku a 25-guinea cup if he could win the 100 metres in 60 seconds, and before the final, Healy heard the American team manager urging Kahanamoku to take this last chance for the trophy. As a result, the Hawaiian raced off at a tremendous pace and, as Healy recollected, 'I saw a streak of foam disappearing over my horizon. I concentrated my worries elsewhere. But after the motorist had traversed about 90 yards, he ran short of petrol, and his form commenced to loom up again in my vision. This occurrence simply electrified me, and minimised my own impending tiredness.'[24] However, the watching Harold Hardwick conceded, 'We would not have beaten the Honolulu chap. He is the fastest man over 100 metres that ever breathed. Mind you, Cecil gave him a fright in the final for that event. The Duke seemed to be tiring as he finished, and Cecil was coming on at a tremendous pace.' The old warhorse's second-place time of 1 minute 4 3/5 seconds was still the fastest time ever swum by a man from the southern hemisphere.

Cecil Healy never expressed disappointment in the choices that may have cost him an individual Olympic gold medal. He now found himself feted for a race he had lost far beyond the adulation he had experienced for any race he had previously won. 'Healy's sportsmanship!' blared the headline in *The Sydney Morning Herald*. 'The Australian's action highly praised!' agreed the *Sydney Stock and Station Journal*. However, it was left to Natator to wonder at the truly unique nature of Healy's action. 'How many similarly placed would act as he did?' mused the commentator. 'Cecil's second under such circumstances is worth a lifetime of firsts scored.'

***

Healy had no time to contemplate the enormity of the 100 metres and its attendant drama. The very next day, 11 July, he was summoned back into the water to contest an event for which he was ill-prepared, given his recent commitment to sprinting—the 400 metres. Boardman had been scratched from the race, but middle-distance specialist Hardwick, who had already picked up a bronze medal in the 1,500 metres, had been reserving himself for the 400, and he now won the first heat in a new world record of 5 minutes 36 seconds, eclipsing the old Beaurepaire mark from 1910 by 3/5 of a second. However, Healy was not considered one of the world's great competitors for nothing. Seemingly unwearied by the physical and emotional trials of the previous days, he carved almost two seconds off Hardwick's time to win the fifth heat in 5 minutes 34 2/5 seconds, a new world record. 'Sensation upon sensation!' screamed the Australia media. 'First Australia's premier representative (Longworth) is forced to retire, and now Cecil Healy, regarded by many as 'having seen his day', breaks a world record. *Good old Cecil.*'[25]

The new mark was, however, short-lived. Two days later, Canadian George Hodgson, winner of the 1,500 metres, took an astonishing 25 seconds off his heat time to win the first semi-final in 5 minutes 25 2/5 seconds, beating the Brit Hatfield by just 1/5 of a second. Hodgson had taken nine seconds off Healy's record set in the heat. Hardwick won the second semi-final in another fast time of 5 minutes 31 seconds from the Hungarian Bela Von Las-Torres and Healy, whose effort of 5 minutes 37 4/5 seconds was aimed simply at making the final the next day. However, the toll of weeks of hard racing was now showing. Nineteen-year-old Hodgson, well accustomed to chilly swimming conditions and with a trudgen stroke Longworth described as 'without equal', won the final in another new world record time of 5 minutes 24 3/5 seconds, drawing away from Hatfield and a determined Hardwick, who was still suffering from ear trouble. Healy 'did not appear in good form', reported the Swedish organisers, and finished fourth in 5 minutes 37 4/5 seconds.

Healy's final chance at Olympic glory came in the only teams event on the swimming program, the men's 4x200-metre relay. Resplendent in their dark-green caps and cloaks on the pool deck, the Australian team of Hardwick, Champion, Boardman and Healy watched the USA win the first heat on 12 July, the powerful outfit of Huszagh, Kahanamoku, Harry Hebner and Percy McGillivray swimming a new record of 10 minutes 26 2/5 seconds to beat strong teams from Hungary and Great Britain. However, the Australians promptly overshadowed that effort with a time of 10 minutes 14 seconds in the second heat, slicing 41 seconds off the old world record to beat Germany by more than 40 metres. The final was swum three days later, and the Australians changed the team order, switching Healy to lead and Hardwick to the anchor role and a likely confrontation with Duke Kahanamoku. Ken Huszagh swam a remarkable first leg for the USA to come in level with a now-weary Healy (whom Huszagh literally pushed right into the side of the pool[26]), but Malcolm Champion quickly put 10 metres on Harry Hebner, a lead that Boardman stretched to 15 metres over McGillivray. Hardwick entered the water nine seconds ahead of Kahanamoku, and although the great man tried desperately to reel him in over the final lap, Hardwick broke from his trudgen into the crawl to win the race by the same margin with which he had started the final leg. The time of 10 minutes 11 3/5 seconds was another new world record. The USA were second in 10 minutes 20 1/5 seconds, with Britain finishing third[27]. It was to be 1956 before Australia won this event again.

The furore over the men's 100 metres had rather overshadowed the entry of women into swimming competition at Olympic level. On the same day as the men's 100-metre final, Fanny Durack and Mina Wylie both won their heats of the women's sprint, Durack using the crawl to set a new world record of 1 minute 19 4/5 seconds. Durack was a well-regarded favourite for the race, with a personal best for the 100 yards of 1 minute 6 seconds, more than seven seconds faster than her nearest rival. The Australian pair won their respective semi-finals, Durack in 1 minute 20 1/5 seconds, some six seconds ahead of the former world record holder, Britain's Daisy Curwen. An attack of appendicitis kept Curwen out of the final on 17 July, which Durack won in 1 minute 22 1/5 seconds from Wylie, who produced her fastest swim of the meet, 1 minute 25 2/5 seconds. Durack was the sole Australian individual gold medallist in Stockholm, and was Australia's only individual female gold medallist in swimming until 1932, when Clare Dennis won gold in the 200 metre breaststroke in Los Angeles. It was 1956 before Australia won another gold medal in women's Olympic swimming. Upon returning home in October 1912 following a successful tour of Europe in which she swam before many crowds of mixed gender, Durack announced that the only remaining objection to members of both sexes swimming together in Australia was the 'strained prudery' that seemed to exist only in her homeland. In late 1912, the Ladies ASA rescinded the rule that required special permission for men to be admitted as spectators to ladies' carnivals. The new system allowed women who objected to swimming in front of men to choose clubs that excluded men.

However, the rule requiring female-only officials remained in place for all sanctioned events.

After failing to win an individual gold medal at the 1912 Games, Healy led the Australasian men's swimming team to gold in the 4x200-metre relay. Left to right: Malcolm Champion, Harold Hardwick, Cecil Healy, Leslie Boardman. [Source: National Library of Australia, call no. PIC/3204].

It was the swim squad that carried the Australasian effort at the Stockholm Games, collecting two gold, two silver and two bronze medals. The only other medal won by an Australasian athlete was the bronze medal won by New Zealander Anthony Wilding in the men's tennis singles. At the end of the Games, the team received diplomas from the Swedish Olympic Committee, Healy for his second place in the 100 metres, Durack and Wylie for their efforts in the ladies' race and Hardwick for his third placings in the 400 metres and 1,500 metres. In addition, special awards of merit were presented to performers achieving a high standard without receiving a prize. These included the Australian rowing eight, Longworth and Boardman for 100-metre swimming and Healy for his effort in the 400 metres[28].

However, long after such tributes had crumbled to dust, the actions of Cecil Healy in the 100 metres at Stockholm would be upheld as being among the noblest gestures of sportsmanship in the Olympic chronicle. Australian Olympic historian Harry Gordon called it 'a sublime gesture', for Healy's action showed the true value of silver in a way now unthinkable in the high-pressure atmosphere of the modern Olympic Games[29].

TEN

A FINAL INNOCENT YEAR

*'To see a world in a grain of sand,
And a heaven in a wild flower:
Hold infinity in the palm of your hand,
And eternity in an hour.'*

—William Blake, *Auguries of Innocence*

***

1913

The British battleship *HMS Dreadnought* steamed through the cold waters separating Britain and the restive powers of middle Europe, eyed from across the Channel by her newborn German sisters, *SMS Ostfriesland*, *Thüringen* and *Oldenburg*. Meanwhile, the young nation of Australia watched wide-eyed as construction of its own capital city began in the rural hills at Canberra. Besieged Macedonia struggled in the grip of its medieval conqueror Bulgaria, and the neighbouring Balkan kingdoms fractured and then burned around it. Faraway in the southern hemisphere, red one-penny stamps featuring a kangaroo on a national map marked the first official postage unit of the new Australian commonwealth.

How far the guileless, youthful nation of Australia seemed from the overheating cauldron of Europe. In that year of dread, as war loomed in the motherland, young Australia celebrated the release of its first national banknotes and welcomed a new place to spend them—the totalisator betting agency, or TAB. Eastern Suburbs won the rugby premiership, Posinatus won the Melbourne Cup, and C.J. Dennis's *Backblock Ballads* feted the rapidly evolving and colourful Australian 'langwidge'.

In December 1912, Cecil Healy and Les Boardman returned from a three-month post-Olympic tour of Europe, having swum at the top amateur championships on the Continent, where Healy preferred to compete because of 'a dread of the short-lapped baths of England', theorised *The Sydney Morning Herald*. However, swimming conditions in Europe had not always been ideal either. In August 1912, Healy had won an international 400-metre race at Spa, in the Belgian Ardennes, where the races were swum in a running river. For half of the 400-metre event, they swam downstream, and then had to turn and swim back against the current. Boardman complained bitterly about his struggles in the swift, cold water, but Healy, with his powerful stroke, simply lifted his shoulders, drew ahead and left his rivals behind.

While Healy had been repeatedly outdone by Duke Kahanamoku in Stockholm, he and his crawl remained enormously fascinating to the European public. When he equalled his personal best for 100 metres at Joinville-le-Pont near Paris on 13 August, the French press were in raptures, marvelling at how Healy 'churned the water into foam with his furious crawl, striking out like a boxer, throwing himself over the water, working his arms with the speed of a paddle-wheel.'[1] Boardman finished a close second in that race. While they had been in Stockholm, Healy had spent considerable time tutoring Boardman in the finer points of the crawl, and the close finish in Paris was material proof of the younger man's improvement. Boardman wrote home that 'Healy never seems to get tired of instructing me. I often feel that I should not worry him so much, but he insists, and already I think I have improved out of sight. He has got me to incline my head on each side as each arm goes into the water. By this means the breathing and roll of the body from the hips up then comes easy ... I seem to hold my own much better, and am twice as powerful at the finish as I used to be.'[2] While in Paris, the pair took time to ascend the Eiffel Tower, 'good training for exploring our own Blue Mountains', Boardman claimed. They also had an offer from a local aviator for a scenic flight over Paris, but Boardman admitted they both 'got cold feet and decided to forego the proffered flight on the wings of the air.'

There was a short trip to Italy at the end of August where Healy won the International 100-metre race at Genoa on 25 August in 1 minute 3 4/5 seconds, a new personal best. The temptations of championship races in Scotland and Ireland finally lured the pair across the Channel in September, where they were guests of William Henry and the Royal Life-saving Society, and of the English Amateur Swimming Club, of which Healy was a life member. On 10 September, Healy established a Scottish all-comers' record by winning the 200-yard championship at Glasgow in 2 minutes 16 1/5 seconds. While in the north, Healy took a trip to Aberdeen hoping for a day of his beloved surf bathing, despite the chilly Scottish weather. So boisterous were the sea conditions that the man at the dressing box would only allow the visitor to enter the water when Healy revealed he was Australian. The man then stood and gaped as

Healy selected a spot where the undertow was racing with the force of a mountain torrent and allowed himself to be swept far out to sea. Then he battled his way back to shore, shrugged and repeated the performance, fighting all the way against treacherous currents and hard-breaking surf[3].

The final outing of the tour was an invitational 220-yard race in Dublin, where Healy and Boardman went neck and neck, with Healy winning by a touch in 2 minutes 36 seconds, a new Irish record. Boardman, whose horizons had certainly been broadened by the trip, marvelled afterwards that 'They absolutely lionised us and when we were departing, they showed the depths of their friendship and warm-heartedness by actually kissing us.'[4]

This European jaunt, for all its excursions and triumphs, was nonetheless a sobering one for the pair, Healy in particular. When they arrived home on 4 December 1912, Natator enthused, 'Cecil Healy is home, looking blooming and fit as ever. His latest jaunt around the globe impressed him more than any prior run, and he brings back ideas and notions which should be of considerable value to swimming in these parts. [But] his observations are also concerned with more serious matters.' Those serious matters were a European continent on the cusp of war.

As the curtain fell on Stockholm and the Western world celebrated a successful gathering of the world's finest athletes, the colour and beauty of these last pre-war Games gave no hint of the bloodshed that would follow and claim the lives of so many of those same young sportsmen and women.

At the Stockholm Games, Healy had been impressed more than almost anything by a speech delivered by the Crown Prince of Sweden at a special supper for the athletes. In tracing the origins of the ancient Olympiads, the Prince had revealed that the purpose of the original Games was not for public entertainment, but rather to 'divert the minds of men from the practice of cutting each other's throats.' The Prince praised the progress of the modern Games for bringing together the cream of the world's manhood to meet in friendly rivalry on the field of sport, and assisting political and diplomatic efforts aimed at preserving peace in the world. Healy himself had witnessed representatives from various countries laughing and joking and toasting one another during the Games, and imagined that these men and women would return home to promote sport as a means whereby patriotic feelings could be expressed without needing bloodshed to honour their flag[5].

However, it was a visit to Hamburg in September 1912 that produced the first cracks in his new optimism. The German sojourn began well. Healy was surprised and touched to learn that a trophy he and William Henry had given for schoolboy swimming in 1906 was still a prize that was highly valued by German school students, and he now witnessed a race for the trophy between lads from 28 schools. When it became known that Healy was present, he was accorded a huge reception, and even plunged into the water for an exhibition of the crawl. Healy's career with Richard Hornsby & Sons had endowed him with a tremendous interest in the manufacturing activities of the big industrial centres he was continually passing through, and afterwards he was politely conducted on tours of the great Hamburg shipyards, which played host to the largest ship afloat at the time, the *Imperator,* and the airfields, where a fleet of airships was tethered. However, despite enjoying the precise and systematic methods by which the Germans produced these marvels, a dreadful premonition of the conflagration to come stirred within. Healy wrote, 'Germany at present is not in any sense of the word a sporting country, and whenever I hear the name mentioned, I associate it with the "tramp, tramp, tramp" of soldiers. The place seems to me to be alive with them, and they give one the idea of being so grim and stern.'

On his first visit in 1906, he had been similarly impressed with the power, strength and resources of the German nation, and he had brought back many ideas on event management and training that had probably contributed to the Australians' success in Stockholm. However, now Healy feared that if the order was given for the German army to march, her battalions would move with a swiftness and sureness that was 'not comforting'. While Healy conceded that the awarding of the 1916 Games to Berlin was 'one of the few hopeful signs of the times', he also noted a new and strong dislike of England among the German people. British army manoeuvres were in progress in the UK while Healy was in Hamburg, and when the war games had to be abandoned after the British forces had become hopelessly mixed up, Healy wrote worriedly that 'Germany grinned from ear to ear'[6].

To Healy, it was plain that Germany's advantages over Britain were growing too rapidly. In a letter to *The Sunday Times* of 3 February 1913, he urged 'all those dependent upon the Union Jack for liberty to awaken to the power and might of Germany' and counteract the complacency and self-satisfaction he felt were the most unfortunate characteristics of Anglo-Saxons.

He fretted that the majority of Englishmen to whom he expressed his views pooh-poohed the idea of being beaten in anything 'by a bally foreigner' and thought that 'British pluck' would always pull them through. 'Little straws', Healy wrote in an ominous portent of things to come, 'have a habit of showing which way the wind is going to blow.'[7]

***

However, during the summer of 1913, concerns on the white peninsula of Manly were not about the possibility of lurking submarines. Eyes were not turned seaward to catch the first glimpse of foreign masts on the horizon or bobbing sea-mines in the clear blue waves. A wholly more domestic anxiety had Manly beachgoers up in arms. Voices were raised and a strident public campaign was launched to improve the state of the beach's dressing sheds.

As captain of the Manly Surf Club, Healy put aside his international concerns for a time to lead the fight for facilities to keep pace with growing patronage of the northern beaches. He described the local amenities in April 1913 as 'ramshackle, crude and dirty' and 'the result of a deplorable lack of foresight, business acumen, and initiative.'[8] Healy also used his new role as special correspondent for both *The Sunday*

Times and *The Referee* to carry public calls for action right to the Minister for Works, Arthur Griffith, writing that 'The public are tired of being told "everything is in order; we will commence work shortly" ... The time for talking is past.' Griffith responded that £20,000 had been set aside for the purpose, but the fault lay with the local councils, who were remiss in applying for access to the funds. However, the campaign paid off, with new sheds being opened in November 1913 at North Steyne, the club Healy had joined that very month, having retired from the captaincy at Manly.

Healy first swam for North Steyne in the surf carnival that accompanied the unveiling of the new sheds. Formed in 1907, the club had won the first three Association Rescue & Resuscitation premierships in the period from 1909 to 1911. Their clubhouse was carved out of the wilderness of bush and dunes on the Manly foreshore, but as a permanent structure, it represented the first move towards the glamourous beachfront development for which the North Steyne area is now renowned[9]. In 1913, the club adopted Healy's suggestion of using a payment system for use of the new dressing sheds, similar to that in use at Bondi, with two pence charged for entrance and a further two pence for use of the lockers.

The move to North Steyne represented a genuine change in focus for Healy in 1913. His travels in Europe had stimulated a desire for new challenges, both in and out of the water. His thoughtful and articulate correspondence had often been published in the press throughout his swim career and now, despite the many demands on his time from Hornsby's, lifesaving and swimming, Healy eagerly accepted an offer from the Evans family newspaper group to join their staff as an expert commentator on swimming and lifesaving.

In the early twentieth century, with no competition from broadcast media, newspapers were the sole food feeding a voracious public appetite for sports news, results and gossip. With a largely male readership, sports coverage was highly selective and dominated by men's sports, often associating the manliness and courage of performance with patriotism. The press rarely questioned the politics of sport and largely stuck to a decorous and conventional cataloguing of sports happenings, It was not until post-World War I that Australian sports journalism moved towards a brasher tabloid style intended to attract a younger, working-class readership[10].

Both *The Referee* and *The Sunday Times*, for whom Healy wrote part-time, were owned by Markham Richard Evans and his sons Henry,

Ernest and Bertie. *The Sunday Times* was a respected Sydney broadsheet and *The Referee* was one of Australia's earliest dedicated sports papers. The phenomenon of publications focussing exclusively on sports was driven by the marginalisation of sport by 'hard news' that had occurred almost since the genesis of sports journalism in Britain in the early eighteenth century. Sport could rarely compete with news in a traditional newspaper environment made copy-scarce by the cost of production and 'taxes on knowledge' (stamp duty). As a result, wholly separate sporting publications such as *Bell's Life in London* (1822), *Sporting Life* (1859) and the French *L'Equipe* (1900) emerged to cater for genteel interests in horseracing, prize-fighting and blood sports.

In concert with these radical publishing moves, sportswriters were emerging as a specialist breed of journalist. However, life as a sportswriter was not all hot pies and free entry to the cricket. Because sports coverage remained largely segregated from hard news, many sports reporters battled against a pervasive stereotype of failed journalists, their status in the newsroom suffering from the perception that sport was a trivial matter in the wider scheme of things. Even within their own sphere, reporters covering working-class sports were often viewed as a lesser species compared with those canvassing the upper-class pursuits of cricket and rugby.

Healy was not employed to cover the 'hard news' of sport, the current affairs, match analysis and results. Rather, he was a sports columnist uniquely placed to produce what those in the trade called 'orthodox rhetoric', a current or former elite athlete using their distinctive voice and experience to discuss the business of sport in their specialised field[11]. Healy used his new journalistic role to write passionately about the surf, promoting the beaches as a healthy playground and spreading a water-safety message among the many new users who congregated there. He wrote on everything from treating bluebottle stings—ammonia, Ricketts' washing blue and a handful of wet sand was his preferred remedy[12]—to the importance of swimming as a survival skill for yachtsmen. 'There is an old saying that those who live nearest to church are furthest from Heaven', Healy mused, recollecting his 1912 encounter with a group of Scottish fishermen who assured him that they had never learned to swim because people who swam were the people who drowned. 'It is a notorious fact that the great majority of people whose existence is spent afloat either cannot swim at all or else are seen to the worst possible advantage in the water.' Healy was convinced that survival at sea was possible given the right skills and attitudes, and suggested an annual 'all-clothes race' for members of yachting clubs to overcome their aversion to swimming. Healy himself happily plunged into the harbour in coat, trousers and leather shoes on behalf of Sydney Ferries to test the efficacy of their life-preservers and demonstrate the survival techniques needed for 'unexpected immersion'.

Healy was now a much sought-after speaker and writer whose opinions were described as 'picturesque, forceful, and correct'. In September 1913, there were even rumours he would stand as a candidate in the NSW parliamentary elections representing the National Progressive Party under Sir George Beeby[13]. A former newspaper editor and barrister, Beeby had been a propagandist for the Labor party before he entered the NSW parliament in 1907. In 1913, he resigned to form the National Progressive Party and at the general election in December Beeby mustered 13 candidates, but all were unsuccessful, including Beeby himself in his tilt for the seat of Waverley. Healy never did officially run, but his former Manly Surf Club teammate Arthur Relph recalled that 'He was one of the finest public speakers I have ever heard. Always a great reader and thinker, Healy made speeches that always commanded rapt attention. He was indeed an orator, and being possessed of a good memory very often embellished his speeches with particularly good quotations.'[14]

However, it was swimming and lifesaving that remained Healy's passions. His 1913 treatise on 'The Crawl Stroke' so impressed the Amateur Swimming Association of England that they distributed 20,000 free copies under their Encouragement of Swimming in Great Britain scheme. He proposed a model of the optimal stroke giving maximum propulsion with minimal physical exertion, primarily achieved using floating to minimize muscular effort. Healy always advocated teaching youngsters the 'dog paddle' until they could stay afloat, before teaching them to lift their arms clear of the water, and not attempting speed until the stroke was properly acquired. He provided very specific technical instructions for teaching the crawl to beginners, including bending the arm at the elbow and thrusting it into the water just beyond the face, 'like a duck's leg', fully extending underwater and relaxing as the limb was about to emerge. The kick was made with the whole limb, especially the lower portion ('flick the instep rather than using a stiff leg'). When breathing, the face was rotated and the head moved back very slightly, but not so far that the legs sank.

Despite the specificity of his technical model, Healy recognised that the crawl stroke was unique to each swimmer who used it, 'just as in the case of fingerprints'. His understanding of the effects of weight, centre of gravity and body dimensions on buoyancy led to a theory of stroke mechanics based on individual variations in body size: 'After all, Nature does not conform to the principles of socialism ... and more often than not, it is necessary to check her tendencies in order to achieve the object desired.' Healy's 1913 treatise was the first thesis on the distinct styles of crawling that had evolved, differentiated by their breathing regime (breathing after every other stroke versus taking four or five strokes between breaths) and motor pattern (use of diagonal arm–leg pairs versus independent arm–leg action). For maximum sprinting speed, Healy concluded that non-regular breathing, a technique favoured by Duke Kahanamoku, with head down, shoulders square and a short arm action, was most efficacious. This body position elevated the legs to minimize drag, and when used in a short pool with vigorous push-offs after a turn, was superior in races of 100 metres or less. However, Healy also noted the difficulties in swimming straight with such a powerful technique, having himself been regularly jostled by the American swimmers in Stockholm. His advice to young would-be sprinters was to 'always consult the watch ... This is the only practical means of finding up to what point any particular stroke is effective.'[15]

In the same year, Healy wrote a seminal article for *The Sunday Times* describing 'a new and startling version' of the origin of the crawl stroke, a much-disputed event. While conceding that the Cavill family were the first to introduce it into competitive swimming, Healy could not be persuaded that they were the inventors of the principle, given the abundance of evidence that the style was in vogue among Pacific islanders 'as far back as the memory of some the oldest traders will take them.' His primary evidence was an assurance from Alick Wickham, 'an intelligent and truthful natured boy, not given to romancing or handling the truth carelessly', that all boys and girls in the Solomon Islands swam the same way, using the crawl or, as Wickham's father called it, *tuppa tup-pala*. While the Cavills gave the stroke credibility—Wickham and his brothers had been dismissed as 'natives who came over here in sailing ships'—Healy's conclusion was that the application for 'Patent Rights' made out on the Cavills' behalf 'cannot be entertained'[16].

***

Following the 1912 Olympic Games, the aging Healy's swimming career was predicted to decline in favour of his business and journalistic interests. However, Healy continued to devote his energies to both sporting and off-field pursuits. [Source: Northern Beaches Council/Manly

Library Local Studies Collection: image number 001/001221].

There was much speculation about the 32-year-old Healy's future in competitive swimming upon his return from Stockholm. Natator reflected that 'None can last for ever at anything, there must come a time when even the warmly ardent might cry "enough" without running the risk of being charged with smothering the flame a moment before it was right and proper to do so.' Healy had previously made murmurings about cutting back his competitive outings, but now firmly stated his intention to compete in the NSW handicap races and, if selected, the national championships, although with his business and journalistic commitments given new and elevated priority.

This announcement coincided with the collapse of his home swimming club at East Sydney. Mismanagement and reluctance to accept executive roles among the younger members had driven the famous old club into a slough from which it could not recover. While Healy had been living in Manly for some years, he was well aware of the tenuous state of affairs at East Sydney, and had maintained his membership there alongside his brothers, but in December 1912 the board voted to wind the club up, and the mighty East Sydney Swimming Club, which had given Australian swimming Freddie Lane, Alick Wickham, Snowy and Son Baker, the Hellings brothers and seven Healys, was no more[17].

Healy now, naturally, threw his lot in with the Manly Swimming Club, with whom he was warmly familiar as the club instructors had supervised much of the swim training while he was at the Manly Surf Club[18]. He had his first swim in Manly colours on 21 December 1912, winning a 220-yard handicap in 2 minutes 35 seconds in a field of 58 starters. He also spent Christmas morning in Manly waters (alongside 132 others) participating in the club's traditional 50-yard festive handicap. His brother Reg, home from New Zealand for the holidays, was also a starter, and *The Referee* reported that Reg had 'fattened up considerably and looked the better for it; [for] there was a Mrs Reg Healy now.'

The Manly club was home to some great up-and-coming crawlers, including nineteen-year-old Harry Hay, who was already covering 50 yards in 25 seconds, Healy's former rival and now great friend Tod Solomons (who was 'training nightly in the ring with the good intention of "getting rid of the superfluous"', Healy noted with a grin) and Steve 'Shark Bait' McKelvey, a sub-minute 100-yard swimmer. However, it was the prodigious young Albert

Barry of the Sydney club who both Healy and Longworth were forced to take note of upon their return from Stockholm. In their absence, Barry had broken Longworth's national 100-yard and 100-metre records, and *The Sydney Morning Herald* accorded him its highest praise: Barry's finishing power and race judgment were 'worthy of being classed with those of Cecil Healy'[19]. There were crawl strokes in abundance at the Manly vs. Sydney interclub carnival on 3 December 1912. Of the 34 competitors in the mile teams race (each man swimming 100 yards), only half a dozen used the trudgen. There were crawls of all descriptions—thehalf-crawl/half-trudgen of Barry, the double-flutter of one leg of Boardman, Hay's extra-vigorous arm action and Hardwick's lifting of one leg clean out of the water.

Healy joined the Manly Swimming Club in 1912 following the demise of his home club at East Sydney. He joined some of the rising young freestylers of the pre-war era, including (back row) Tod Solomons, Steve McKelvey, (front row) Harry Hay, C.D. Bell, and Len Murray. [Source: Northern Beaches Council/Manly Library Local Studies Collection: image ID: man01879].

Healy eventually eschewed the 1913 national titles, attending them only as a correspondent, as he remained much-occupied with his work. In addition to his role in the print media, he continued as a travelling salesman for Richard Hornsby & Sons, roaming as far afield as Tamworth in northern NSW to spruik the firm's irrigation products and to Gundagai in the south, where the locals found him 'a most interesting cuss'[20]. His 1913 visit to the little southern town had painful consequences, however. Healy was riding into Gundagai on his motorcycle when, as he approached Five Mile Creek north of the town (the site of the now-famous Dog on the Tuckerbox monument), the bike skidded on the unsealed road and Healy was flung from the saddle, his foot becoming entangled in the machine as he fell. His lower leg was badly mangled and Healy was forced to limp several miles into town for treatment and respite at the Royal Hotel. As a result, he only swam in the Flying Squadron teams event at the NSW State Championships in 1913, where the Manly outfit finished third behind new powerhouse club Rose Bay (with two Longworth brothers and two Wickham brothers in their team) and Sydney (whose squadron included three Boardman brothers and Albert Barry). Healy, swimming alongside Tod Solomons, promised the public that 'my little bit of fluff will be in at the kill', but he took the Flying Squadron event extremely seriously, describing it as 'the grand parade of our best swimmers' and 'from a club point of view, the most important thing of the year'. He felt the event should 'appeal to a higher instinct, sinking one's own selfish motives and looking upon the honor (sic) of the club as the first consideration'[21].

With public interest in the Olympic Games booming on the back of the dramatic events in Stockholm, Healy now urged Australian swimming to 'get to work at once to prepare the ground' for the 1916 Berlin Games. After the convincing victory of the men's relay team in Sweden, Healy was sure Australia's best hope for gold in Berlin once again lay in the teams event. He also knew the sort of hard physical preparation that was required to swim fast over the 220-yard legs of the relay. His main concern was that Australia's elite speed swimmers, raised almost exclusively on a diet of sprinting, saltwater baths and beaches, would be unprepared for the length of race and the freshwater conditions they would encounter at the Berlin Games. Despite his own golden career as a sprinter, Healy now called for the rapid identification and nurturing of talented middle-distance swimmers[22].

Likewise, Healy knew that a couple of weeks in Germany prior to the Games was insufficient time to adapt stroke and style to swimming in fresh water. In 'The Crawl Stroke' treatise, Healy had identified the technical differences of swimming in salt water, where one kick per arm stroke was sufficient, to the less-buoyant fresh water, where additional support was necessary. 'At Stockholm, it was punch, punch all the time and drag back', he remembered. 'That gliding motion that you get in salt water was lacking; you sink too deep.' Now, in February 1914, Healy called for a freshwater training centre to be quickly established in Sydney to begin specific preparation for the Games. A swimming enthusiast in Parramatta directed Healy's attention to the dam below The Kings' School in Parramatta Park. Upon inspection, Healy was delighted to find the water between six and fifteen feet deep, the width more than 100 yards and the river straight[23]. ASA representatives visited the course on Healy's recommendation and found it 'admirably suitable', and appointed Healy through the Australasian Representation Fund Committee to arrange a special fundraising carnival in April 1914 to promote the venue. This became an instant reunion of the 1912 Olympic team. Boardman, Longworth, Durack, Healy and Wylie all appeared, as did Harold

Hardwick, although he had now retired and was working as a boxing instructor in Snowy Baker's gym.

Perhaps all this talk of Olympic glory re-lit the competitive fire in Healy. At the end of 1913, the East Sydney Club was re-established, with Healy, Alick Wickham's younger brother Ted (a 24-second 50-yard swimmer) and the upstart Tas Jones from Rose Bay all on the membership roster. Even the aging Freddie Lane was willing to strip down for a teams event at his new-old club. Healy was back in the water at the end of December, still swimming off scratch for 100 yards and giving some of his clubmates up to 50 seconds start, but felt he hadn't regained sufficient sprinting power to put his name in for the 1914 state championship on 5 January, which Barry won from Longworth and Solomons. Healy only swam in the 100-yard club handicap, producing a time of 58 2/5 seconds, which would have won the open championship. He also entered the 440 yards against Longworth, which the youngster only won by a yard after a terrific struggle. The papers marvelled that 'Healy was behind all the way but never gave up hope of being first to touch the board and made repeated dashes against his rival.'[24]

The pair resumed their rivalry the following week in the state 220-yard championship at the

Domain. Compared with the round-faced 'boy of the bulldog breed' Longworth, *The Referee* enthused that Healy looked 'the picture of rugged health ... Bigger and much browner than the others, he was very conspicuous, his fine physique being generally commented upon.' Healy and Longworth were drawn on opposite sides of the course and Healy got the best start, putting two yards on Longworth by the 25-yard mark with his shorter, quicker stroke. After 40 yards, Longworth had caught up, but Healy stayed with him until his usual terrible turn saw him lose ground to such an extent that the task of catching Billy seemed hopeless. By the 150-yard mark he was three yards behind and looked in danger of slipping out of the places, but his head went down and those massive brown arms were brought into play more vigorously than ever. With 40 yards to go, the gap was half a yard, and with two yards to go, the 'grand old man' came at Longworth, but his efforts proved fruitless, with Longworth winning by an arm's length. When the veteran climbed the ladder, however, he was the recipient of a volume of cheering that was rarely heard for a second-placegetter[25].

On the back of that performance, Healy was selected to represent NSW at the Australasian championships alongside Longworth and Barry.

Healy finished fourth in the 100 yards behind his two team-mates, with the surprise packet, E.G. Finlay, the breaststroker from Western Australia, touching him out for third. He then placed third in the 440 yards, again behind Longworth. His final glory came on 19 February 1914, when the absence of Longworth from the Eastern Suburbs 100-yard championship allowed Healy to annex that title.

However, there was sadness for Healy in the winter of 1914 when his long-time coach and mentor, George Farmer, died after a lengthy illness. It was Farmer who had first hailed Healy from the East Sydney pool deck in the 1890s with a 'Cec, try Cavill's new splash stroke' and thus spawned one of the greatest generations of crawlers in swimming history with his adoption of Alick Wickham into the East Sydney club. As the long-time proprietor of the baths at Woolloomooloo Bay and a founding member of East Sydney, Farmer had passed on his skill and knowledge to the likes of Freddie Lane, George Reid, Longworth, Wickham and Snowy Baker. Farmer had represented New South Wales as a goalkeeper in water polo, was secretary of the NSW ASA, and as far back as 1898, had received the East Sydney club's gold badge for service rendered[26].

A further blow came on 23 June 1914. The self-proclaimed 'spinsters of Manly', a gay group of young unattached women and their obligatory chaperones, put on a dance at Sargent's ballroom in the seaside village. The hall was gaily festooned with trails of pink roses and the red berries of sarsaparilla, and among the *femme sole* present, resplendent in crepe de Chine, butterfly sashes and lace overdresses, was Miss Olive Maitland, accompanied by her mother Victoria[27]. Cecil Healy was part of the crowd of young men feigning coolness in the face of this perfumed onslaught, but search as he might, scanning the room over the lip of a glass or across the crimped and curled head of a partner, Muriel Maitland was nowhere to be seen. The beady eye of Victoria Maitland almost dared him to ask after her, but Healy, who, as his swim career waned, had returned to live at the Darling Point home of his mother to be closer to the offices of Hornsby & Co. and the Evans group, could only guess at the reason for her absence. It could be just a bad cold, for the winter *had* been cool, or perhaps measles, mumps, a sprained ankle, a library book to finish, or late apples to preserve? The ubiquitous headache? However, the more troubling conclusion was inescapable; perhaps, after all the long silences and absences as a result of the ambivalence of feelings that he himself could not understand and could not bring himself to act upon, Muriel had given up, perhaps even married someone else. Her place may now at the head of a household, not the head of a line of waltzing girls in pink and white and blue.

Ultimately, Healy's own emotional barriers had proved insurmountable to all the complicated feelings, half-offered, half-retracted, between him and the feisty Muriel. For all his polish in public speaking, profound technical knowledge of swimming and worldliness in international travel, Healy was still ruled by the anxiety and insecurity that had stymied many of his early swimming performances. He had not written to Muriel during his long sojourn in Europe, half-hoping that the extended silence might convey the message he could not bear to deliver in person—that it could not be, not with her, not with any woman. For all his golden achievements in and out of the pool, none had been sufficient to silence the voice inside him insisting that he was unworthy of love and respect, the voice that had dogged him since his mother had shipped him off to the cold Southern Highlands as a lonely, bewildered child almost a quarter of a century earlier.

Now, as he conducted a sad, silent survey of the crowded room, Healy thought that perhaps, at the next dance, if he could just get

Olive on her own—*why did these giggling misses always have to travel in packs?*—he might find out where Muriel had gone, or with whom. Healy had no way of knowing that there would be no next dance—that this was to be Manly's final social splash before the world changed forever. In just five weeks, the world's skies would be clouded by war.

ELEVEN

WHITE FEATHERS AND OSTRICH PLUMES

'Is your "Best Boy" wearing Khaki?
If not, don't you think he should be?
If your young man neglects his duty to his King and Country,
the time may come when he will neglect you!'

—To the Young Women of London (Army recruiting poster, 1915)

***

ASSASSINATED. Heir to Austrian throne. Archduke and Wife.

At 3.10pm on Sunday 28 June 1914, the fateful telegraph reached London. The heir presumptive to the Austrian throne and his wife had been murdered in the Bosnian capital Sarajevo. Archduke Franz Ferdinand, son of Archduke Charles Louis and nephew of Emperor Franz Joseph, had been shot dead while inspecting the imperial forces in Bosnia and Herzegovina, both former Ottoman territories annexed by

Austria-Hungary in 1908. His killer, Serbian nationalist Gavrilo Princip, had struck after the Archduke's motorcade took a wrong turn, and now Europe, already teetering and torn by civil wars and internal strife, held its collective breath for the fallout.

Prussian statesman Otto von Bismarck had once predicted that 'A great European War will come out of some damned foolish thing in the Balkans', and his forecast proved correct. War was declared on 4 August 1914, after Austria-Hungary blamed the Serbian government for the assassinations. Russia immediately backed the Serbs, and the Austro-Hungarian parliament received their own assurance of support from German leader Kaiser Wilhelm. Within a week, Russia, Belgium, Britain and Serbia had guns aimed towards Germany and Austria-Hungary, and Europe was at war.

Australia's offer to send 20,000 men to back the British effort, 'a magnificent manifestation of patriotic enthusiasm', was immediately accepted. Volunteers came from all over New South Wales and even New Zealand to besiege Sydney's Victoria Barracks, 'adventurous spirits ready to play their part in the world cataclysm'. On 17 August 1914, *The Sydney Morning Herald* announced that 'Almost all the required number of men for the infantry regiments have already applied; there will probably be only a few days left in which to volunteer.'

Destruction of Dinant—More German Savagery: The Germans have by shell fire destroyed Dinant, on the Meuse, fourteen miles south of Namur, in Belgium. The destruction of the town was accompanied by the barbarisms that have already become a customary feature of German methods in this war. Frightened women took refuge in convents while hundreds of men were summarily shot. A hundred prominent citizens of the town were rounded up and were then ranged in line in the Place d'Armes and shot. M. Hummers, manager of a large weaving factory employing 2000 hands and M. Poncelot, son of a former senator of Belgium, were both shot, the latter in presence of his six children.
—The Age, 9 September 1914

Within weeks of the call to arms, Les Boardman's brothers Phil and Bert, along with George Hill and Chas Helsham of the Sydney Swimming Club, had signed on with the Army Medical Corps. Ten members of the Surf Bathing Association immediately volunteered, and the NSW ASA contributed to the Patriotic Fund by donating the proceeds from an intraclub handicap on 31 October. At the East Sydney club's annual general meeting on 21 October 1914, a resolution was passed making those members who had joined the Expeditionary Forces honorary members during their absence; eight of the club's 47 members had already signed up.

Among the first Australians to enlist was Cecil Healy's cousin, Nicholas Healy III. Nicholas had some of his convict grandfather and namesake's wild spirit. Instead of entering the legal practice of his late father in country Cootamundra, NSW, Healy had become a self-described 'bushman', and enlisted in far north Queensland, where he had been mustering and prospecting, in August 1914. Like his paternal grandfather, Nicholas was dark-complexioned with 'the blackest' hair and Celtic grey eyes, and was also combative and ever-ready for an adventure. He sailed on 16 August 1914 with the 2nd Australian Naval and Military Expeditionary Force in a pre-emptive attack on German New Guinea, where armoured cruisers stationed with the German East Asia Squadron posed a threat to Allied shipping in the region. However, a mutiny by the stokers over short supplies aboard Healy's ship, the *Kanowna*, saw it turned back to Townsville in an attempt to restore order, and as a result, Healy never saw action in New Guinea. Undeterred, Nicholas immediately shipped out for the Middle East with the 5th Light Horse Regiment, but was medically discharged home in September 1915[1].

Germans Driven Back Exhausted and Demoralised. Flight from the Marne. Panic-stricken Germans. The Allies in Pursuit. More Austrian Defeats. Servians (sic) Join Russians.
—*Newcastle Morning Herald, 14 September 1914*

In England, the factories of Richard Hornsby & Sons were seconded for the production of munitions. The 'caterpillar' tractors and automobiles Hornsby's had produced between 1906 and 1910, with their unique chain-tracks instead of tyres, had briefly interested the British army for their ability to cross tough terrain, but these early progenitors of the tank were considered underpowered to pull a heavy gun, and so Hornsby's sold the track patent to the USA in 1911[2]. In addition, in 1914 the United Kingdom abandoned all swimming championships, international water polo matches and inter-association visits between England and France, and in December 1914 there was talk that the Australasian swimming championships would be similarly cancelled 'in view of the unsettled state of affairs in consequence of the war'. Healy reflected that the public mood was 'dull and depressed', but also that it served 'no useful purpose to brood unnecessarily, and thereby make the burden harder to bear.' Healy and Tod Solomons organised a charity water polo match in November 1914, which Healy felt would have additional benefits beyond fund-raising for the war effort. The game, he wrote, was 'fought out more in accordance with Marquis of Queensberry rules ... I have always thought that water polo develops a man's fighting instinct.'[3]

British in Action—Fierce Fight at Langemarck: At Langemarck, they entrenched. During the night a shrill whistle was suddenly heard, and a lot of bushes which had been soaked with petroleum by the enemy broke into flame. Simultaneously, masses of Germans sprang from the beet crops a few hundred yards away from the British position. The British hurriedly manned their trenches and opened fire on the advancing troops with machine guns. In addition, volley after volley was fired with rifles. The Germans replied with cries of 'Hoch, hoch' and rushed onward, but fell in hundreds. The British sprang out of the trenches with their bayonets ready and hand to hand encounters took place in the dim glare of the burning bushes.

—Chronicle, 31 October 1914

The *Herald's* prediction in August that Australia's recruitment quota would be full and there would be little need for more men beyond the initial twenty thousand proved to be incorrect. As 1914 drew to a close, Europe's raging bushfire of a war had spread to east

Africa, Asia Minor and Mesopotamia, and calls for more men became increasingly strident. Eleven hundred Australians enlisted at Sydney's Victoria Barracks in the first week of November alone, largely through the issue of free railway passes to men from rural areas. Many of the new recruits were shearers, 'the strong and wiry type ... [who] can not only ride and drive, but can shoot well', said the *Herald*. However, urgent calls came for more motor drivers, mechanics, horsemen for the Veterinary Field Hospital division, and female volunteers to conduct ambulance and first-aid classes. Thus, enlistments continued to decimate the ranks of Australasian elite sport, with swimmers, rugby players and golfers all leaving their playing fields and heading off to face bombardment in the sands of the Middle East and the freezing mud of western Europe.

News reached Healy on 11 November 1914 that New Zealand swimmer Lt. Bernard 'Tiny' Freyberg had been severely wounded while fighting in Europe. Freyberg, who had won the New Zealand 100-yard championship in 1906 and 1910, was a great friend of Healy's, having visited Australia in 1905 for the ill-fated national titles in Brisbane. Healy remembered him as 'one of the most humorous sportsmen it has been my pleasure to meet', and felt sure that the first utterance to pass Freyberg's lips after the wretched missile found its mark would have been a joke[4]. Freyberg survived his wounds and later became the youngest general in the British Army during the War, winning a Victoria Cross and three Distinguished Service Orders (DSOs).

Worse news came in December, the peak of the Australian summer and the depths of a hellish French winter. Healy received a letter from the front from his friend, the French swimmer George Borocco, who was now a sergeant in the 33rd regiment French Territorials. The pair had met during Healy's 1906 trip to Europe, and when Healy and Boardman returned to Paris in 1912, Borocco treated them with characteristic French hospitality, placing his apartment at their disposal. Borocco's letter, dated 10 October 1914, advised that he was on the front with the English and awaiting comrades from Australia. 'A few months and Germany will be death for the world' was his chilling assessment. He told Healy that many swimmers of their mutual acquaintance had already been killed[5]. The fallen included Austria's 1906 Olympian Leopold Mayer, 1900 medallists Charles Devendeville and Andre Six of France and Hungarian Oszkar Demjan, a breaststroker at the 1912 Games.

***

At the conclusion of the Stockholm Games in 1912, Cecil Healy and Duke Kahanamoku had parted as firm friends, Duke conveying the great compliment to the Australian that he had 'the aloha spirit', a kind of warmth and affection with no obligation in return, a joyful sharing of life energy. In return, Healy invited the Hawaiian to visit Australia and give a series of surfing and swimming exhibitions to encourage the growing public appreciation of both sports. This, Healy reported, was an invitation Kahanamoku was 'very anxious to accept', but despite strenuous efforts by the NSW ASA, the visit was twice delayed, first in late 1912, when Kahanamoku had a finger bitten off by a large eel, and then again in December 1913 for private business reasons[6].

However, in a move that was destined to boost the morale of Sydneysiders who were worried about the war, in October 1914, a tour by the Duke was at last locked in, encompassing Sydney, Brisbane, Melbourne and New Zealand. Kahanamoku arrived in Sydney on 14 December 1914, accompanied by 19-year-old surfer-swimmer George Cunha and manager Francis Evans, and was met by a gathering of prominent swimmers and officials for a reception at the luxurious Hotel Australia. Kahanamoku spoke calmly and deliberately at this function, and all Healy's 'glowing impressions' of the man were reinforced when the pair met privately afterwards. 'I cannot conceive the thought of anyone taking other than an instant liking to him', Healy said warmly, and the Australian public did exactly that. On 19 December, the tall, dark Duke was welcomed rapturously at the Coogee swim carnival by hundreds of fans, and in return, proposed three cheers for the Australian crowd with his famous broad, white smile. His kindness and modesty charmed the curious locals, and he didn't even have to enter the water to become a firm favourite. Healy theorised that the title of 'Duke' was not one of aristocracy, but a term of endearment, conferred upon him as 'a prince of good fellows'[7].

While Australians were familiar with Duke's achievements in the pool, a demonstration of the Hawaiian's other great skill was arranged for 24 December 1914 at Freshwater Beach. Healy had hoped that Kahanamoku might give a surfing demonstration during his visit, but upon his arrival, Healy looked about his person and noted with keen disappointment that the Duke had not brought a surfboard. 'We were told the use of boards was not permitted in Australia', Kahanamoku explained, but noticing the sorrowful look on his friend's face, he quickly added, 'But I can easily make one here.'[8] He was as good as his word, and duly appeared at Freshwater toting a slab of local sugar pine 8 feet 6 1/2 inches long, 23 inches wide and 2 3/4 inches thick, a board so hefty that, at 78 pounds, it had to be towed out beyond the break by a surfboat. The event was intended to be a private demonstration of his surf-riding skills for invited media only, but when rumour of Duke's appearance got out, thousands of fans crowded the beach and it had to be postponed until an undisclosed time the next day. Healy, who had stoked the public's appetite for Kahanamoku by proclaiming that 'His extraordinary skill as an exponent of the old-established pastime of surfboard riding made him a well-known Hawaiian identity long before he had an opportunity of demonstrating his pre-eminence as a speed swimmer', was not actually present, having been detained by work commitments, but those lucky enough to be invited marvelled as Duke subjugated the dumping shore break, even proceeding backwards for a time on one wave. The Freshwater Club members were fully cognizant of the honour conferred on their beach, and a commemorative statue now stands on the site[9].

Duke Kahanamoku's visit to Australia in 1914 at the invitation of Cecil Healy aimed to raise the morale of a young nation newly beset by war. Kahanamoku (centred) is pictured as an interested spectator at a mock boxing match between two of Australia's great pre-war swimmers, Snowy Baker (left) and Frank Beaurepaire (right). [Source: State Library of NSW, Davis Sporting Collection part II: swimming. IE no.946050].

It was not until early February that the public had a chance to see the great man among the waves when Kahanamoku gave a surfing exhibition at Dee Why in front of a packed crowd, catching waves from half a mile out and performing all sorts of acrobatic feats on the board for nearly an hour. He was accompanied at intervals by fifteen-year-old Isabel Lethem after calling for a volunteer to aid in a demonstration of tandem surfing. That performance gave Healy his first look at Kahanamoku on a board, as he was competing in the Surf Brace Relay race representing North Steyne, paired with Tod Solomons[10].

Kahanamoku's 1914 visit was eulogised as the introduction of surfboard riding to Australia, but young men had been surfing the northern beaches for at least two years before Duke's arrival, in fact his first exhibition was believed to have been held at Freshwater because too many surfers were crowding his waves at Manly. Surf historian Mark Maddox identified North Steyne Surf Lifesaving Club president Charles Paterson as the father of surfing in Australia. Paterson had imported a redwood surfboard from Hawaii in 1910 and launched the board at his home beach with fellow lifesavers Jack Reynolds and Tommy Walker in eager attendance. While the unwieldy plank disliked the steep shore break and was soon consigned to the Paterson household for use as an ironing board, the stunt produced a ripple that would grow to become a multi-million dollar industry in Australia. Kahanamoku himself endorsed the view that North Steyne members had been riding the waves long before he arrived: 'The Walkers were the first', he said, and generously presented Tommy with his own handmade board at the end of the tour. While not the formal genesis of the sport in Australia, Kahanamoku's demonstration proved critical in popularising board-riding and his link to the Freshwater and Manly beaches helped both to gain recognition as national and world surfing reserves[11].

The one disappointment of the tour was the lack of a rematch in the pool between Healy and Kahanamoku. When Duke lined up at the NSW State Championships in the 100 yards, it was against titleholder Albert Barry, Manly prodigy Geoff Wyld and Ivan Stedman, the champion of Victoria. Billy Longworth was the only survivor of the 1912 Olympic team to make the field. Even using the six-beat kick more suited to fresh water, Kahanamoku dominated the race, winning by more than a body length in 53 4/5 seconds. Cuhna was second, with Barry and Longworth some way back. Duke also won the 220 yards over both Longworth and Boardman, but the great surprise came in the 440-yard event, in which he was beaten by an unheralded youngster from Manly, Tommy Adrian. Adrian was a slender youth who had received some tuition from the old stager Freddie Lane, although Healy hoped that Lane would spare the boy his vegetarian leanings: 'Tommy looks as if it would be to his advantage to wrestle with a fat steak occasionally.'[12] Healy could not have known how prophetic this quip would prove, with little Adrian's fortitude about to be tested behind a Howitzer on the Western Front in the most savage and tragic manner imaginable.

***

The voice of Commander Dix broke the silence. 'Tell the colonel', he shouted, 'that the damn' fools have taken us a mile too far north.' There was deathlike silence for a moment. Then suddenly: 'Look at that!' said Captain Leane in one of the northernmost boats. The figure of a man was on the skyline of the plateau above them. A voice called on the land. From the top of Ari Burnu, a rifle flashed. A bullet whizzed overhead and plunged into the sea. A second or two of silence ... four or five shots as if from a sentry group. Another pause—then a scattered irregular fire growing very fast. They were discovered.
—C.E.W. Bean, *Landing of the Australian 1st Division at Gallipoli, 4.30am, 25 April 1915*

The whirl of ukulele music and saltwater dreams accompanying Duke Kahanamoku's tour could not subdue the horrors of war that were creeping closer to Australia. In April 1915—just days before the dreadful baptism of fire for the Australian forces at Gallipoli—public calls for sportsmen to justify their non-enlistment reached an early peak. *The Referee,* doubtless mindful of their own Cecil Healy's non-enlistment, tried to defend the local sporting population. The Manly Swim Club had 26 members in khaki, several dozen oarsmen and scullers had enlisted, along with 20 members of the East Sydney athletic club, 70 Melbourne boxers, Tony Wilding and Stanley Doust from the Australian Davis Cup tennis team and no fewer than 300 rugby players, including 34 from Manly and 32 from Eastern Suburbs. Some athletes were so eager to enlist that they resorted to self-mutilation to make the grade. South Steyne lifesaver Albert Rein, turned away for an overlapping toe, checked into the Manly Cottage hospital to have the offending digit removed before presenting himself again at the barracks. Fifty-two of Bondi Surf Club's 87 members were at the front[13], 'where every single surfer should be', declared the *St George Call.* By mid-May, eleven surfers had either been killed in action or died of their wounds[14].

However, Australia continued to call upon its athletes simply for the fact that they were indeed athletes—men with the necessary physical attributes for easy conversion into military prowess, men who knew and accepted discipline. The Royal Sydney and Killara Golf Clubs had formed rifle associations, and their members were liable for service as part of the reserves, but joining a Rifle Reserve Club or National Guard was soon decreed insufficient sacrifice for an able-bodied athlete. Such associations, the papers adjudged, should be reserved for those whose age, family ties, or employment exempted them from the firing line in Europe.

In a new era of national austerity and belt-tightening, there were also severe public admonitions to curb the hedonism associated with sport, both in participation and spectating. *The Methodist* trumpeted that 'Pleasure must not be the rival of duty, but its servant. If football, for instance, prevents men from enlisting who ought to enlist, the game becomes unpatriotic and evil. If surf bathing and race meetings absorb either the time or money that just now might be placed to better advantage, they should at least be suspended.' On 27 June 1915, NSW Premier W.A. Holman called for a blanket suspension of professional sport: 'Those who play it should be at the front, and those who watch it should be in training', he declared. 'Every man is needed, badly needed. The resisting power of the enemy has apparently been much underestimated.' That call received wide-ranging support in both the business and sporting communities. The Rev. Wentworth-Shields, vicar of St. James in Sydney, decreed that 'Money for sport is money for the Germans!' Richard Teece, general manager of the AMP financial group, called for all capable men to be forced to fight, and rugby great Dally Messenger advocated that all football fields be turned into rifle ranges. Mr L. Ormsby, secretary of the Surf-bathing Association, agreed that 'all those in a position to go to the war, and those who may ultimately have to go, should spend their spare time making some kind of preparation.' The Sunday Times accompanied this report with a photograph of the bodies of drowned children recovered from the Lusitania under the caption 'The Germans did this.'[15]

There was a scramble of feet over the parapet, the sound of falling earth, and the knocking of accoutrements. The peck-peck of Mauser rifles from the trench opposite had already begun, and it gradually swelled into a rattle. A man fell past me into the trench, bleeding from a wound in the mouth. Out in the scrub, a line of our old 'peasoup' Australian khaki was racing, jumping the low bushes and wire straight for the enemy's trench.
—*Capture of Lonesome Pine, The West Australian, 28 August 1915*

The biggest recruitment news in the swimming world came on 14 May 1915, with the enlistment of Frank Beaurepaire. He was followed into khaki by fellow Victorian champions Matthew Griffiths (200 yards), Stanley Crane (diving), W.B. Bennett (100 yards) and Louis Grieve (220 yards). In New South Wales, ASA president William Hill moved that all swimming activities be reduced or suspended 'until the time had arrived when every available swimmer had found his way into khaki'. The annual meeting of the Association turned into a recruitment drive, with Hill endeavouring to make swimmers aware of the seriousness of the crisis. *The Referee* estimated that 300 swimmers had already answered the call, 'but there are others that could go', and prominent public men were dispatched to club meets to appeal to swimmers to do their duty[16].

By August 1915, public calls for sportsmen to enlist were intensifying. Fifty-three men from Healy's North Steyne Life Saving Club had signed up for war, but Healy was not amongst them. [Source: Sportsmen's Committee, State Parliamentary Recruiting Committee, Enlist in the Sportsmen's Thousand, Chromolithograph on paper, 1917. Australian War Memorial, collection ID: ARTV00026

By August 1915, 72 of the 81 members of the Manly Life Saving Club had volunteered; of the remainder, most were under the nominal 18 years of age. North Steyne had 53 of its 71 members enlist, while 108 joined up from Bondi. However, absent from the ranks of swimming and surfing volunteers were Cecil Healy and Billy Longworth. On 8 August 1915, the pair were the targets of a waspish attack in *The Sunday Times* by Mrs Gordon Lowe, wife of the noted English tennis player and mouthpiece of the 'white feather movement', in which militant women publicly waved white feathers in the faces of men they perceived as shirkers. Boys as young as ten had been targeted by these radicals, and suicides had been linked to the humiliation of such attacks. The headline accompanying her treatise in *The Sunday Times* demanded that Healy and Longworth explain 'why they are still civilians', lambasting them as 'bloodless heroes'.

Healy and Longworth were, however, stoic in the face of Mrs. Lowe's hostility. Longworth claimed to have had 'quite serious thoughts of joining', and had only been put off by the 'Liverpool part': the loss of freedom that came with camp life. He now stated, however, that 'while the war (is) not Australia's quarrel, the outlook is a serious one.'

Healy's feelings about the war had also undergone a dreadful revision, independent of Mrs Lowe's malicious intervention. Before the disaster at Gallipoli, Healy saw sports participation and patronage as vital to public morale, but the release of the first casualty lists in April 1915, which included the names of friends including young Manly swimmer Carl Adelt and lifesaver Norman Roberts, both killed at Gallipoli, altered the whole aspect of the war in Healy's eyes: 'Each succeeding addition to the Roll of Honour we have been made acquainted with has tended to confirm my conviction that it is not altogether seemly, and perhaps savouring somewhat of ingratitude, to indulge in sport as a public amusement whilst our fellow countrymen are being laid low by shot and shell, particularly after their imperishable deeds of valour.'

The war had clearly been weighing on Healy, for his journalistic pen, previously so earnest and cheerful, had fallen almost silent. Healy wrote his final sporting story for *The Referee* on 31 March 1915, marvelling at a new world record for the 500 yards set by Fanny Durack: 'Only her tresses betrayed her—Miss Durack's style and evident strength in the water have caused her to be mistaken for a specimen of the sterner sex.' Now, cornered by the militant Mrs Lowe, Healy spoke only of a new and terrible reality. His long career at the top of elite sport had taught him expediency, the knowledge that 'there is nothing so unsubstantial in life as so-called "glory".'[17] The litany of loss among his friends, colleagues and team-mates only confirmed this knowledge: that bullets and bombs did not discriminate between the great and glorious and the nameless and humble. Healy would don khaki expecting nothing less.

After the Mrs Lowe article, the war seemed to subsume Healy from all sides, like a foaming breaker in a North Steyne storm. Sydney swimmer George Hill, who had corresponded with Healy from Egypt, and Jack Reynolds, with whom Healy had shared so many surf rescues, were both killed in the Dardanelles. The Legion of Frontiersmen were in camp at Dee Why, just around the corner from Manly, where they were drilled in scouting, skirmishing and signalling. On 22 August 1915, 120 recruits from Manly, mostly athletes, marched to Holsworthy Barracks to join 'A Company', Tommy Adrian among them, as was Edward 'Happy' Eyre, the professional lifesaver, and local cricketers, footballers, surfers and yachtsmen. The men marched through Manly to the wharf accompanied by the local band, watched by over 20,000 locals. 'Manly sports have done their share', declared the *Farmer and Settler*[18].

Within a week of Mrs Lowe's attack, Longworth was in uniform. Healy waited just a little longer, stung by the viciousness of the Lowe assault and perhaps resisting so as not to affirm her vitriolic intimations. On Wednesday 15 September 1915, Healy joined 51 other men at Victoria Barracks and signed his name to the *Australian Imperial Force Attestation Paper of Persons Enlisted for Service Abroad*[19].

TWELVE

DIGGERS

*'My name is Ozymandias, King of Kings.
Look on my works ye Mighty and despair!
No thing beside remains. Round the decay
Of that Colossal Wreck, boundless and bare,
The lone and level sands stretch far away.'*

—Percy Bysshe Shelley, *Ozymandias*

***

HMAT A23 *Suffolk*
Indian Ocean
23 December 1915

The punch was a savage roundhouse left.

It whistled past Healy's chin as the huge sergeant rushed at him, arms flailing, bellowing like a wounded bull. Healy swayed clear and then swivelled on the balls of his feet to keep his assailant in sight, his own guard instinctively lifting. The bare-knuckled sergeant was two axe handles across the shoulders and burned to mahogany by the Indian Ocean sun, and as he set himself like a pig dog for a second assault, Healy saw that his eyes were misted red with rage. He braced himself to duck the left that he knew would come again and to follow it with his own straight right to the big man's jaw. *He didn't want to hit this bloke, for all his unschooled brutishness, but with that reach and that killing madness....* There was a roar from the crowd of watching men and, with a sinking heart beneath his sweat-dampened shirt, Healy ducked his head and met the oncoming rush with his own right fist.

The impact was like a bolt of lightning through his arm; the great lantern jaw was as hard as a block of wood and, for a terrible moment, Healy thought his hand had given way, but the sergeant stopped as though poleaxed. His eyes, which had been fixed doggedly on Healy's, now glazed over and the meaty arms dropped to his sides as he swayed, pirouetted in a slow half-circle, and then crashed to the deck on his back.

That put an end to the day's boxing entertainment aboard *HMAT Suffolk*. The men buzzed with chatter and laughter, and Healy heard the crinkle of ten-bob notes being slapped onto grudging palms. Roy Hendy threw a towel around Healy's shoulders and clapped him on the back as the men dispersed, some drifting below to their hammocks, while most sought places on deck to lounge, smoke and discuss the fight.

It was December 1915, two days before Christmas. The *Suffolk* had been at sea for nearly a month and in that time her payload of Australian troops had sighted neither land nor passing ship. They were steaming west across the Indian Ocean, but taking a path nine hundred miles south of the traditional route via Colombo and Port Said, a secret path to Africa intended to avoid German submarines and warships. To combat the twin perils of boredom and confinement, Healy and four others had drawn up a program of boxing and wrestling to entertain the men. Healy was quickly elected boxing referee, despite protesting ignorance of the Queensbury pastime. A ring erected on 'B' Hatch beneath the bridge allowed nearly the entire complement of troops to find a vantage point and the contests were spirited, with professional fighters such as Queenslander Charlie Godfrey in the ranks. Godfrey won the ship's middle-weight championship in a points victory over Pope of Western Australia, a fight of such quality that Healy said afterwards, 'I will always recall my having constituted the third person in the arena for this match with pleasure.' Many of the bouts were not so skilled, with a good deal of what Healy called 'Slather-em Whack', which saw him 'smeared a vermilion hue'[1].

Healy's close friend Sgt-Major Roy Hendy told *The Sunday Times*, 'On the way over, he (Healy) was immensely popular ... There was a good deal of regret that he was the third man in the ring instead of being there as a contestant.' However, on one occasion Healy did heed the calls to don the gloves, specifically in response to an old bare-knuckle scrapper who taunted him 'to have a go, old style versus new style'. The result was demoralising for Healy's adversary. While he had clearly underestimated the efficacy of Healy's right hand, it was probably the 33-year-old staff sergeant's footwork that saved his features from rearrangement. As Hendy recalled, 'Had Cecil caught some of the swings that came his way, I doubt if he would ever have got on his feet again.'[2]

Healy had now been a member of the Australian Imperial Force (AIF) for three months. Basic training at Liverpool in western Sydney was as far removed from Healy's old life in Manly, all clean and salty and breezy, as the *Suffolk* was from a luxury liner. The camp was a canvas city, with hot and unshaded rows of conical white tents stretching along the eastern bank of the Georges River. At 5 feet 8 1/4 inches tall and weighing 198 pounds, the tanned, dark-eyed Healy was described as a 'fine stamp of a man', well within the AIF stipulations of being aged 18–45 years and a minimum of 5 feet 2 inches in height. His strapping 42-inch chest measurement was a full nine inches above the AIF average. Recruits were examined like horses in a dealer's yard—mouths forced open, and feet, legs, arms and eyes checked for dysfunction or deformity. Their skin was scanned for British army tattoos, particularly the revelatory BC (bad character) or D (deserter) insignias[3]. Healy had always been keenly interested in rifle sports, having met many European shooting champions during his international travels. Now he was thrust into a world of bayoneting, sighting and grenade throwing, an endless round of marching and musketry accompanied by the non-stop haranguing of drill sergeants, his feet aching in new boots that could only be broken in by daily lashings of castor oil.

Almost everything was done in the open under the baking November sun, from ablutions at rows of outdoor taps to barbering and eating (both seated on a box), with food ladled from huge buckets and billies onto tin plates. There were first-aid classes, gas defence drills, and marksmanship and physical training. Then there was the 'bull', which many felt crushed any individual initiative among the men: the incessant dusty marching up and down, the never-ending cleaning of rifles and boots, snap inspections of tents and feet and teeth, and endless saluting, parading and kowtowing.

New Australian Infantry Force recruits entering the army camp at Liverpool, NSW, where Healy completed his basic training. [Source: Australian War Memorial, collection ID: H03357. Donor E.K. Burke].

Healy was in camp with Billy Longworth and Eric Fox, the 1913 national breaststroke champion[4]. The *Westralian Worker* speculated that Longworth and Healy would be sent to Gallipoli, 'where they might emulate Leander by swimming the Hellespont'. However, while they were in camp at Liverpool, swimming was far from their agenda, in fact the greatest challenge for the former Olympians was the physical training itself: the mindless repetitive drill and tedious group runs around the compound, all of it lacking the elite competitor's daily striving for improvement and perfection, strengthening the body but wearying the mind into the dull obedience of the carthorse. However, outside the army, there was little for Australia's remaining unenlisted swimmers to compete or train for. The 1916 Berlin Olympic Games had been cancelled, and in October 1915, the Australian Amateur Swimming Association annulled all championships, both local and interstate, as most of the leading swimmers were in khaki and 'it would be extremely unfair, to say the least, to give an opportunity to the stay-at-homes to gain the highest honours which the association is capable of conferring.' In Healy's absence, the Anti-Lunch Brigade had continued to turn out, although there were suggestions that the name be changed to the 'Dainty Lunch Brigade' due to the cups of tea and piles of food now being consumed after the daily dip. In lieu of regular racing, many clubs were now holding memorial events for their fallen, including Fred Doodson from the Pyrmont club and Sydney swimmers Blair Swannell and George Hill[5].

Conditions were basic at the Liverpool army camp, with bathing, barbering and meals all conducted outdoors. [Source: Australian War Memorial, collection ID: H03366. Donor E.K. Burke].

Healy was appointed a Lance Corporal on 15 October 1915, and on 1 November he was assigned to the Australian Service Corps as a Quartermaster Sergeant (warrant officer second class)[6]. At the end of the month, on Tuesday 27 November, he and more than 1,200 other troops embarked on *HMAT A2 3 Suffolk* to finally head for the theatre of war[7]. At the time, the East Sydney Swimming Club had 20 men, or 35% of its members, enlisted, including their captain Healy, 'whose absence (would) be greatly felt'. Healy had been re-elected as captain while he was in camp, with young Reg Joyce to stand in his place until what the club felt was Healy's inevitable return.

On the eve of his departure, Healy's impending absence was remarked upon by his colleagues at *The Referee*, whose staff publicly wished him 'the best of good luck'. Healy was granted leave to attend a dinner at the NSW Sports Club on 24 November, at which he was presented with a 'souvenir of esteem' and his health drunk by friends including Tod Solomons and Vicary Horniman. Healy had formed a close friendship in camp with twenty-six-year-old Roy Hendy, who swam for the Waverley Club at Bondi and had enlisted on the same day as Healy. Hendy had been an alderman with Randwick Council, and both he and Healy were treated to supper by alderman Douglas Maxwell Cooper in Coogee on 25 November, with a number of eligible young ladies present.

However, Healy's final act before embarkation concerned two other ladies. He visited the family solicitors Lambeth & Manning in the city to make a will, in which half of his not-inconsiderable estate—some £344—was left to his mother, Annie Louisa. The other half, in the event of his death, was to go to 'my friend Muriel Maitland'[8].

On 27 November 1915, Healy and more than 1,200 other Australians sailed for Egypt and the European theatre of war. [Source: Northern Beaches Council/Manly Library Local Studies Collection: Series: 2006-07-27(23), image ID: 1100003406].

***

While the war was now almost eighteen months old, Sydney still rallied to every khaki column of men marching its streets before departure. Windows and balconies were hung with Union Jacks and Australian flags, and thousands of well-wishers waved handkerchiefs as the men in slouch hats and ostrich plumes passed by, bayonets gleaming in the sun, headed by a brass band bravely proclaiming *Advance Australia Fair*. Some of the boys were achingly young, with the barest hint of fluff on their cheeks, while others, like Healy, were worldly veterans of life, but all were sailing to an unknown destination and fate. In November 1915, so many streamers were flung to loved ones on the quay from the decks of the *Suffolk* that she was quite swathed in their coloured web. Then she began to move, and one by one, the streamers broke.

The men aboard the *Suffolk* were told little of their mission or target. Not only was their route across the Indian Ocean a clandestine one, but many of the diggers had no idea on which beach, peninsula, cove, or even in what country they were destined to land. Pt. E.A.D. Hill wrote home that 'All sorts of rumours are abroad about our ultimate destination, a fair number of them naming England.'[9] For all the ferocious reputation of the Indian Ocean for tropical cyclones and even sea monsters, their passage was mostly hot and torpid, with a long, lazy swell and little seasickness. Conditions below decks, with the men accommodated in hammocks, were close, but while on deck the men were permitted some relaxation in dress standards to seek some relief from the sultry tropical climate. Shorts were the order of the day, a liberty that appealed to Healy, who observed that travel on a troopship had one distinct advantage over a P&O liner—'one can go about as one likes in the tropics ... and regaining his wonted mahogany tint made [him] feel more at home.'[10]

The Australian troop-carrier SS Suffolk (HMAT A23) passes through the Suez Canal. [Source: Australian War Memorial, collection ID: P00998.027].

As the *Suffolk* steamed inexorably toward 1916 and Egypt, the crossing of the Equator was celebrated with a traditional ceremony and Healy was railroaded into taking a prominent role, donning the garb of Father Neptune. Preceded by buglers playing the royal salute and followed by a retinue that included the champion sportsmen and other notables on board, 'the sovereign of the seas' made a mock inspection of the ship amid flights of rockets and fireworks. The ceremony itself saw first-timers dunked in a small canvas tank erected on deck, with the immersions presided over by the royal party. 'A good deal of laughter was created', Healy said, 'and I gave an original (if nothing else) interpretation of the character.'

However, for all the moderations in dress code and efforts to provide entertainment, the days were mostly hot, tedious and crowded. 'It is easy to imagine how we live our lives: just day after day with nothing but water', wrote Sergeant A.J. Braybrook, perhaps recalling Coleridge's *The Rime of the Ancient Mariner*. 'Soldiers on a transport feel very much like a mob of cattle, not only from the general treatment, but from the cramped way we are compelled to live. Privacy is a term whose meaning I have forgotten.'

Boxing matches were among the entertainment that was organised in an attempt to relieve the heat and tedium of life aboard the transport ships. Healy was drafted in as both referee and competitor while aboard the Suffolk. [Source: Australian War Memorial, collection ID: C01577].

The first sight of *terra firma*—the barren coast of Somaliland in east Africa—came in January 1916 after six long weeks at sea, and the *Suffolk* now turned north, her prow facing the conflict zone for the first time. Two days later, she eased along the hazy coast of Arabia, passing through Hell's Gate (*Bab-el-Mandeb*) into the Red Sea at midnight, *en route* to her destination at Suez. For Healy and the men who had boarded in Sydney, it would be the first time they had set foot on land since departing. The ship had paused only in Fremantle to board more troops, and the men who were already on board had not been allowed to disembark.

Their arrival in Egypt, however, was not a happy one. At Suez, the port was full of horse transport ships that had to be unloaded first, forcing the men aboard the *Suffolk* to wait for three hot and cheerless days before disembarking on 6 January 1916. Various destinations were allotted to the various Australian detachments. At the commencement of hostilities in the Great War, the British had established a military government in Egypt to protect the vital Suez Canal and had erected massive Allied training camps at Mena, Maadi and Heliopolis, with a training school at Zeitoun, north-east of Cairo[11]. When they finally disembarked, Healy's unit took a third-class train to their temporary consignment at Zeitoun. The train left Suez at 1.30pm and did not reach Zeitoun until 2.30am the next morning after a teeth-rattling journey. 'Under ordinary circumstances, the trip takes about seven hours', Healy recounted, 'but our progress was continually being stopped in order to permit troop-laden trains making Canal-wards to pass. It was bitterly cold when we arrived in camp. Our equipment had been wrongly directed and I shall long remember the wait we had until sunrise without blankets. It is not that the temperature is very low, but the atmosphere at this time of year has a damp chilliness in the early hours of the morning that seems to freeze the marrow in one's bones.'[12]

The desert nation held many surprises for the Australians. Healy and four other sergeants occupied a disused officers' hut at Zeitoun, derelict but a cut above the tents erected for the enlisted men, as at least the roof attempted to keep the rain out. The Egyptian winter of 1915–16 was, according to the locals, unusually wet, boasting the extraordinary total of 'two or three heavy ten-minute showers', Healy marvelled. It was just the first of many culture shocks in this sensuous, riotous land, with its antiquities and slave markets straight out of the Old Testament. As strange as stage scenery, Egypt was a hedonistic swirl of veiled women and clamouring Arabs, stately camels and overloaded donkeys, white sand and brilliantly green fields fringing the mighty Nile.

Healy's unit soon moved to the Australian camp at Mena, ten miles south-west of the capital. Frowned over by the massive pyramids of Khufu, Khafre and Menkaure, the camp was also in the line of sight of *Abu al Hul*, The Terrifying One—the Sphinx. This largest Australian camp had grown up around the old Mena House luxury hotel, itself converted to a military hospital as casualties from Gallipoli flooded in. The main camp, on a sandy flat sandwiched between the ancient monuments, bristled with tents, horse lines, wagons and guns painted in bright reds, blues and yellows, supposedly to blend in with the local desert traffic. Conditions were even more basic than those at Zeitoun. Official war reporter C.E.W. Bean recollected that the tents occupied by the best part of a thousand AIF officers at Mena were 'easily recognisable in the line of any battalion or unit as being generally the most ramshackle constructions within sight ... tall, naked scaffolding poles tied together with ropes and knots and with what appear to be the remains of aged carpets hung up over the lower portion of the framework.'[13]

An enormous shanty town had risen from the sands at the camp entrance, its alleys awash with inky Arabic coffee, mind-numbing *zibib* (a cloudy drink made with aniseed) and strange local delicacies including *falafel* and stuffed pigeon. Visitors to the town were besieged by eager throngs selling tomatoes, 'orangies' and 'eggs-a-cook'. Bizarrely, there were also four cinemas among the tin and hessian shacks, showing nothing less than the very latest Hollywood releases. The troops had been cooped up for months in transports, and now they poured into the slums and beyond to the sordidness and vice of Cairo, pockets full of British currency and ready for anything. It was not Healy's first visit to Egypt—his 1906 Olympic journey to Athens had included a stop in Suez—and he was wise to the Arabs who pestered the men yelling '*Backsheesh, backsheesh!*' Just as they had targeted tourists pre-war, the locals now preyed upon novice soldiers until the men learned to swear forcibly in Arabic (which, Healy observed, only took the Australians a day or two). Beside the camp itself was the palace of the Sultan's brother and its harem, whose 'darling little inmates' often peeped from the windows and waved to the men. Healy noted that any attempted incursion by the Australian boys was thwarted by armed sentries who 'attain[ed] the size of giants' and who were almost as fascinating to the Australians as the girls. However, amid this bewildering cacophony were also small glimpses of home. Some Australian units had smuggled kangaroos, koalas and possums into Egypt as battalion mascots. The marsupial expats subsisted on a diet of soldiers' biscuits and horse chaff, and were a great source of morale to the homesick troops.

The seemingly mandatory activity for every serving Australian was having a picture taken while aboard a camel at the Pyramids. Healy was no exception, and the photograph, in which he is accompanied by Roy Hendy, the requisite camels and the frowning Sphinx, appeared in the *Pastoral Review* journal, edited by his own brother Harold, in 1918[14]. However, as the final stop for most of the men before the front, life at Mena was primarily a hard slog of drill, rifle practice, trench digging, tactical schemes, night bivouacs and, above all, route marching with full packs. Men slogged for miles around the Pyramids through soft sand, weighed down by full kit and drenched in perspiration that, after they cooled down in the incessant desert wind, caused many deaths from pneumonia.

Life at Mena camp was a hard slog of drill amidst the soft sand, hot wind and tension awaiting a call to the bloody battlefields of Europe and the Middle East. [Source: Australian War Memorial, collection ID: PS0718].

As a sergeant in the Army Service Corps, Healy and his unit shared responsibility for everything from transport to postal services and foodstuffs to petroleum. Much of the supply came via camel and donkey trains driven by an army of motley Arabs and Nubians, and life was a long and dusty round of haggling, packing and stacking. Camp life soon developed into an exquisite torture for Healy. During his travels before the war, he had observed the German emphasis on swimming instruction in the defence forces, and he called for the Australian soldiers to be similarly tutored in order to reduce casualties after shipwrecks or river crossings. He praised the 'up-to-date and business-like Americans', whose officers were required to prove competence as swimmers before being granted a commission. However, such instruction was not forthcoming for the Australian troops, and Healy's skills as both a swimmer and pedagogue remained unutilised. Worse, the mighty Nile river was out of bounds to all troops, greatly disappointing Healy, who thought it looked 'bonzer for a dip', despite the grubs that were said to attack white men daring to enter the water.

Healy's role in the Army Service Corps in Egypt included management of transport, postal, fuel and food supplies for the camps at Zeitoun and Mena. [Source: Australian War Memorial, collection ID: PS0665].

Having not swum a stroke since the previous November, the earthbound Healy and Hendy launched a research campaign that soon determined that the nearest swimming pool was the sulphur baths at Helwan, a 45-minute train journey south of Mena. The troops were allowed recreation time from late afternoon on most days, so Healy and Hendy set off one evening to investigate this tantalising possibility. The pair were bitterly disappointed to find that the baths—an Egyptian centre of therapeutic tourism since the pharaonic era—had now been emptied and dismantled. Undeterred, the incorrigible two stripped off and engaged in a nonchalant sun-bath by the non-existent pool. Two members of the Coogee Surf Club—each known to both Healy and Hendy—happened by this cheeky spectacle, as both were attached to the army medical unit at a nearby hospital. Healy and Hendy, after resuming their dress, joined the two for tea at the former convalescent home now serving as a medical post in Helwan. The site commanded a view of the Saqqara pyramid, the world's first large-scale stone structure.

It was another two months before the pair finally managed a dip in the briny. Aware of the likelihood of being shipped out at any time, Hendy and Healy took the train to Alexandria during a rare period of leave in March 1916 with the sole objective of a swim in the Mediterranean. While the weather was cloudy, the sated pair still enjoyed the swim immensely.

***

By early 1916, the war had spread like a bloodstain from Europe to Africa and the eastern reaches of the Ottoman Empire. German airships raked the skies from Paris to the British coast in late January, and submarines hunted in packs throughout the Mediterranean, the Black Sea and the English Channel. The Austro-Hungarian army now occupied Montenegro and Albania, and was deadlocked with Italian forces over control of the Isonzo Front in Slovenia, where 12 battles were fought between June 1915 and November 1917. Russian forces had launched a devastating winter campaign against the Turks in Armenia and the Caucasus region, capturing the strategic fortress town of Erzurum and re-taking Kirmanshah in West Persia during a two-week assault in late February. On the Western Front, the 21 February assault of the German Fifth Army on forces in north-eastern France marked the commencement of one of the longest and bloodiest conflict in Europe, the Battle of Verdun. Almost half of Germany's million-strong force, along with 540,000 French troops, were killed or wounded during that ten-month battle of attrition.

British forces were now stretched by air and sea attacks on both their own coastline and fronts in German East Africa, Constantinople and Kut in modern-day Iraq, where an unsuccessful attempt to relieve the besieged city saw 10,000 British troops forced to surrender. On 27 January 1916, the British parliament passed the Military Service Act, imposing conscription on all single men aged between 18 and 41. Exemptions were granted only for ministers of religion, men involved in essential war work, the medically unfit and conscientious objectors. In Australia, two plebiscites to overturn the Defence Act 1903 and introduce conscription were defeated in October 1916 and December 1917, although the October vote was lost by a margin of only two per cent. Australia remained one of only two nations not to introduce conscription during the war (South Africa was the other). However, a total of 416,809 Australian men, almost forty per cent of the white male population aged between 18 and 44, signed up voluntarily[15].

By March 1916, calls on the home front had re-intensified for sportsmen to enlist, despite the multitude already laying down their lives to protect the liberty that allowed sports at all. A reader of *The Sunday Times* harangued boxer Les Darcy for his plans to tour America in 1916, bellowing, 'Is he so devoid of manhood as to lend his support to any attempt to get him out of the country whilst all around him thousands of men with far greater ties are gladly offering themselves as sacrifices on the altar of liberty?' Darcy snuck out of the country anyway, retorting, 'I wouldn't mind being killed right out'. His greatest fear was that he might come home maimed, his boxing career ruined. However, after a disastrous tour of a war-focussed USA, Darcy enlisted as a reservist in the American Flying Corps, and then promised to return and enlist in the Australian Army 'after a few fights', but it never happened. Darcy took ill and died, at just 21 years of age, while still in the USA. Cecil Healy's former clubmate at East Sydney, Snowy Baker, was one of Darcy's most virulent critics. Baker himself had tried three times to enlist in 1916, but had been ruled unfit due to injuries sustained in a motor vehicle accident. Fellow swimmer Harold Hardwick had vigorously defended his own non-enlistment on the basis of unspecified 'obligations', but finally signed up in August 1917. Ironically, his became a decorated military career that spanned both world wars, Hardwick rising to the rank of lieutenant-colonel.

On 17 July 1916, Cecil Healy's younger brother John also joined up. Like his sibling, John Henry Healy was a mature recruit at 31 years of age, and he too was unmarried, having been working as a wool classer in northern New South Wales. Their mother, Annie Louisa, was now 70 years old and, with her sons all grown, married, or moved away, was living alone at her home *Killua* in Darling Point, Sydney. While both boys had listed her as their next of kin upon enlistment, Harold Healy requested that he be first informed in the event of misadventure, to reduce the potential nervous shock to the elderly woman. On 8 November 1916, Private John Healy shipped out with the 22nd Reinforcements, 13th Battalion, 4th Infantry Brigade, bound for the winter hell of trench warfare in France.

***

In March 1916, the Egyptian days were growing hotter and the men's few pleasures had begun to pall. Training was a weary litany amid the heat and tension of waiting for their call-up. A biographical sketch of Healy appearing in Sydney's *Lone Hand* magazine on 1 March 1916 speculated that Healy's first engagement would be in Greece, possibly in Olympia, the original centre of the Ancient Olympic Games—a dreadful irony, as this had been a place where young athletes met in friendly rivalry and fought out their contests in a chivalrous spirit. Greece was now subsumed into the conflict as part of the Allied campaign against Bulgaria[16]. However, when orders came for both Healy and Hendy on 20 March 1916, they were assigned to the British Expeditionary Force in France. With just 24 hours to prepare, the atmosphere became electric as men rushed about, packing and preparing, shaking hands, passing on the superfluous that could not be carried and scrawling last letters to loved ones.

From the port of Alexandria, they boarded the *HT Oriana* for Marseilles in France, a nerve-racking seven day crawl across the Mediterranean with every available eye straining for the telltale wake of a torpedo or bob of a sea-mine. The German submarine campaign had begun on 1 March, and no vessel was sacred, with the Russian hospital ships *Portugal* and *Vpered* torpedoed in the Black Sea and the civilian ferry *Sussex* sunk in the English Channel. It was on the third day, with land out of sight and a thin mist obscuring the sky, that the searing white wake hove up on Healy's side of the ship, carving through the freezing waves on a deadly and unwavering course toward the *Oriana*'s thin steel sides. Cries of terror rose as the scrambling men realised there was nowhere to run, that the lumbering ship had no hope of outmanoeuvring the dreadful aquatic thing that was tearing towards her hull. They were prisoners on a wallowing steel island, caught squarely in the crosshairs and forced to watch their own doom scything through the ocean to blast the decks from beneath their feet.

The wake seemed to sink, and every man braced against a bulkhead, rail or lifeboat waiting for the terrible impact ... and then a puff of silvery water vapour rose, incongruous as fairy dust, beside the ship. A great grey head, the sliding arc of a wet, barnacled body and a tremendous fluked tail lifted out of the waves as a whale rose beside them, exactly amidships. For a frozen moment, there was absolute silence. Then, the small knowing eye seemed to find

Healy and his shipmates as the creature rolled onto its side to observe them, and a great gasping roar of laughter and relief erupted into the winter sky.

THIRTEEN

DOWN AND OUT IN ETÁPLES

'If I were fierce and bald and short of breath,
I'd live with scarlet Majors at the Base,
And speed glum heroes up the line to death.
You'd see me with my puffy petulant face,
Guzzling and gulping in the best hotel,
Reading the Roll of Honour. "Poor young chap",
I'd say—"I used to know his father well;
Yes, we've lost heavily in this last scrap."
And when the war is done and youth stone dead,
I'd toddle safely home and die—in bed.'

—Siegfried Sassoon, *Base Details*

2nd Australian Division Base Depot
Etáples, north-eastern France
23 December 1916

It was a third straight Christmas for many Anzacs in *bloody-western-bloody-Europe*, where there was no sunshine or backyard cricket or cold salads, no dozy beers on a hot verandah while the children rioted on sweets and new toys.

There was only driving rain and sucking grey mud, a foxhole with a sheet of tin on top for the lucky ones and shell craters full of black water and dead men for those preparing to go over the top. For the Australian diggers fortunate enough to be rotated away from the front, the big divisional base at Etáples was scarcely far enough, for they could still hear the big guns from their cold barrack bunks, and many of them cried and thrashed in their sleep at the echoes.

'Sir, it can be done. It *must* be done.' Every morning, the grey faces of the returned infantry swam before Cecil Healy in his own shaving glass. The haunted eyes were truly dreadful, but worse were the haggard, resentful stares directed at his own well-fed features. The way they walked or limped wide of him, or talked loudly of 'Ally Sloper's Cavalry'[1] as he passed, for Cecil Healy was far behind the lines, while they took the thwack of bullets and sweated and shook and screamed under shellfire at the front.

Now the weight of anger and shame made Healy land both palms on the C.O.'s desk. 'Sir....'

The commanding officer finally put down his pen and looked up. '*Sergeant* Healy', mimicking the younger man's inflection sarcastically, 'the men are provided for. Even if we wished to increase their rations over Christmas, it is simply impossible. We have U-boats in the Channel and tanks on our doorstep. You, I'm sure, are well aware of the grace with which we must already receive our weevily flour and mummified vegetables; procurement of anything further at any time, let alone at this late hour, cannot be done.'

'Give me two men and a wagon, sir. Just for a day.'

'Sergeant, this really is quite out of the question. If the other depots have not managed to secure so much as a Christmas cracker for the men, what makes you think we can feed our two thousand on turkey and ice-cream? The budget alone....'

'We have to.' The dark eyes were unwavering, and Healy was leaning across the ramshackle desk like a preacher, his intensity magnetic and overwhelming. The C.O. could suddenly see how this man, for all his unassuming façade, would be first into a thunderous Manly surf when no other swimmer would dare. He was one of the quiet ones who burned with an inner rage, the ones who would charge a machine-gun post or dive headlong into a trench full of Boche when the regulation soldier held back as a result of a desperate desire for self-preservation. Healy's eyes burned into his own as they faced each other, their breath misty in the cold warehouse.

The C.O. gave in. However, he kept his tone stern. 'Sergeant Healy, I do not for one moment condone this outrageous scheme. Do I make myself clear? Should this venture fail, I am holding you personally—and financially—responsible. *Do you understand?*'

However, after half a salute and a whisking sound, Cecil Healy had already gone.

The horse was a wall-eyed creature with a shifty visage, and it pinned its ears as Healy slipped the collar over its neck. Healy knew little of horses, but now, afire with something positive to do at last, he pushed its leering face aside with his elbow and thrust the bit into its mouth. With one sentry on the seat beside him and one in the back, they were away, at no great speed in the creaking old cart to be sure, but headed east nonetheless, beyond the barbed wire and out of the camp in search of Christmas.

At the regulation cry of *'Jippo*, boys!' from the mess tent, the men would normally arrive grumbling, and poke morosely at the dreary fare, all greasy and grey and boiled beyond recognition. However today, Christmas Day, there was a collective pause in the doorway, and then a tremendous shout followed by a rush and a dive. The trestles fairly groaned beneath the weight of sizzling roasted poultry, golden-skinned with butter and basting, heaped around with snowy white potatoes and glistening onions, no less than a whole ham for each mess of 16 men, salty and pink and sweetened with three tins of pineapple, fresh bread with not a weevil in sight, slathered with farm-churned pats of white butter, and sticky luscious dates, beer, and tea by the gallon, and just when they thought they could gorge no more, half a pound of plum pudding heaped upon every plate. The men of 2nd Division, battle-hardened survivors of Gallipoli, Pozieres and Flers, were nearly beaten to a standstill by this generosity, raising incredulous toasts to whatever Christmas spirit had provided such bounty. When the plates were finally sopped with the last of the custard, they staggered back to their tents to fall asleep for the remainder of the afternoon, their slumbers, for today at least, undisturbed by the creeping barrage. The commanding officer, when presented with an account for *poulets* worth a few centimes but charged out by the village farmers at 6 francs apiece, never turned a hair[2]. He just grinned, shook Cecil Healy very firmly by the hand, and offered him his last piece of brandy-soaked pudding.

***

Before 1914, Etáples had been little more than a minor fishing port in the Pas-de-Calais region of northern France, not far from Boulogne and the Belgian border. Sacked five times by the British during the Hundred Years War, the town was noteworthy for little more than an outbreak of plague in 1596. By the turn of the twentieth century, it was home to some five thousand souls who trawled peaceably for cod in the muddy Canche River, and a colony of artists attracted by the enigmatic seascape of dunes and marshes. However, in 1916, this bucolic lifestyle was rudely uprooted and flung to the winds, the estuary village groaning under the weight of one hundred thousand British, Australian and Canadian soldiers and enemy prisoners of war. Allied troops arriving in France, whether fresh reinforcements or men returning from convalescence, proceeded to their units via base depots such as those at Etáples, itself a vast military camp with twenty hospitals, barracks and a holding facility for prisoners. The camp was built along the local rail line and connected to both southern and eastern battlefields in France and to ships carrying troops and supplies across the Channel. The AIF established five divisional depots around Etáples in March 1916, and while all were moved west to Harfleur near Le Havre in June 1917, many of the hospitals remained and were bombed by the Germans in May 1918.

It was to Etáples that Cecil Healy came in March 1916 as a quartermaster sergeant at the 2nd Australian Division Base Depot (ADBD). Described by Lady Olave Baden-Powell as 'a dirty, loathsome, smelly little town', Etáples resounded to the continual *tramp-tramp* all day of men on their way 'up the line' or marching to the so-called Bull Ring for drill. To British poet Wilfred Owen, Etáples was a dark place, 'a vast, dreadful encampment ... a kind of paddock where the beasts are kept a few days before the shambles.'[3] And for many of Owen's Allied compatriots, it was a place of neither peace nor respite. Nurse Elsie Tranter wrote in 1917, 'Today I had to assist at ten amputations, one after another ... We see the most ghastly wounds and are all day long inhaling the odour of gas gangrene. How these boys suffer!' The misery intensified in the winter of 1916–17 when a wave of respiratory infection swept through overcrowded Etáples, Healy himself falling victim[4]. The camp, with its barracks crowded full of soldiers compromised by gas attacks on the Somme battlefields, was ripe for an epidemic, and the threat of disease was further intensified by the presence of a piggery on site and the purchase of live poultry from surrounding villages. In 2005, *The Lancet* speculated that the virulent infection that swept Etáples was a cross-species transfer of avian influenza virus, and possibly even the genesis of the worldwide Spanish Influenza pandemic in 1918–19.

However, beyond the squalor and sickness and overcrowding, Etáples was most notorious during the war for the unremitting tension between the infantrymen and the camp officers. Many of the depot officials had never served at the front, breeding an atmosphere of contempt and ill-feeling among the troops. No imagination or military textbook could replicate their own dreadful experiences of pain and disfigurement, of their mates blown to pieces, horses with legs shattered and guts strewn across the mud, men sent mad by the unceasing, unbearable noise of bombardment. At the depot, there were wards full of men who no longer knew who they were, men with melted faces, legless men, tongueless men, hopelessly crippled and maimed men, and outside the hospitals there were barracks full of men who were resigned to the same fate. Their anger towards and disdain for the officials around them was only exacerbated by the remoteness of the staff officers, who did not feel obliged to explain what was happening at the front, and the brutal training regimes to which the already exhausted troops were subjected: gas drill, bayonet drill, and endless slogging marches through sand dunes swarming with biting insects.

It was the junior officers and NCOs such as Cecil Healy who often became the managers, teachers and father figures the enlisted men craved. In late 1918, when it was all over, Australian commander John Monash recounted that 'Our success was due in large part to the devotion and skill of our junior officers.'[5] Nonetheless, chronic tension dogged Staff Sergeant Healy during the nineteen months of his tenure at the 2nd ADBD. His role with the Army Service Corps—managing the stores and post, and the resupply of food and weapons—was entirely behind the scenes. The Corps, with their good pay, comfortable conditions and comparative safety, were particularly shunned by the troops and savagely satirised in the popular media. Even when the Corps acquired their well-earned *Royal* prefix in 1918, their service acronym of RACS was quickly lampooned as 'Run Away, Someone's Coming'.

The inherent security of his backroom role with the Corps was a source of torture for Healy. As the battles of the Somme set new standards for slaughter around him in July 1916, from Albert and Delville Wood to the terrible carnage at Fromelles and Pozieres Ridge, Healy began a quest to be assigned to an active fighting role. 'Men are dying in the effort to stem the Teutons' onward rush', he wrote home. 'My conscience would not permit me to occupy a safe job indefinitely, notwithstanding that I was assured by my Commanding Officer that I was doing good work where I was.'[6]

Nevertheless, while he sought—and was repeatedly denied—his transfer to the front, Healy did manage to shake off the disdain and derision the enlisted men reserved for their non-fighting compatriots. Much against his wishes, his action in scouring the bombed-out countryside to provide Christmas dinner for the troops in December 1916 became public knowledge, and went a long way towards securing the respect of the exhausted and traumatised diggers. Healy's reputation for humanity and empathy towards the troops was warmly noted in many letters home. Jim Bourke, who captained the South Sydney football team in the early 1900s and spent two harrowing years in France, spoke of Healy in high terms, praising his extraordinary kindness towards the men at the base. Such consideration from regimental officials was, sadly, rare, particularly in the darkness of Etáples, where the undercurrent of tension exploded on 28 August 1916. Private Alexander Little of the 10th Battalion AIF abused a British NCO after the water was cut off while he was showering. Little was backed up by three mates, and the quartet were all court-martialled, convicted of mutiny and sentenced to death. The three Australian combatants were spared by AIF regulations, which prohibited capital punishment, but New Zealander Jack Braithwaite was shot by firing squad on 29 October 1916. The incident sparked a further year of festering unrest in the camp, culminating in the Etáples Mutiny on 9 September 1917. The little holiday resort by the Canche estuary, Le Touquet-Paris-Plage, was out of bounds to enlisted men, but on that fateful day, several infantrymen bypassed the pickets to enter the village and were apprehended as deserters. When an angry crowd gathered, military police fired into the ranks and one corporal was killed. By the next morning, more than one thousand angry diggers were pursuing the police, with furious demonstrations continuing for days and causing great damage to the camp infrastructure.

While the Australian depots had been moved to Le Havre before the Mutiny occurred, such episodes only made Healy more determined to both connect with the men and join them at the front. After the summer slaughter on the Somme in 1916, Australian troops had sunk into the worst winter in living memory as the dreadful campaign in north-eastern France raged on towards 1917. When it was not snowing it was raining, and 'when it rains here, it forgets to stop', wrote Staff Sergeant A.J. Braybrooks grimly.

This was a war of massive industrial technology, of long-range rifles, machine guns, barbed wire and shelling, the troops mired in a barren lunar landscape mazed with trenches and shellholes. Tiny French hamlets that nobody outside Europe had heard of now took on global significance: Guillemont, Ginchy and Flers-Courcelette, where tanks saw action for the first time, and Thiepval Ridge and Ancre Heights[7]. Many of those returning to Etáples at Christmas 1916 were shell-shocked, gassed and traumatised from months of unremitting mud and horror. The noise of the shelling was deafening, the vibration unnerving, the terror of being blown to pieces unceasing. Infection raged through the wounded in those pre-antibiotic days. Mustard gas, with its reek of onions and garlic, attacked the skin and eyes, causing temporary blindness, blistering, fever and pneumonia, destroying the lungs, genitals and skin. The men were beset by trench fever, lice and scabies, unprotected from rain and glutinous mud, and exhausted from heavy trench-digging, sentry duty and sleep deprivation. When Healy went to his C.O. with his proposal for a genuine Christmas dinner for the troops, the battle-shattered men were already restive after a cross-country race between teams from Scotland, England, New Zealand and Australia scheduled for Christmas Eve at Etáples had been cancelled without explanation. Healy's approach was scoffed at, in particular the idea of procuring sufficient poultry to feed two thousand men, but Healy personally scoured the district, door-knocking, entreating, flattering and stockpiling, to provide a banquet that was a rare warmth for Australian troops in the winter hell that was Christmas in 1916.

Despite the overwhelming success of this scheme, Healy himself remained low-spirited. His old inner monologue of the perfectionist and overachiever kept up its constant whisper that, safe behind the lines, he was far from doing enough. His appeals for a transfer to the front had been ignored or refused, and his misery was compounded by the news that Billy Longworth, preparing for the front at Salisbury Plain in England, had won the 220-yard Empire Services' swimming championship in October, while Healy had not swum a stroke for months and now weighed close to 15 stone. 'I remember Cecil Healy saying it was essential for him to swim all the year round to keep himself from becoming too weighty', Longworth recalled, and now Healy's misery and confinement had seen his weight balloon dramatically. Old friends Healy encountered in France, including Manly golfer Roscoe Collins and Australian boxers Larry Lassan, Roy Bailey and Harry Punch, seemed cold and distant, and wrote home dismissively of Healy's cushy job and expanding girth.

Healy was also terribly lonely, even amongst the tens of thousands of men crowding the base. He had struggled with social isolation since he was a child, marooned in the midst of his much younger and older siblings. Despite the accolades heaped upon him during his swimming career, social, emotional and religious barriers had always separated Healy from those around him. His enforced business career had differentiated him from his swim counterparts, with their wealthy patrons and unlimited training time, athletic success had set him on a pedestal that denied him a true connection with the working men who idolised him and his own family's fall from grace had barred him from the upper echelons of society that otherwise might have embraced him. His Catholic upbringing forbade him a relationship with the only girl he had allowed even a sliver of attachment to, yet the intensity of his male *camaraderies* hinted at a sexual ambiguity that remained deeply suppressed and unfulfilled. Healy's uncertain place in society—neither here nor there, not belonging anywhere—had only served to feed that desperate childhood need for acceptance that, in adulthood, warred with his native shyness and fear of failure and rejection. Now, on the cusp of war, Healy was cut off by rank and station from the enlisted men whose respect he craved. He would not write to Muriel, and the powerful male friendships that had sustained him before the war were now far out of reach—Roy Hendy was at the front, as was his brother John, and Harold, Reg and Arthur Relph were all thousands of miles away back at home, so far away that the very seasons themselves were reversed.

'Never before in my life have I felt so disinclined to commit my thoughts to paper', Healy wrote on his allotted two sheets at Christmas in 1916. 'I regard my present existence as something akin to that of those oxen one sees in Egypt, blindfolded and attached to an apparatus for drawing water that necessitates them going around and around and around, their destiny decided by circumstances over which they have no control.'

***

As the year 1917 dawned, cold and dank and dark, Healy decided upon a plan of action to regain control of his destiny and self-respect. If he would not be sent to the front immediately, he would train as though he were leaving tomorrow. On 14 February 1917, digger Harry Punch wrote to *The Referee* from Dorset, where he had been invalided, to say that he had seen

Healy again at Etáples and he looked 'very fit'. Roy Bailey's brother Charles wrote home that Healy was 'getting into training again, and expects to be doing things shortly' and had, with Roy's assistance, resumed organising sporting contests to entertain the boys. There was boxing, athletics on the dunes and interdivisional cricket matches (with one wag scrawling across the sightscreen '13,000 miles to good old Sydney Cricket Ground'). Rumours even reached the Australian press that Healy was in training for an attempt to swim the English Channel, an extremely unlikely endeavour given the presence of sea-mines, dreadnoughts and marauding U-boats[8].

In January 1917, the prospect of peace seemed further away than ever, with the Austro-Hungarian and German governments declaring their intention to prosecute the war to its successful end. The United States entered the conflict on 6 April 1917 after Germany unleashed destroyer fire on the British coast and set its submarine fleet to targeting Allied hospital ships. Healy's view that Yankee brains, wealth and resources would turn the war was received with incredulity by the men around him until Healy related his 1912 Olympic experience of underestimating American abilities: 'Theirs is a shrewd and business-like system ... equipped with everything that brains could suggest and money buy', he explained. 'In most instances, we received a sound trouncing at their hands.'

The entrance of American troops into the war was timely, with fighting now raging in Gaza, Armenia, East Africa and northern Italy, air raids on Britain and the Western Front torn apart by the Battles of Vimy Ridge, the Aisne and Bullecourt. The Russian summer offensive coincided with German counter-campaigns on the Eastern Front that stretched all the way from Romania to the Baltic Sea. By mid-summer of 1917, the conflict was truly global, with Thailand, Liberia and Brazil all declaring war on Germany. The toll on Australian swimming continued to mount. Vice-president of the Royal Life-saving Society NSW, Major General William Holmes DSO, was killed at Messines and Melbourne swimmer Ivan Stedman was invalided to England with multiple gunshot wounds. Alick Wickham's younger brother Ted was killed in action in November 1916 and Manly Swim Club's Alick Buckley arrived home in December 1917 with the Military Medal but without his right arm. Jim Thompson, a fine backstroker from Brisbane, lost a leg, Frank Beaurepaire was invalided back to Australia with trench fever, his Victorian compatriot Frank Fitts was so severely gassed that he would never swim again and the north shore's exciting young sprinter Albert Barry, destined to be a successor to the great Cecil Healy, had his left leg blown off at Messines in June 1917. 'The toll of war is hitting swimming in this country', mourned *The Referee*. 'Its one agreeable aspect is that it shows how thoroughly the swimmer has shown his mettle in the great conflict.'

The courage of the swimmers in bearing their wounds affected the public profoundly. Kindly William Henry had been watching over Albert Barry during his convalescence in London, and was moved almost to tears by a note from Barry saying he hoped to 'hop in' shortly. A photograph of Barry taken on 26 June 1918 showed him on the pool deck in London, where a swim club had been formed at AIF Headquarters by 'a score or more of the halt and lame'. When Barry produced a 50-yard swim in under 29 seconds and a 100-yard swim in 64 seconds[9], Roy Hendy joked that Barry might make a champion yet, since the leg he had lost had obviously been a drag on his stroke. On 2 January 1918, the Melbourne Swimming Club 50-yard Christmas Handicap featured the touching sight of the club's former champion, Tom Mason, hobbling to the start line on crutches, also with a leg missing. He and Frank Beaurepaire had been in rehabilitation together, and not only did Mason swim in the race, he was only beaten by a few inches. Beaurepaire, too, made a remarkable comeback to swimming after the war, winning two medals at each of the 1920 and 1924 Olympic Games and five Australasian titles in 1921. In 1940, he was elected Lord Mayor of Melbourne and played a pivotal role in bringing the Olympic Games to Australia before his death in 1956, just weeks before the opening ceremony in his beloved Melbourne.

The AIF swimming team that competed at the Inter-Allied Games in Paris in 1919. Albert Barry (front row, left) was missing a leg. Also pictured are Healy's clubmates and friends Tod Solomons (rear, centre), Harold Hardwick (rear, right) and Bill Longworth (front, second from right). [Source: Australian War Memorial, collection ID: D00657].

With the parade of the wounded and damaged slowly returning to a wounded and damaged nation, conscription was debated more hotly than ever in Australia in 1917. In May 1916, a second Military Service Bill extending compulsion to married men had been passed by the British House of Commons, but with a generation of young men already wiped from its infant towns and cities, Australia was wavering as to the worth of its involvement in the conflict. The 1917 Australian referendum on conscription was duly defeated, and the recruitment effort flagged as news of mass casualties on the Western Front rolled in waves over the horrified populace. Healy's image, instantly recognisable from his swimming and surfing achievements and his perceived sacrifice for his country, was appropriated into a new mid-war enlistment campaign urging young sportsmen to sign up, and in April 1917, standards in relation to age, height, and dental and ophthalmic fitness for enlistment were again reduced, with previously ineligible men now urged to re-apply. The tone of the propaganda posters became more trenchant: *'Would you stand by while a bushfire raged? Get busy and drive the Germans back!'* and *'It's nice in the surf, but what about the men in the trenches? Go and help!'*

***

Few men, and even fewer soldiers, have the privilege of reading their own obituaries.

In late 1917, Cecil Healy was still with the Service Corps in Le Havre after ten months of fruitless struggle to obtain a transfer. Not even a brief reunion with his brother John, who had spent several weeks in hospital in Boulogne and was now *en route* through Le Havre back to the front, could drag Healy's morale from the mire into which it had sunk. He seemed destined to spend the war behind a desk, sorting the post and filling out requisitions while the big guns boomed just beyond the horizon. Daily, he wrestled with the clanging conflict of his heart and head. As his desire to prove himself at the front grew more desperate, so too did his abhorrence of the armed forces and the senseless slaughter. 'I hate and detest everything associated with the machine', he wrote. 'I have seen too many inconsistencies perpetrated in it, and too much of the seamy side of it. But', he continued quietly, 'I am influenced by a desire to live up to the best expectations of my personal friends....'

A small measure of relief came on 11 October 1917, when a grinning corporal summoned Healy to the commanding officer's quarters. 'Well', said the C.O., handing the previous day's sheaf of newspapers to Healy across the desk. 'I'm not sure whether to congratulate you or commiserate.'

'Sir?' Despite spending two years in France, Healy did not read French, and almost skipped past the French paper *Sporting* on top of the pile before the word *nageur* in the headline caught his eye. He flipped quickly to the *London Sportsman*, which had been folded neatly open at page five and saw the reason for all the grins. 'Famous Swimmer Killed', bellowed the headline.

Healy's eyes widened as he read multiple accounts of his own alleged demise during the Battle of Messines in June. *Illustrated Sporting and Dramatic News* had even accompanied their version of the sorrowful story with a photograph, albeit of another swimmer entirely. John sprawled upon his brother's bunk in a most unofficial manner to read the obituaries aloud, and punctuated the accounts with laughter so infectious that Cecil, too, could not help but grin. 'The remarkable Healy has run 100 yards in 10 1/5 seconds', John quoted with one eyebrow raised, 'was an international footballer of high degree ... conqueror of the redoubtable Kahanamoku on three occasions' ... Jeez, where can I meet this bloke? He's a bloody god ... or he was, 'til he got blown to Kingdom come.'

Twelve months earlier, Cecil Healy would have been shocked by both the erroneous story and the frank humour with which his brother crowed over it. Now, he held the *Illustrated*'s erroneous photograph up beside his own face and grinned. 'Death has done good things for my career—and my hair.' Cecil patted his own thinning hair and grinned at the unknown man in the photograph with his luxuriant dark locks. 'At least I didn't die bald!'

Despite this rakish enjoyment of his own demise, Healy did quash the false report with a note to the respective editors, denying his own death and reassuring them that both he and John, who *had* been at Messines, were indeed extant. He also gently refuted the exaggerated tributes that credited him with running 100 yards in Olympic time, alongside 'other claims to immortality'[10].

His intervention, as it turned out, did not prevent the story permeating the Australian press, from the metropolitan broadsheets right out to country settlements from Albany to Zeehan. However, fortunately for the Healy family, the antipodean press spoke only of the mix-up, not of Healy's supposed demise. However, while assuring the Australian public that their champion was very much alive, these domestic reports still contained errors, with many referring to Healy and his brother Reg chuckling over the obituaries, when Reg was in fact safe at his new home in

Brisbane with his newborn daughter, who had been christened Cecile in tribute to her uncle. Such misinformation was, sadly, common during the Great War, with unverified death notices for soldiers often appearing in the press and causing great distress to loved ones at home.

***

In 1916, the ravages of war invoked not only conscription in Great Britain in the search for more enlisted men, but also the establishment of twenty training schools to upskill regular soldiers into officers and NCOs. Over six intensive months, candidates were schooled in military tactics, man management and the use of and defence against new war technologies such as tanks, gas and aircraft. On 7 December 1917, Cecil Healy finally escaped his perceived humiliation in the backrooms of the war when he was accepted into the 5th Officers Cadet Training Battalion at Trinity College in Cambridge.

The softness and greenery of the English countryside was in stark contrast to the ravaged monochrome of northern France. The white limestone spires of the ancient university and its green playing fields were untouched by shells and bombs, while Europe lay in smoking ruins after another sustained and dreadful campaign on the Western Front, including at Verdun and Ypres.

The offensive at Passchendaele alone had cost 600,000 lives. While the armistice between Germany and Russia of 3 December 1917 suspended hostilities on the Eastern Front, the war raged on in western Europe and Palestine, and Britain was also still under direct attack, with its coast shelled by submarines and destroyers and London held hostage by raids from German planes and zeppelins.

The city of Cambridge played host to the 1st Eastern General Hospital and several convalescent homes for Allied troops, in addition to housing 300 officer cadets from the AIF in training at the various colleges. Roy Hendy, who was reunited with Healy at Cambridge in February 1918, reported his friend as 'most serious in his study in order to pass with flying colours for his commission.' Healy had caught the imagination of Cambridge with both his intellect and physical prowess. The article Healy had published on the crawl stroke in 1913 that had been so well regarded when first published that 20,000 copies had been distributed to swimmers throughout Britain was now reprinted in *The Blunderbuss*, a paper issued by the 5th Officers' Cadet Training Battalion at Cambridge. Hendy grinningly recalled the impact Healy's physical powers had on the locals. 'He has shocked not only the natives of Cambridge, but all the young people who are training to be officers, by having a swim in the River Cam every morning during the past Winter', Hendy wrote to William Henry. 'Snow or ice did not deter him. His method of procedure is to undress in the open, don a swimming costume, then skip for twenty minutes, after which take several headers, and finish up with a couple of hundred yards swim. As a result, he is in perfect condition—absolutely physically fit—but all of this has not made a hair grow on the top of his head.'[11] Lt. Quentin Spedding, a former *Daily Telegraph* journalist, added admiringly, 'Cecil will not age ... He astonished the dons and others by, every morning, before breakfasting, plunging into the then icy Thames. Other cadets, tight wrapped in mufflers and British 'warms', were present on occasions to witness his 'devotions'. They did it well up the bank, however.'[12]

Members of B Company of the 5th Officer Cadet Battalion in training at Cambridge University, May 1918. Healy (seated fourth from right) received his commission a month after this photograph was taken. [Source: John Oxley Library, State Library of Queensland. Image number: 702692-19180921-0023. Original image appeared in page 23 of the Queenslander Pictorial, supplement to The Queenslander, 21 September, 1918].

Now 36 years old, Healy drove himself like a much younger man, his weight plunging from 15 stone (95kg) to 11 1/2 stone (73kg) as he won the Cambridge cross-country championship and blitzed his younger rivals in an exhibition sprint swim at the Automobile and Bath Club. He rowed in the company and platoon boats, played rugby and even reassumed the gloves as a heavyweight boxer to contest the college championship. After a first-round bye, Healy drew a Guardsman standing well over six feet tall—'a hefty-looking customer', Healy wrote home to his brother Eric. Cecil promptly skittled his rival with two punches, a performance that caused him to be hailed as a veritable 'White Hope', with onlookers wagering as much as £100 on him for the final. His opponent, a big Tasmanian Anzac named Durney, did not impress Healy much, although he admitted that Durney was exceedingly tall and vigorous looking. As soon as the gong went, Healy barrelled over to finish him off in the same manner as he had dispatched the Guardsman, but Durney evaded the oncoming left hand by ducking low, and then swung a mighty, bony fist, not aimed anywhere in particular, he later told Healy, but dispatched with enough force to fell a bullock. The blow landed square on Healy's chin, after which proceedings were a blank for the wannabe-boxer. The spectators groaned as Healy went down but cheered as he rose again almost immediately. However, the dark eyes remained hopelessly glazed, and there was little Healy could do but stand wavering in the face of some further 'unmerciful bashes' before the referee finally called a halt. It later emerged that Durney was an experienced wood-chopping competitor, which accounted for the weight behind his punches, and Healy was left with his arm in a sling and both eyes blackened. While the crowd had roared their approval for his ability to take Durney's punishment, Healy felt that this was little consolation for the humiliating and ruthless thrashing he had sustained[13].

The whirl of study and Healy's punishing self-imposed physical training regime saw the six months at Cambridge fly by. The Russian armistice collapsed in February 1918 and the German army swept through the Caucasus and the Baltic states, simultaneously launching a spring offensive on the Western Front. The first long-range shells, fired from Crepy-en-Valois, 75 miles away, fell on Paris on 23 March 1918. German forces sacked the provincial towns of Bapaume and Peronne, and Noyon and Neuve Chapelle on the Somme, with dreadful casualties on both sides. The losses forced Britain to pass a third Military Service Act on 10 April 1918, raising the military service age to 50 and extending conscription to citizens of Ireland as Field-Marshal Sir Douglas Haig issued his 'Backs to the Wall' order to the British army in France. Spearheaded by tanks, in late April German forces captured Villers-Bretonneux, which Australian forces had fought so hard to protect just weeks earlier. Immediate retaliation under cover of darkness drove the Germans from the village and nearby woods in a memorable triumph for the Australian 13th and 15th brigades, but on 31 May, the German forces reached the Marne River outside Paris.

On 1 June 1918, Cecil Healy was appointed 2nd Lieutenant in the Australian Imperial Force and on 12 June he sailed back to France and the firing line. Those final weeks in Cambridge were bright, fine and sunny, the countryside awash in greenery and flowers. His final letter from England, dated 9 June, came from the upper reaches of the Thames in Wiltshire, where he spent a solitary weekend camping, swimming to his heart's content and enjoying the picturesque surrounds, while from overhead came the constant drone of aircraft engines and the distant *thud-thud* of Barking Berthas across the Channel. 'The world was not as peaceful as one might have been led to imagine from appearances at that particularly favoured spot', Healy wrote. 'I am prepared for the worst, and am quite resigned to my fate ... It was against the repeatedly given advice of officer friends that I transferred from the A.S.C. to the infantry. But I cherish the hope that I will be able to sell my life dearly, and earn the respect of the men whom I command.'

FOURTEEN

THE FOG OF DOUBT

'Keep that bottle of sparkling stuff on the ice, on the off-chance of my having the good luck to come through the ordeal.'

—Cecil Healy, *in the field, France* (13 August 1918)

***

The French summer of 1906 was beautiful, as French summers are born to be; iridescent green leaves and blossom-strewn meadows, and lazy boulevards ripe with slow, golden sunshine. A young Cecil Healy was in France during the summer of 1906, just 24 years old, tanned and eager in his flannel bags amid the gay, pleasure-seeking crowds of Paris and the Riviera. France then was yachts and flowers, royals and barons and palatial hotels, Sobranies and sidewalk cafes, an idyllic paradise to which the shattered and smoking ruin of France in the summer of 1918 bore no resemblance.

On 13 June 1918, Healy returned to his old station at the 2nd Australian Divisional Base

Depot in Le Havre, but only for the briefest of stays. Three days later, his convoy left for the village of Rivery, near Amiens in north-eastern France, to join the 19th Battalion AIF: the 'Fighting Nineteenth'. Raised at Liverpool, NSW in March 1915 as part of the 5th Brigade (2nd Division), the 19th was a Sportsmen's Battalion, a type of fighting unit pioneered in World War I in the belief that competitive sport provided the ultimate preparation for war[1]. Healy privately doubted whether the 19th was any more entitled to the 'Sportsman's Battalion' epithet than any other unit in the AIF, given the gigantic contribution of Australia's sportsmen to all battalions, but acknowledged that the 19th had more than its quota of prominent athletes[2]. These included Edward 'Happy' Eyre, Australia's first professional lifesaver, Olympic rower and Wallabies international Syd Middleton and NSW rugby player Les 'Dodger' Seaborn.

The men of the 19th were seriously battle-hardened. Many had fought with the Australian Naval and Military Expeditionary Force to capture German New Guinea at the dawn of the war in 1914. The 19th were on the front line at Gallipoli during the attack on Hill 60 in August 1915, and from the arid wastes of the Dardanelles they marched to the wet hell of France, where they fought in the bloodbath of

Pozieres, and the mud they encountered at Flers was described by Charles Bean as the worst ever met by the AIF. They drove German forces back at Lagincourt in 1917 while outnumbered five to one, and led the fighting at Bullecourt, Menin Road and Poelcappelle[3].

Group portrait of officers of the 19th Battalion. Healy stands ninth from the left, middle row. [Source: Australian War Memorial, collection ID: E02595].

The 19th were now in reserve at Rivery, training in rapid-bolt rifle fire and bayonet fighting, and undertaking close-order drills with gas masks and live gas. The village and nearby town of Amiens were within range of the German heavy guns, necessitating the rapid evacuation of the civilian population, who had fled with only what they could carry. A letter home from Lt. Ernest 'Ess' Wright of the 19th claimed that some ten thousand shells had fallen on the Amiens district so far: 'It is rotten to hear [one of] these big shells go howling over your billet, and hear it go through a couple of streets before the shell bursts and then hear the falling debris.'[4]

Healy was one of 31 officers overseeing the 654 men of the 19th who, after the evacuation of Rivery, enjoyed the unusual luxury of sleeping in real beds with real linen in the abandoned houses. The troops drew lots for rooms and beds, and while the unlucky ones slept on the floor, there was compensation in the form of well-stocked wine cellars in most dwellings. Ess Wright marvelled that 'The lads can talk two or three kinds of Australian and five or six kinds of French language "fluidly" when they have sampled a few bottles. I am almost sorry at times I am still a T.T. [teetotaller] when I see a nice sparkling glass of champagne, but I am of a different mind when I look at the lads on parade next morning.'

Rivery, with its deserted streets and shell-damaged boulevards, lay beside the Somme River, where the men swam and dabbled with the abandoned canoes once used for carrying produce to market. This was, technically, a banned activity, and not without reason, for

Lance Corporal Peter Kelly had drowned on their first day in Rivery after his canoe overturned in the cold water. The men would also 'fish' in the canal using hand grenades to stun the fish for easy collection, although Ess Wright complained that 'So far I have not been able to get enough for a feed.' Lt. Les Seaborn defended the men for these small mischiefs and indulgences: 'The Australian lad and his unselfishness in the things that count here in this war cannot be described—it has to be seen and gone through with him to really understand. One thing always is in my mind—that the "dinkum" Australian soldier boy should be forgiven a lot, for he has done much and has by his unselfishness and courage made it possible for people over there to sleep and eat and make money in comfort and safety. As one who has seen it and been with him in the greatest adventure of all, I tell you he is pure gold.'[5]

In Rivery, Healy was reunited with two of his oldest and closest friends, now both serving with the 19th. He had known 'Dodger' Seaborn since their school days, when the pair often spent holidays together at Sydney's Vaucluse beach. 'I knew him very well', Seaborn remembered, 'and when we met in the same battalion, in which Sydney Middleton was second in command, we had many a yarn.' Major Sydney Middleton DSO was a dual Olympian, winning rugby gold at the 1908 London Games and then representing Australia in the rowing eight in 1912[6]. Middleton and Healy had been team-mates in Stockholm, and had cemented their friendship when both became contributors to *The Referee* on their respective sports after the 1912 Games.

Seaborn and Healy were now platoon commanders in the 19th, and Healy quickly endeared himself to the men. 'He was a great spirit among the lads, and helped on the sport with a will', said Seaborn. 'He was very popular, and the boys were proud to have him in the battalion.' Another of the 19th's officers wrote, 'His men liked him and (he gained their) complete confidence through his winning personality, his fearlessness, his devotion to duty, and his absolute fairness.'[7] As had been his wont in Etáples, Healy handled his men the only way he knew how—with kindness and humanity, endeavouring to understand the trauma and battle-weariness of his troops, some of whom had been in harness for four years. Others were barely half his age, and Healy recognised that they looked up to him as a father or older brother. Healy wore his mask of command so convincingly that he gave them no glimpse of his natural anxiety, which was now ramping up under the extra responsibility of command, or the wild recklessness that sometimes erupted to disguise it.

In late June, the battalion marched three miles to Blangy-Tronville, where they camped on the banks of the Somme, expecting at any moment to be called up to relieve in the Villers-Bretonneux sector. Even encamped a few miles behind the front line, they were in range of the German large-calibre shells, which the Australians wryly referred to as *billets doux* (love letters). As the Australians had just penetrated a mile into German territory and captured around 1,500 prisoners at Hamel, Healy speculated, 'The Hun was evidently greatly enraged over another one of those splendid successes achieved by our boys', and wrote of that assault, 'It is beyond comprehension how anyone lives through such terrific and concentrated gunfire ... Every now and again pieces of shell strike the roof of my dugout which, by the way, does not happen to be a very substantial one.'

Healy went with Middleton, who was acting company commander, on forward reconnaissance during a brief lull in the shelling, and on their return journey they came under heavy extended fire. The Germans were using a new form of shell, which the troops termed a 'Rubber Belly', a high-velocity projectile that only took a second between the ear detecting its approach and the explosion, infecting the troops with 'a beastly state of uncertainty'. 'I do not relish the idea of being knocked in a rearward position', Healy wrote, 'but very often nowadays the strain on one's nerves in such places is more severe than in the actual front-line trenches.' This place of barren shell-blasted fields, wrecked and deserted towns, and roads that rumbled with the metallic tread of tanks, was far from his old life of blue waves and free-wheeling silver gulls. Exertion was no longer a pure physical contest with the foaming breakers; here, the burning in his lungs and limbs came from sprinting for cover against the dreadful upswell of mustard gas, sulphur, mud and blood.

A month after his arrival, on 13 July 1918, Healy was sent to the Australian Corps School at Aveluy for a four-week infantry course. The School was a small military teaching institution, with each division sending 20 officers and 45 enlisted men to each course. The training included machine-gun and Lewis-gun firing, trench mortar, bombing and bayoneting, intelligence, signalling, cooking and sanitation[8]. While Healy was at the school, the war raged in all its ferocity around him, quite literally. Aveluy, between Arras and Amiens, just north of the Somme River, was surrounded by infamous battlefields—Pozieres, Dernancourt, Courcelette and

Villers-Bretonneux. On 15 July, German forces launched a second offensive on the Marne designed to draw Allied troops out of Belgium and allow the Axis powers to take Flanders in their absence. The Germans, after a bloody three-week campaign that cost more than 280,000 lives, were ultimately driven back and the Australian forces pursued them, chalking up in big letters through the re-taken villages, '13,000 miles to Bushell's Tea' and 'This way to Australia'.

A letter to E.S. Marks dated 13 August 1918 further highlighted Healy's revulsion towards the war. 'War, in my opinion, is a putrid game, but, of course, I realise someone has got to do the dirty work, and I try to make the best of it. I am away from the front at the moment, but return again in a couple of days' time. The news recently has been most encouraging, and I really think the prospects of finishing next Spring (if not before) are promising, to say the least of it. Yankee money, resources, and men have been the deciding factors, as I have always imagined would be the case. Keep that bottle of sparkling stuff on the ice, on the off-chance of my having the good luck to come through the ordeal, and we will discuss old times together whilst we dispose of it.'[9]

On 8 August, the Allies had launched the Hundred Days Offensive with an assault on Amiens that would ultimately lead to the end of the war. Germany lost 30,000 men in a single day, and John Monash was knighted by King George V in the days after that battle. One week later, on 16 August, Healy rejoined his battalion at Fouilloy, where they were recovering from a bloody assault on the village of Rainecourt east of Villers-Bretonneux, following which no less than 14 men were recommended for the Military Medal[10].

A swimming carnival for the Allied troops was arranged on 22 August in a lagoon off the serene, slow-flowing Somme River—a fantastical scene given the terrible carnage the battalions had experienced in the preceding weeks. Men flowed in from many of the nearby units to participate and spectate, and the carnival had all the air of a holiday, with a comical fancy-dress parade, the cheerful honking of the battalion band and not a single shell falling in the vicinity. Healy, as unofficial master of ceremonies, gave a short lecture and exhibition of the crawl, but he saved his true efforts for the open 100-yard event, which was headlined by an Englishman who boasted of defeating the great Jack Hatfield, winner of two silver medals in Stockholm. The 19th decided to take this tall poppy down a peg, and invited Healy to represent the battalion against him. No one put 'Tommy' wise as to who he was up against. When the request reached Healy, he pondered, 'Well, if he could defeat the Middlesbrough wonder, the job would be a very ugly one, to say the least of it. However, I decided to rush in, as it were, where angels fear to tread.'[11]

Sporting competition between divisions, units, or even nations was used to fill the hours and days between front-line engagements for Allied troops. Healy competed in several match races and swimming displays while on active duty in France. Pictured here are Australian swimmers and servicemen (left to right) Bill Longworth, Harold Hardwick, J. Dexter and Ivan Steadman during the Inter-Allied Games in France in 1919. [Source: Australian War Memorial, collection ID: E05367].

The course was a straight 100 yards, as though purposely selected to suit the Australian hero. Healy was naturally very curious to cast a gaze on the British leviathan awaiting him, but there was only time for a hurried introduction before the field was ordered to toe the mark. Also on the start line was Private Alfred Henry of the AIF Field Ambulance, who wrote home that he had actually beaten Healy in an impromptu 50-yard race two days before, a defeat, Lt. Seaborn said, that 'Healy took in the way he could take it always.' It was Henry who led the race until halfway, before Healy made his traditional late and irresistible charge at the line. 'Much to my surprise, when I had breasted the rope and looked round', Healy said, 'there was what might be termed a fairly wide expanse of water separating me from the next cove; and lo and behold, it was not the conqueror of Hatfield ... I need hardly add that it was my firm conviction that the self-termed vanquisher suffered from hallucinations. But what makes the incident more amusing is that he disappeared after the race, and I am still ignorant of how or when or where he won his title to fame.'

It was Healy's final public appearance in the element he loved so well and in which he was so conspicuously successful. As one ever anxious to see the sport progress in popularity, Healy was delighted with the success of the carnival, and in saying goodbye to young Henry, he promised that 'when the stunt was over, we should have some more dips together'[12].

***

On 25 March 1918, the towns of Bapaume and Peronne, ten miles east of Aveluy, had been taken by German forces. Letters found in captured German trenches addressed to the British read 'Dear Tommy—You think you are beating us. Wait till our scheme is complete. You will find everything changed.' The second phase of the offensive began on 21 August as the Second Battle of the Somme, with the Third and Tenth French armies, First and Third British armies and ANZAC forces aiming to recapture Bapaume, Arras and Peronne and to drive the German forces further back towards the Hindenburg Line. On 26 August 1918, the 19th received orders to move to the front and assault Peronne and nearby Mont St Quentin as part of the Hundred Days Offensive[13]. North of the fabled mountain stood German machine-gun posts on the Bouchavesnes Spur, which looked down on the district of Clery and the Somme River west of Peronne. Monash's forces could not take Peronne, nor safely cross the river at Clery, until they took the mountain and the ridge, both of which were held by the crack 2nd Prussian Guards[14]. On this day, Healy would lead his platoon into action for the first time.

The Somme Canal and, across the water, the town of Peronne, lying in the shadow of Mont St Quentin. Between the Australians and their goal on 29 August 1918 lay open fields scattered with woods and thickets concealing heavily armed German troops, artillery and sniper posts. [Source: Australian War Memorial, collection ID: E03212].

Suddenly, all the diligent study and training seemed for naught. Healy, secretly tortured for months by the responsibilities of command, was now consumed by the old self-doubt that had dogged him throughout his swimming career. Failure in this moment meant more than a second placing or the loss of a record—the lives of his men were in his hands. The way they looked at him with such trust, even men like Harold Vaughan, who had been wounded no less than four times and, at 24 years old, was an encyclopaedia of the Front when Healy himself felt like no more than the opening page. With his battered wristwatch ticking remorselessly toward Zero Hour, Healy at last confided in Seaborn. 'Poor old chap!' Seaborn wrote later. 'He was of a very sensitive nature. He said to me—maybe two or three days before the stunt—"I feel I'll never be a soldier in the sense of dealing out drill. I feel very nervous in front of the lads, whereas on ordinary occasions I haven't any such feeling." It was a thing he could not conquer. I knew the feeling well, but I said, "After all, Cec old chap, that's all very well in its way, but just now it counts for very little, and it's the other part of the game you'll count in."'

As the night wore on, talking among the men died away. Faces became set, rifle bolts were fingered, bayonet edges silently caressed. Some men slept, some lay silent but open-eyed, contemplating the inescapable order that would set them moving forward like clockwork to face death head-on. Would it be death by the massive concussion of shellfire, or being burned up and melted away like a candle, or by the mortal thud of a bullet? Many, indeed most, of these men knew the pain of wounds, but none could answer the greatest question of all: did death hurt? Would it be messy and painful and prolonged, or just as simple as falling asleep? For Healy, his own endless question revolved in the dark: *what would the first moment feel like—the first 'Let's get 'em, boys', the first stride into open country with all those trusting men behind him?* Sometimes he feared the men at his back as much as he feared those in front.

Healy wrote his final letter before the assault to the English essayist and playwright John Boynton Priestley. While at Cambridge, Healy had enjoyed a short sojourn in Newcastle-upon-Tyne, where he had met the 24-year-old socialist writer. Priestley himself was in khaki, having served with the Duke of Wellington's Regiment, and then the 10th Battalion of the Devonshire Regiment, who were billeted at Newcastle in early 1918[15]. The burly, black-haired Priestley had introduced Healy to the Knights of the Round Table, a society to which many authors, actors and artists belonged. Charles Dickens is reputed to have been a member, and the Society's statutes aimed to 'promote Knightly good fellowship' in the spirit of the legendary British King Arthur. 'My Dear Jack', Healy wrote on 26 August, as carefully casual as always, 'we move up tonight to take our position in the orchestra stalls, and long before this reaches you I will have hopped the bags and I trust have won my spurs ... Recounting our many and enjoyable little escapades makes me long to some day re-visit your good self in particular and 'The Knights of the Round Table' in general. My impression is anyone who has the luck to be still going six months hence, will have an excellent chance of reading about the last shot being fired.'

The 2nd Division, of which the 19th Battalion was a part, planned to take Mont St Quentin as part of the approach to Peronne. Major-General Rosenthal's plan was to have the 7th and 5th Brigades (including the 19th) cross the Somme River on the morning of 29 August, with the 5th advancing between Feuilleres and Herbecourt to take the high ground of the mountain. The 19th would take the right flank and move across open farmland towards the junction of Canal du Nord and the Somme opposite the village of Halles. When the 19th, with the 17th, 18th and 20th in support, were across the river, they would assault Mont St Quentin in a converging attack.

On the morning of 28 August, Monash ordered a general advance, and the 19th pushed ahead, pursuing the German troops falling back from the river to the villages of Halles, Omiecourt-les-Cléry and Cléry-sur-Somme. The

19th followed the southern bank of the river towards Salmon Wood and the little town of Cappy, but the movement was spotted and the area shelled with tear gas and high explosive. The men remained hunkered down around the wood, under fire for most of the night.

Dawn on 29 August brought a widening and flattening of the riverbanks as the 19th moved east, the river a sheet of still, brown water more than half a mile wide, marshy and studded with little islands. The grey seventeenth-century ramparts of Peronne rose above the river on the opposite bank, solid as iron, ensconced by the river like a medieval moat. In the hazy north stood Mont St Quentin. It didn't look much, just a hillock, bare and green with a few trees on the summit, but it commanded Peronne, the river and the land to the east that stretched away to the Hindenburg Line. Between the Australians and their target was unwelcome clear ground scattered with woods and copses, and then the swampy river fringed with thick vegetation—a landscape weighted heavily in favour of its German defenders. In the dark shadows lurked platoons of hand-picked Hun troops, and beyond lay entrenched heavy artillery and machine-gun posts.

He had not shaved in three days. His face felt gritty and dirty in the dark. Healy's feet were damp in his boots, cold and clammy like the earth beneath his body. He could smell sweat, the sweat of fear and expectation, even in the sleeping men around him. Or was it just himself, the only one with eyes open and heart wriggling like a bag of worms? Were they truly all sleeping, knowing what must come tomorrow?

He closed his eyes and wished for a cut-off switch like the one on a big Hornsby engine, but the wish did nothing to slow his mind's relentless recall of everything he had learned at Cambridge and Aveluy. Strange disjointed flashes of tactics and weapons drill and command flickered on and off like a badly tuned radio, instructors' voices blending in and out in an exhausting and bewildering litany. Healy lay rigid, trying to breathe slowly but hyperaware of the men around him. He could feel Tommy Cravino's elbow in his back, and could hear young Carl Bentin mutter something in his sleep that sounded angry and scared.

If it were not for these men, it would be so simple. Go forward alone, to either die or not die. But these men would wait for his instructions, they would go where he sent them like obedient chess-men. A mistake, his mistake, and the checkmate would be fatal—not just for him, but perhaps for them all.

Another flare of shellfire briefly lit the thicket where they lay, the platoon from C Company. The earth trembled distantly and Healy felt a stir among the sleeping men, as though they sensed both the fall of the shell and the rise of the impending dawn.

Reveille. Zero Hour, 5am, 29 August 1918. Bully beef and cold water.

The sky was pearl-grey in the east, a faint glow of day echoing above the crouching bulk of Mont St Quentin. Across the river, the bombed-out villages seemed to smoke in the cool, rising mist. At the front of the khaki column of the 19th, a hand was raised and swung in a slow, silent arc. *Forward.*

It was the same commitment as was needed to enter a big sea—you couldn't call time out and turn back if you didn't like how the waves were coming. Hesitation could mean death—your own and that of the drowning man screaming and spluttering for rescue. Now there was nothing but forward, a relentless tramp-tramp in no other direction but forward. Rifles and helmets, boots and bullets, Mont St Quentin a smudged and crouching monster across the river, the red-tiled roofs of Peronne huddled at its base and men—*his* men—at his back.

The ground sloped gently upwards as they picked their way cautiously toward the river with its heavy cloak of foliage, platoons dispersing right and left like shadows to provide covering fire, eyes swivelling, ears straining. Sweat was freezing on Healy's back, and his shirt stuck to him like glue. The rifle felt like a clumsy toy in his numb fingers. The distant rooftops were growing larger—*was that a glimpse of the bridge through the trees?*

Australian soldiers taking a German trench at Mont St Quentin. Mont St Quentin was a pivotal German defensive position on the line of the Somme, and by August 1918, was the last German stronghold in the region. This illustration is by cartoonist and illustrator Cecil Percival, who contributed to 'Aussie', a paper for troops in the trenches. [Source: Australian War Memorial, collection ID: ART03291].

The machine-gun rattle was as rude and savage as barking laughter in a church. Suddenly, men were yelling and falling, and bullets were shredding the canopy of leaves and snicking and ricocheting off trees so it was impossible to tell from whence they came. Healy found himself lying full-length on the soft earth, a handful of Carl Bentin's shirt still clutched in his fist. The ashen-faced young private met his eyes with his own white-rimmed with terror, gasping, 'Thanks, sir!'

'Move, son. For God's sake, move!' Healy's voice was ragged, but the words were authoritative. He wondered if that was simply spontaneous recall of the long months of command training, because his heart was beating so hard he thought it must surely burst. He looked around for the rest of his platoon, and jerked his head furiously to them. 'Those trees! Heads down and go!'

There were already men in the coppice of pines, panting and shocked, backs pressed to the ancient trunks, one clutching a bloodied arm. 'They've got us pinned', the officer with them said as he crawled towards Healy, and then pointed as he lay among the dry fragrant needles. 'Bastards are up there on the left, and near the road too.'

'We can't get round them on the right', Healy glanced over his shoulder. 'There's no way we can cross the river down there. Half of these fellows can't swim.'

The group lay flat on the aromatic, damp earth, eyes barely visible above the carpet of fallen needles. 'There', Healy's companion whispered with a little nod towards the road. 'If we can knock off that gun near the track, we might get through. How are your blokes?'

'They're game.'

'I'll leave three of mine here to cover us.'

It was surprisingly simple after that, as though the incident had at last warmed his anxiety-chilled limbs and pierced the fog of doubt in which he had marched until the first bullet pinged past his ear. His feet now moved softly through the trees, and when Harold Vaughan stuck a rifle against the back of the German machine-gunner and told him to drop it or die, Healy was the first to turn his gaze further up the slope towards the river. 'We'll push on and clear this place right out.'

They left three Huns trussed up like turkeys and, stepping over the bodies of the fallen with a quick and silent prayer, slipped through the trees, splitting left and right as they reached the edge of the wood. Healy turned briefly to watch his fellow officer, whose name he still did not know, slide away into the shadows with the remains of his own platoon. He was now alone with his men—in sole command. Their eyes were on him, awaiting instructions, and his heart rate, which had slowed while the prisoners were taken in hand, began to gallop upwards again.

A camouflaged German machine-gun post such as that encountered by Healy's platoon in Sword Wood on his first foray in command on 29 August 1918. [Source: Australian War Memorial, collection ID: E05208].

A swathe of open meadow lay before them, the rising sun catching pale highlights on the summer grass. Beyond was the dark belt of vegetation fringing the river. Healy drew a deeper breath, half turning away from the expectant eyes. 'Wait here.'

'What're you gonna do, sir?'

'Cover me. I'll go for a look.'

'Sir....' It was Vaughan, dark eyes intent, a strong brown hand reaching for his arm. Their eyes met and held. *If he turned back now, meekly accepted Vaughan's restraint, his leadership bubble would burst: the platoon would be a rudderless flotilla with him bobbing somewhere helpless in the middle. And they would all die.*

'Just cover me. I won't be long.'

A small scrubby copse was the only shelter in the meadow stretching between himself and the tree-lined river. Healy took it at a run and flung himself full length as he reached it, expecting the rip and whiz of bullets, but nothing happened. He lay briefly winded and feeling sick with coursing adrenaline, and then crawled slowly forwards on his elbows to peer through the foliage.

At that instant, he saw it. A glint of sunlight caught the metallic gleam of a machine-gun barrel through the trees on the riverbank. It crouched like a tiger in the shadows, smug on its tripod among the sandbags, waiting to scatter haughty death through the boys awaiting orders behind him. Then the cold, grey barrel began to rotate slowly towards them. Healy turned and looked back. He was sure he could see them, khaki smudges, terribly unaware. *His boys, his responsibility.* He could hear the roar of the surf in his ears, the heavy thunder of waves, his heart pounding hammer blows in his chest.

Then he was up and running straight at the gun post, steel helmet flung to the wind, struggling to drag the rifle strap over his head, his tear-blinded gaze never leaving the single red eye peering like a cyclops from its nest. *The fog of doubt was gone—the way ahead was, at terribly long last, clear.* A welter of voices ... voices crying alarm ... amazed Boche voices in the darkness....

***

They found them together, tangled and torn and grey-faced, five of them, for the boys had seen him go, and seen him hit, and they had gone to him, and in so doing, had gone to their own deaths.

Carl Bentin and little Tommy Cravino, cut down by Healy's side, Harold Vaughan a little behind but with one arm flung out across the grass as though trying to reach his lef 'tenant. The medic was still alive, curled in a foetal position and trying to hold his own intestines in place. Healy, too, was alive. He lay on his back, and beneath the reddened swathe of dressing the medic had begun to wrap about his head before he too was hit, Healy's eyes were open to the blue sky, wisps of cloud reflected in their hazy darkness. Each breath came with unnatural slowness, accompanied by a soft whistling sound from the open wound in his right breast. The diggers called his name, even shook him a little, but Healy never spoke, just looked up unseeingly at the sky. Then the dark-shadowed eyes very slowly closed.

Stretcher bearers frequently had to cross open ground to reach casualties, often becoming casualties themselves from snipers, crossfire, or shelling. [Source: Australian War Memorial, collection ID: E03105]

The temporary grave created for Healy and his fallen comrades near Peronne. In 1919, their bodies were relocated to the New British Cemetery at Assevillers, five miles south-west of the town. [Source: Australian War Memorial, collection ID: E03362].

They carried the wounded medic out, but it was evening before the four cold bodies could be borne away from Sword Wood. They were buried in a single grave, shoulder to shoulder, in a battlefield cemetery within sight of Peronne. The site was marked by a white cross bearing the inscription, 'In loving memory of Lieut. C. Healy, 6523 Pte. C.F. Bentin, 3732 Pte. C. Cravino, 1669 Pte. E.W. Vaughan. 19th Batn. A.I.F. Killed in action. R.I.P. 29.8.18.'[16].

The loss of the only Australian Olympic gold medallist ever to fall in battle was noted on

Army Form B.103: *Casualty Form, Active Service:* Healy, Cecil Patrick: Killed in Action[17].

6523 Private Carl Frederick Bentin was a member of Healy's platoon and died alongside him at Sword Wood. He was just 19 years old and had seen 18 months of service, including being gassed at Hangard Wood. [Source: Tasmanian Archive and Heritage Office. Original image appeared in The Tasmanian Mail, 13 March 1919].

Later, the remainder of Healy's platoon killed every German manning a gun around Sword Wood.

On 1 September, Peronne and its guardian mountain were retaken in what was counted among the greatest of Allied victories in the war[18]. 'We had', said General Hobbs, 'to pass through trenches filled with Boche; check 'em out and then get through belt after belt of barbed wire 20- to 30-feet thick, uncut, without any artillery support, under machine-gun and artillery fire, all the time in full view of the enemy. How it was done I can't say.'[19]

Australian soldiers in a street strewn with the wreckage of houses in Peronne. On 1 September 1918, the town was taken and Australian forces went on to capture Mont St Quentin, driving the German forces east back towards the Hindenburg Line. [Source: Australian War Memorial, collection ID: E03763].

***

Surfers say heaven is an ocean—in life, the rough waves push you back, but once you pass them, endless peace and calm opens ahead.

FIFTEEN

'IT HARDLY SEEMS POSSIBLE...'

'Where I shall fall upon my battle-ground
There may I rest—nor carry me away.
What holier hills could in these days be found
Than hills of France to hold a soldier's clay?
Nor need ye place a cross of wooden stuff
Over my head to mark my age and name;
This very ground is monument enough!
'Tis all I wish of show or outward fame.'

—Ray Gauger, *Monument Enough.*

***

When Cecil Healy had returned to Australia from the 1906 Athens Olympic Games, having finished a disappointing third in the 100-metre swimming final, he was nonetheless honoured with a reception in Sydney that included a banquet and much toasting of the health of the young swimmer. After the plates were cleared, the vice-president of Healy's East Sydney Swimming Club, Lawrence Campbell, rose to recite the following poem in honour of their beaten son.

> 'Did you tackle the trouble that came your way
> With a resolute heart and cheerful?
> Or hide your face from the light of day
> With a craven soul and fearful?
> Oh, trouble's a ton, or trouble's an ounce,
> A trouble is what you make it;
> And it isn't the fact that you're hurt that counts,
> But only—how did you take it?'

This composition, cheerfully entitled *How Did You Die?*, was no doubt intended to highlight Healy's graciousness in defeat despite going into the Games as a world record holder and race favourite. However, it would also prove eerily prophetic when in 1918, within sight of the Armistice, the only Australian Olympic gold medallist ever to give his life on a battlefield was shot dead by a German sniper, and the Australia nation plunged, as Healy once had into the Manly surf, into an outpouring of grief unprecedented for an amateur sportsman[1].

The dreaded yellow telegram arrived at 22 Roslyn Gardens, Darlinghurst, in early September 1918. Harold Healy then walked for fifteen minutes to carry it to *Killua* in Darling Point, following the shore of Rushcutters Bay with the envelope fluttering in his hand. The spring breeze curled little white-capped waves, and small yachts bobbed in the water. How *blue* the harbour was! It stung his eyes, that blueness, that breeze, it made his eyes sting and prickle so painfully....

Annie heard the distinctive squeak of the gate, which was unusual at this hour. *Too late for the post, too early for the rabbit man....* Her straight-backed, dark-haired son was ashen. Annie's hand went to her heart as Harold came up the path toward the small, bare terrace house, the flimsy yellow piece of paper he was holding the only spot of colour in the grey streetscape. *Which of her boys...?Jack, Cec...?*

On 23 September 1918, it became inescapably official. There came letters transmitting the regret of their Majesties the King and Queen for Annie Healy's loss and the Governor-General's sympathy on the death of a gallant young officer 'who fell fighting for country and empire'. These two terrible missives did not detail the circumstances of Cecil Healy's death, and the family were left to piece together his final hours from newspaper reports published more than two weeks earlier. Many, as was common amid the confusion and poor international communication of the war, got it wrong. In 1918, Australia's newspapers contained few accounts of parties or socials, picnics or engagements or weddings. They were instead a sad litany of 'word received'—of sons, brothers and husbands killed in action, died of wounds, or captured. *The Referee* of 4 September 1918 contained a blithe description of a forthcoming swimming contest between the Australian diggers and the Americans in London and mentioned that Healy was 'busy with the infantry at the front'. Healy was, in fact, already dead. As news of his death filtered slowly around the world, one widely published report claimed that Healy had been killed while swimming the Somme River, leading up to 500 troops at the time[2]. Others cited an account from a private in the Australian Medical Corps who said that Healy had been struck on the head by a piece of shell and killed almost instantly[3].

It was not until a letter from the Commanding Officer of the 19th Battalion arrived on Harold Healy's desk at the end of September that the family knew the tragic details: 'He died well in front of his platoon looking for machine guns, and by his fearlessness gave the enemy too good a target to miss', Sydney Middleton wrote. 'He was, indeed, a great loss to the battalion, and was a very promising young officer. For his first time under heavy fire, he displayed wonderful coolness and any amount of courage. He died a true soldier, leading his men, and with his face to the enemy. He has left in the battalion a name that will be cherished by all who knew him, just as his record in the athletic world can always be recalled with feelings of admiration and respect.'[4] Middleton wrote to William Henry in London with the same report: 'Cecil was doing very gallant work, leading his platoon, and met his death by rushing a machine gun that was holding his men up. It was a very gallant act, as we would expect of him, but he was shot through the neck and fell, when a further burst of machine-gun fire went through his chest. Though he lingered for an hour, he never spoke after being hit.' Middleton assured Henry that his old friend 'made good from the day he first joined the battalion as an officer and that he (Middleton), as well as all his comrades in arms, felt his loss most keenly, although [we are] expected to be accustomed to such things.'[5]

More accurate accounts of Healy's death did not reach the Australian press until late September, when *The Sun's* correspondent embedded in France, Keith Murdoch, reported that 'The story of Cecil Healy's death, as learnt from his battalion, does not confirm the Paris correspondent's picturesque account. Healy led his platoon in the first stages of the Mont St Quentin attack on 29 August, and when approaching a machine-gun position, was killed by a bullet through the head.'[6] The 434th Australian Casualty List of the war was published in *The Sydney Morning Herald* on 15 October 1918. Among the inventory of those who had Died of Wounds, been Accidentally Killed, Wounded, or were Prisoners of War was 'Killed—2Lt. Cecil Healy, Darling Point.'

A requiem mass for Healy's life was held at St. Mary's Catholic Cathedral in Sydney on 23 September 1918. The mourners were led by Healy's mother Annie and brothers Claude and Harold, his cousin, digger Nicholas Healy Jr, and many representatives of Australian sport, including E.S. Marks and Vicary Horniman, W.W. Hill from the Rugby Union and Ossie Merrett from North Steyne Surf Club. The panegyric was preached by the Rev. Father J. O'Gorman, who had been a personal friend of Healy's. 'I have seen boys sitting around him and looking up to him with a sense of wonder, so charmed were they by his kindly disposition and amiable nature', O'Gorman told the packed cathedral. 'He was their hero, who had fought Australian battles in the athletic competitions in Athens, Stockholm, and many other capitals of Europe. Everywhere, and in all competitions, the genuine sportsmanship of Cecil Healy had won for him the greatest respect and esteem. There was no blot on his escutcheon, for he was honourable and uncorruptible in all his doings ... He was not attracted by the panoply of war, for he had a horror of it. Neither was his motive that of adventure; it was the desire to help Australia and the Allies because disaster to them would mean everything to his native land.'[7]

This tribute, while sombre and understated as befitted Healy's conservative middle-class Catholicism, nevertheless unleashed an outpouring of unprecedented national mourning. Even after the years of carnage and loss, of an entire generation of young men gouged from Australian society, of yellow telegrams that did not discriminate between the humble and the notable, few had expected a man like Healy to fall. It was just not to be thought of. Healy was national property—his achievements were owned by everyone from small children peering through the pool fence to men who pointed him out on the beach or stopped to shake his hand in the street. 'He did much, both by precept and example, to encourage the moral development of the younger generation', read one tribute. 'His fine spirit, both as a man and as a soldier, will not die with him.'

Cecil Healy was the first, perhaps, in a great tradition of Australian athletes that later included Don Bradman and Dawn Fraser, who made both a significant contribution to sport and a lasting contribution to Australian society. 'Australia is particularly proud of her sportsmen, and especially of those who combine a kindly nature with unusual skill in their special branch of athletics', mourned *The Sydney Morning Herald*. 'When the average man declares that a particular champion is a "true sport", he infers that his idol is one who, in the heat of contest, does not forget that he is a man, or that to win is but a secondary consideration to that of "playing the game". It is such a man as this that we envisage when we recall the late Lieutenant Cecil Healy. His death on the battlefield, within sight of Mont St Quentin, and almost within reach of the waters of the Somme, was the crowning point of a career which all lovers of true sportsmanship cannot fail to admire.'

Tributes came from all echelons of the military, from the supreme commander of the Allied forces, Lt.-Gen. William Birdwood, who wrote of the qualities that made Healy conspicuous, 'even in the large body of magnificent men of which our Force is composed'[8], to American Consul-General J.I. Brittain, who expressed his appreciation of Healy's 'kind actions and words on behalf of my countrymen in France.' Brittain also recalled Healy's astuteness in the years leading up to the war, as 'one of the voices raised to warn the world long before the great bulk of Englishmen could be induced to realise what Germany had in view.'

The Australian sports community was rocked by Healy's death. Public eulogies revisited his many achievements in the pool, including the records over 110 yards, 150 yards and 200 metres, which still stood. *The Referee* anointed Healy's race with Charles Daniels in England over 100 yards in 1906 as his greatest, reminding readers that while Healy had lost that race through his habitual slowness in the turns, 'kicking-off was not swimming'[9]. After all, *The Australian Worker* proclaimed, 'Cecil Healy, one of the Big Scrap's latest Australian victims, was, bar perhaps Barney Kieran and Dick Cavill, the best swimmer this hunk of the earth has produced ... When he wasn't victorious, he compelled the winners to hurry more hurriedly than they ever hurried before.'[10]

But for all Healy's luminous achievements in the waters of the world, regret echoed most of all for the man he had been. 'There are some people who imagine the surf lifesaver one who goes onto the beach for the conspicuousness he earns', said *The Sydney Mail*. 'Men like the late Cecil Healy—perhaps the greatest of all surf lifesavers—did not rush into the surf four and five times a day to help people out of difficulties to become conspicuous.'[11] *The Arrow* stated simply, 'A man of very sensitive nature and of fine mental qualities, war was repugnant to him. But like thousands of other Australian athletes, he went forth to fight against the barbarians of our times, only to fall gallantly, with his face to the foe.'[12] While Death had won the race, Healy had his laurel wreath, dying as he had lived—playing the game for all he was worth.

None were so heartfelt and heartbroken as the tributes that flowed from Healy's close friends. William Henry grieved, 'It seems only the other day when we were together, just after he passed his examination for his commission, when we had a swim, a talk, and a chat: I was also with him at the railway station to say adieu when he was off to France, and heard from him from across the Channel a few days prior to his battalion entering the firing line. It hardly seems possible that we shall never meet again or exchange views on our favourite topic.' Les Seaborn, who was wounded and awarded a Military Cross for his actions at Mont St Quentin, learned of Healy's death while in hospital in France. 'He went in the same way as all the sportsmen have gone—face to the foe, doing his bit up to the hilt', he wrote to *The Referee*. 'He was, if anything, too daring, right out in front of his platoon, making for a machine gun. He died as such a chap would die—a champion of the world.'

For some, the news was not to be borne. Swimmer Tommy Adrian, who had been a clubmate of Healy's at Manly, was told of Cecil's death while at Villers-Bretonneux and became 'terribly despondent'. Adrian had always been of a nervous disposition and Healy himself had written of Adrian's mental collapse before the Australian mile championship of 1914, when the well-wishes of friends so burdened the young man that 'his hopes of defeating the champion (Longworth) were pulverised'. Adrian never recovered from the news of Healy's death or his own awful experiences as a gunner on the Somme. In 1924, as coach of swimming champion Andrew 'Boy' Charlton *en route* to the Paris Olympic Games, Adrian threw himself over the side of their ship in a fit of unrelieved mental anguish. He was rescued, but remained a traumatised victim of war until his death in 1948[13].

Gunner Tommy Adrian, who had swum alongside Healy in Manly, never recovered from the shock of Healy's death or his own terrible experiences on the Somme. He remained beset by mental anguish until his death in 1948. [Source: Northern Beaches Council/Manly Library Local

Studies Collection: Series: World War I soldiers (619), image ID: 1100017659].

Despite only having had a brief acquaintance, writer Jack Priestley was shattered by Healy's loss. He was the recipient of Healy's final letter, which only arrived, full of his thoughts and hopes and fears, after Priestley had already learned of Cecil's death, a truly dreadful experience for the young scribe. Priestley later wrote to Harold Healy, 'If there was one man in the world that I thought 'summit of', then it was your brother (dear boy) Cecil. Some people laugh at the thought of a man expressing himself as if in love with a man—to me they are silly devils—but anyone who knew of a piece of human mechanism the same as your brother, knew him as I did, and did not think the world of him, then there must have been a kink in the brain, eyesight, or they were blind. No words of mind that I may write could express to you and yours my sorrow when I got the news which has touched me ever since ... There was something about him that one cannot describe, although it cannot pass from memory—something that many had not.'[14]

Some even sensed the fatalism that accompanied Healy to Mont St Quentin—that Healy was secretly but assuredly convinced there was no escape from either the war or his own terrible self-doubt but death. Lt. E.E. Booth, who had helped Healy organise many military games and sports while in France, wrote sombrely, 'He always imbued me personally with his very strong intuition that if he got his commission he would be 'pipped over', to use his own expression. Nothing could shake this from his mind.'[15]

***

Cecil Healy's death came just 74 days before the Armistice was signed on 11 November 1918, ending the war. The Australian victory at Mont St Quentin was named by British commander Sir Henry Rawlinson as 'the finest single feat of the war'. The flank and frontal attacks of which Healy had been part saw the undermanned Australian forces push into Peronne on the night of 29 August 1918. They consolidated their hold on the city the following day after six hours of bloody fighting amid the smoke of shellfire that rose continuously like a dust storm. The subsequent assault on Mont St Quentin caught the occupying forces unprepared after Australian sappers threw up a bridge across the Somme to transport heavy guns, but the savage combat resulted in 3,000 Australian casualties from gas, shrapnel and snipers. Three Australians who died in the onslaught, Albert Lowerson, Edgar Towner and Robert MacTier, were posthumously awarded the Victoria Cross for their roles in the battle.

The casualties of 1918, combined with long-term leave for 1914 enlistees and dwindling new enlistments, had sapped the strength of the AIF to such an extent that on 10 October 1918 the 19th Battalion was disbanded to reinforce other battalions in the brigade. Fierce fighting continued in Belgium and northern France, and around Homs and Mosul in the Middle East, despite a proposal by Germany for an armistice in early October. It was 9 November before German chancellor Kaiser Wilhelm II abdicated in line with US President Woodrow Wilson's demands to deal only with a democratic German bureaucracy, and two days later, on 11 November, the Armistice between the Allied powers and Germany was concluded. The guns on the Western Front fell silent at 11am.

SIXTEEN

LEST WE FORGET

'They shall grow not old, as we
that are left grow old:
Age shall not weary them, nor
the years condemn.
At the going down of the sun
and in the morning,
We will remember them.'

—Laurence Binyon, *For the Fallen*

***

It was March 1919 before Healy's personal effects were forwarded to his mother in two parcels. They were poignant in their ordinariness: his dog-tags and wallet, a silver pencil, photos, letters and receipts, a wrist watch with a damaged strap, a safety razor and an old brown valise containing his official tunic and breeches. His war medals, including a Victory Medal, a 1914–15 Star and a British War Medal, were presented to Harold in 1921.

In 1919, Harold was the manager of a monthly agricultural journal called *Pastoral Review*, and he used his journalistic expertise in the months following his brother's death to produce a book memorialising Cecil's life. *Cecil Healy—In Memoriam,* a collection of newspaper stories and tributes, was printed just in time for Annie to read it before she died on 2 June 1919, at the age of 73[1]. She lived just long enough to see her other son, John Henry, repatriated from Europe in March 1919, but that young man was not the same vigorous, handsome wool-classer who had donned khaki three years earlier. He came home afflicted by neurasthenia, a nervous breakdown precipitated by the dreadful trauma of war. While often physically unmarked, the neurasthenic soldier was racked by physical and mental symptoms ranging from complete paralysis to deafness, stammering, vomiting, delusions and depression[2]. Already weakened by the loss of one son, Annie Healy died soon after John's sad return, her meagre body falling prey to the worldwide Spanish influenza pandemic[3].

John followed her to the grave shortly after, in 1926. Many neurasthenic patients were unable to stand the noise and crowds of cities, and were tortured by loud sounds and sudden movements. Dr E.W. White, Emeritus Professor of Psychological Medicine at King's College London, recommended that they live as much as possible in the open air, in the country if circumstances allowed. John was one of many returned servicemen who fled the city for the blessed silence of the outback. He returned to his pre-war employment as a wool-classer in north-western NSW and married Mollie Ryan in 1923 in what seemed a promising move toward rehabilitation. But even before his marriage, he was suffering from terminal testicular cancer, and in 1926, he died at Harold's home—the old Healy home—at 22 Roslyn Street in Darlinghurst. John was just 42 years old[4].

As a beneficiary of Cecil Healy's will, Muriel Maitland received half of his estate, savings to the value of about £170. However, such comparative wealth was no balm for a heart shattered by Healy's death. For all the ambivalence of their affair, with its unspoken and bewildering emotions, Muriel had continued to hold fast to the little that Healy had given her. Despite all of Healy's half-fearful speculations, Muriel had never married, but remained at *Karoon* to care for her aging parents until her father died in 1936 and her mother in 1940, after which the big house on the corner of Addison and Darley Road was demolished and replaced by a block of apartments[5]. The development was financed by Muriel herself and her sisters Vera Targett and Clari Emblen, and the trio lived in the apartments for the rest of their lives.

However, even amidst the comings and goings of that little microcosm of Manly life, Muriel remained very much alone. Vera had married Boer War veteran Harold Targett in May 1915, a wedding Healy probably attended before his enlistment. Targett and his new wife were both keen on sports and Targett worked as a sports correspondent, writing on golf for *The Referee*. Muriel lived alone in Flat 9 until she died in 1959 at the age of 71. She was by that time a rich lady, with more than £13,000 in assets from her share of the *Karoon* flats, but her old age was Spartan, without watches, jewellery, cars, or luxuries, and with grief as her only companion[6]. She had spent the remainder of her life in Manly beside the ocean Healy had loved so well, where he had found sustenance, hope and rejuvenation, where they had both heard its wooing and crooning.

In 1940, the Maitland home Karoon on Darley Road was demolished and replaced by modern apartments. The development, financed by Muriel Maitland and her sisters, provided a home for Muriel for the remainder of her long but lonely life. [Source: Northern Beaches Council/Manly Library Local Studies Collection: Series: 2009-06 (307), image ID: 1100005157].

***

In faraway France, Healy's body lay alongside his three companions in the cold earth of Sword Wood, on the rise of a hill about 500 yards from where he was killed. Les Seaborn visited the site, with its white timber cross bearing the names of the fallen. 'He lies in good company among several of his comrades—Australian Diggers', he wrote. 'He and they are well worthy of each other and, could we but know it, are mutually proud of the comradeship.'[7]

In 1919, after their original grave marker had been destroyed by shellfire, the bodies of Healy and his men were relocated to the official war cemetery at Assevillers, five miles from Peronne. [Source: author's own collection].

The original grave marker was destroyed by shellfire in the final battles of the Somme, and in late 1919, the remains of Healy, Bentin, Cravino and Vaughan were exhumed and moved to the New British Cemetery in the village of Assevillers, five miles south-west of Peronne[8]. Healy's life and sacrifice are now commemorated in the museum at Assevillers as one of the many Anzacs who, 'with soft hats and easy-going manner', came from the other side of the world to liberate Europe[9]. In Australia, the Cecil Healy Memorial Fund was established by the NSW Amateur Swimming Association within weeks of Healy's death. The Fund was used for the purchase of War Loan Bonds, and the accrued interest, supplemented by profits from sales of the *In Memoriam* book, was devoted to the encouragement of junior swimming. Healy's alma mater, St. Aloysius College, still awards the silver Healy Plate to the school's champion house at the annual swimming carnival. Cecil Healy was inducted into the International Swimming Hall of Fame at Fort Lauderdale, Florida in 1981 and the Sports Australia Hall of Fame in 1986. His name also appears on the Manly Pathway of Olympians, the NSW Hall of Champions Honour Roll at Sydney Olympic Park and the East Sydney Amateur Swimming Club and Australian War Memorial Rolls of Honour.

The lifesaving community was also quick to honour their fallen associate. Healy is a nominee on the World War I Honour Board at both North Steyne and Manly Surf Clubs, and in July 1919 Manly honoured their former captain with a shield valued at 65 guineas to be competed for by clubs over a period of 10 years. The first contest for the shield was held at North Steyne on 6 December 1919, and the Alarm Reel race featured Healy's old comrades Harold Hardwick and Harry Hay, Hardwick having just returned from active service himself. The shield was eventually won—ironically—by Manly Surf Lifesaving Club.

The lifesaving community was quick to honour the life of one of its favourite sons with a memorial carnival held in

Healy's honour at North Steyne in December 1919. [Source: Northern Beaches Council/Manly Library Local Studies Collection: Series: 2006-07-27(23), image ID: 1100003424].

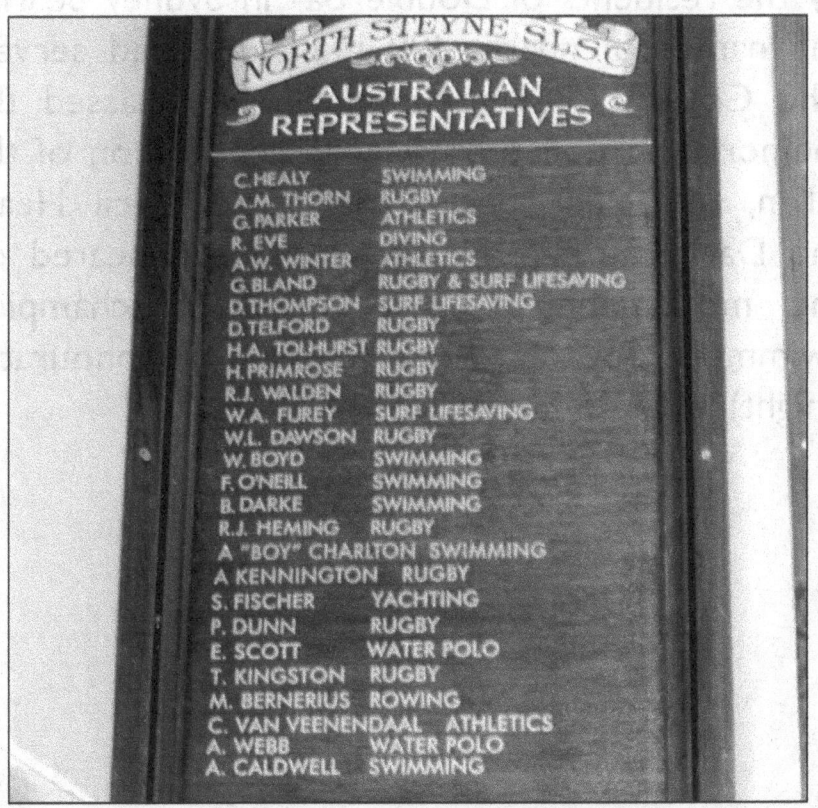

Honour board in the North Steyne Surf Lifesaving Club clubhouse listing its Australian sporting representatives. Healy's name heads the list. [Source: author's own].

Meanwhile, in the parks, streets and squares of Australian towns and cities, sad memorials to a fallen generation began to grow, like beautiful but unwanted flowers. These cenotaphs of bronze and stone listed the names of local men who had served, and became a place of congregation and reflection for a wounded young nation. In August 1919, the NSW State Governor Sir Walter Davidson unveiled a monument erected by the residents of Double Bay in Sydney bearing the names of nearly 400 men who had served. The Governor called upon all who passed the memorial to doff their hats in recognition of the fallen, and paid special tribute to Cecil Healy, the Darlinghurst boy whose name appeared on the monument, as 'not merely a champion swimmer, but a *preux chevalier* (honourable knight).'[10]

The Manly Surf Club honour roll lists the names of 61 members lost during the Great War, amongst them their former captain Cecil Healy. [Source: Manly Surf Club].

In recognition of his place of birth and long-time residence, Cecil Healy's name was included on the Double Bay war memorial in inner-city Sydney when the monument was erected in 1919. [Source: Sandra Brown].

The Cecil Healy shield for proficiency in lifesaving was first awarded by the Manly Surf Club in 1919 in the hope that those who competed for it would 'ever bear in mind the splendid example of the great amateur in whose name it is given'. [Source: Manly Surf Club/Manly Surf Lifesaving Club].

However, more than 90 years would pass before Healy's own wishes were fulfilled. Despite his upbringing in inner-city Sydney, his heart remained on the city's north shore, amongst its blue waves and white sand. Notwithstanding Healy's emotional and sporting connection to Manly, his enlistment record gave his place of residence as his mother's home in Darling Point, and Cecil Healy's name was not initially included on the Manly cenotaph that now stands at the intersection of Belgrave Street and The Corso[11]. In 2007, the North Steyne Surf Lifesaving Club launched a campaign for Healy's name to be added to the monument, including a march through Manly's streets calling for public support for the move. North Steyne surf historian Mark Maddox cited a previously unknown letter from Healy to his brother Harold, written just before he left Cambridge for the front in 1918 and expressing the wish that he be 'remembered for a year or two (in Manly)' as demonstrative of Healy's genuine affiliation with the peninsula, and on 25 April 2007, Anzac Day, Healy's name became the 464th to be added to the Manly cenotaph. The North Steyne Surf Club formed a guard of honour and laid a wreath in his memory. Mr Maddox concluded simply that 'His name is among his swimming and surfing mates. I think he would appreciate that.'[12]

The memorial cenotaph on The Corso in Manly, to which Cecil Healy's name was added in 2007 in honour of his service and residence in the area. [Source: author's own collection].

Cecil Healy's name was added to the Manly cenotaph in 2007 after a public campaign by the North Steyne Surf Lifesaving Club to have his final wishes recognised. [Source: author's own collection].

EPILOGUE

Cecil Healy never won an individual Olympic gold medal, and minor medallists usually fade quickly away, outshone by the golden glory of their conquerors or swept aside by the erratic current of public interest. While Healy did capture gold as a member of the Australian 4x200-yard relay team at the Stockholm Games of 1912, it was his silver medal performance in the 100-metre freestyle that saw him upheld as 'the very best type of an Australian sportsman'.

Such adulation for a non-winner is not unusual in Australia, which has an atypical relationship with the accomplished and influential. It is characteristic in Australian society that so-called 'tall poppies'—those who achieve success, power, or influence—are frequently criticised or resented because their achievements distinguish them from their peer group, and battlers or underdogs are elevated in the public's affection instead. One theory suggests that the early days of domination by British colonial rulers instilled in Australians an inherent distrust of status, rank and privilege, with their associated reek of domination and repression[1]. Writing in *The Sydney Morning Herald*, political editor Peter Hartcher observed that 'According to the unspoken national ethos, no Australian is permitted to assume that he or she is better than any other Australian. But it isn't success that offends Australians. It's the affront committed by anyone who starts to put on superior airs.'

In a nation that takes a dim view of the flaunting of wealth, intelligence, or achievements, Cecil Healy's native humbleness and the sportsmanship that underpinned his 1912 defeat in Stockholm helped his poppy to escape the public scythe. Psychologists refer to a theory of 'deservingness': the degree to which a tall poppy is judged to have earned their high status and its associated rewards[2]. In keeping with that model, Healy was probably judged to have deserved his success because he trained hard to achieve it and was publicly understated about his achievements. Furthermore, his defeats equally endeared him to the nation through the Australian cultural peculiarity of favouring the 'battler'—the one whose success is not defined solely by the outcome of his or her endeavours but the attitude with which they were undertaken.

While championing the runner-up and the 'never-had-a-chance' is not an exclusively Australian trait—after all, the plot of virtually every Hollywood movie seems to feature a small fry doing battle with an evil empire or superhuman rival—Australian support is distinctive in that it is not conditional on the protagonist emerging triumphant. On the contrary, if they have tried their utmost, never surrendered and undertaken their effort without pretence, Australians still consider them a success. This espousal of the battler is a recurrent theme throughout Australian history, from the Eureka Stockade to Ned Kelly's last stand and the disastrous military campaign at Gallipoli, and is again surmised to date back to the convict era and the stoicism of those who endured great affliction with little hope of escape or reprieve. Others have speculated that support for the battler is a product of the unremitting, harsh environment in which Australians labour, a continued salvo of drought, flood and fire that has forced generations of farmers to reshape their goals from conquering the earth to trying their best and never surrendering[3].

Whatever the genesis of his public support, Cecil Healy remained an unwavering favourite in Australia throughout his life, almost irrespective of whether he won or lost in the pool. Although he didn't fit the mould of the larrikin Digger whose notorious disregard for military discipline forms such a part of the contemporary Australian identity, Healy the Olympian, the bronzed lifeguard from Manly, still embodied many of the mythic values associated with the Anzac legend: masculinity and mateship, discipline and sacrifice, humanitarianism and public duty[4]. While Healy won many a contest in the pool, even 'to the point of monotony' as *The Referee* once groaned, and was awarded honours for feats of bravery and selflessness in the boisterous Manly surf, it was his sacrifices in both Stockholm and on the battlefield of the Somme, his concern for the men around him, his flaws and self-doubts and his awareness of his own mortality that brought such a collective wail to Australian throats upon news of his death.

Cecil Healy's plaque on the Manly Pathway of Olympians honouring Healy's selection for the 1912 Stockholm Olympic Games while resident in the town. The plaque was sponsored by the North Steyne Surf Club, of which Healy was a member before he enlisted to serve in World War I. [Source: author's own].

Of a population of less than five million, more than 62,000 Australians were killed in World War I, and many more returned home spiritually broken and physically incapacitated to a society in shock at such a devastating reshaping of the world. Many of the casualties came from the ranks of Australia's sportsmen, who had flocked from the playing fields and sun-kissed beaches to take the high ideals of sport into the fighting arena. Those making the supreme sacrifice included Geelong centreman Joe Slater from the Victorian Football League, rugby league players Frank Cheadle and Bob Tidyman and swimmers Arthur Rosenthal, Stanley Crane and Clarence Powell. The Manly region lost dozens of lifesavers, including Carl Adelt, Jack Reynolds and George Hill. Australia's representative cricket ranks were decimated by the loss of Albert 'Tibby' Cotter, Australia's fastest bowler, and NSW batsmen Gother Clarke and Arthur Callaway, who was blown to pieces in France. Also joining the army of phantom sportsmen were Davis Cup tennis ace Tony Wilding and Australian Open champion Arthur O'Hara Wood, rugby players Jim McManamay and Blair Swannell, Sydney cross-country champion Fred Flowers, international rower Fred Kelly and Clyde Pearce, winner of the NSW Open golf championship.

The Olympic memorial in Sydney's Hyde Park commemorates the lives of all Olympians who have perished in or as a result of armed conflict and the hope that the Olympic Games will encourage the peaceful resolution of conflict. [Source: Peter F. Williams].

Forty past and future Australian Olympians fought in the Great War, of whom three—Healy, rower Keith Heritage, who was credited as the first Australian to volunteer and who won a Military Cross in France, and runner Claude Ross—were never to return. Healy continues to hold the sad distinction of being the only Australian Olympic gold medallist killed on active duty. While one of the prime motives of Olympic competition is to foster friendship and goodwill between nations, war has forced the cancellation of three Games (1916, 1940 and 1944) and hundreds of Olympians have lost their lives as a result of armed conflict. World War I alone took a dreadful toll on the international Olympic movement. History records 135 Olympic representatives killed, from countries as wide-ranging as Canada, Finland, South Africa, Serbia and Haiti. On 7 September 2000, eight days before the opening ceremony of the Sydney Olympic Games, flags were flown at half-mast to pay tribute to the hundreds of Olympic victims of the Great War and subsequent conflicts, and a plaque commemorating the fallen Olympians was unveiled in Sydney's Hyde Park by IOC President Juan Antonio Samaranch.

Healy's deeds at Stockholm, his gallantry and democratic ideals and the heart-tearing tragedy of his death are part of the fabric of the Australian identity, the very essence of the mythology that makes up the great Anzac tradition[5]. War propaganda espoused the theory that sport befitted a man to fight for the honour and safety of his country, imbued him with innate discipline, soundness of wind and limb and the sportsmanship once thought essential to earn honour on a battlefield. It is tempting to view stories such as that of Cecil Healy and the many other international Olympians affected by conflict as a convergence of the twin battlefields of sport and war. Despite the harsh disparity in objectives—one amity, the other annihilation—both are driven by a desire for victory, unmasking the greatest good and the greatest evil in mankind. A common end-product of both sport and war is the hero, but Healy, a member of the 'Fighting 19th' Sportsman's Battalion and for so long cast as the ultimate soldier-sportsman, argued consistently against the juxtaposition of sport and war. He wrote from the front line in the weeks before his death:

> I am afraid there is very little of the sporting element in modern warfare. The terrible engines of destruction and diabolical accessories, such as poison gas, now employed, resolve the issue for the individual into being not one of the survival of the fittest, but sheer luck, nothing more or less.[6]

Healy's service and death lifts the veil on the myth of the blithe larrikin Anzac, charging grinning at the enemy with bayonet flashing. The honesty of his correspondence from the front—remarkable in one so reticent—about his desperation to do his duty and his fear of accepting a command position he didn't feel he could honour, of wanting to live up to the expectations of his friends and of his almost certain death exposes the terror and uncertainty of many servicemen for whom heroism was no prize to be sought.

Healy's death, too, is emblematic of the tortured private lives of many male sportsmen, driven to self-destructive behaviour by both internal and external expectations, playing not for glory but for a critical measure of self-worth. Pretending to be tougher—or saner—than you really are is central to life as an elite sportsman. Tales of self-destruction through drink and/or drugs, fast cars and gambling are distressingly common among male professional athletes. Suicide rates among sportsmen have been reported as being over two and a half times the male average in Britain[7]. For one such as Cecil Healy—emotionally unresolved, unsparing, as brilliant in the water as he was doubt-ridden out of it—the theatre of war offered the most complete and final escape from his unrelenting search for self-respect.

In his post-war *Notebooks*, American writer F. Scott Fitzgerald mused, 'Show me a hero and I will write you a tragedy', and it was for this reason that poet Wilfred Owen penned his own dreadful commentary on the futility of war: *dulce et decorum est, pro patria mori*—what Owen called 'the old lie', that it is sweet and right to die for your country. Healy's death echoed the eternal unanswered questions of war—the injustice of robbing a nation of its finest, the futility of raising man's hand against man.

ABOUT THE AUTHOR

Rochelle holds a Ph.D. in Sports Science and has worked with some of Australia's leading elite athletes. She has also worked as a journalist and medical researcher in Australia, Europe and the United States, and represented Australia in women's fencing. This is her second biography of an Australian sportsman.

ENDNOTES

Prologue

[1] The 19th had followed the southern bank of the Somme towards huts on the eastern side of Salmon Wood and the village of Cappy. The movement was spotted by the enemy who shelled the area with several calibres of artillery in the afternoon of August 28, 1918. The 18th and 19th Battalions remained in position around Salmon Wood but the Germans shelled the area again during the night with a mixture of tear gas and high explosive. Matthews, W. and D. Wilson. (2011). *Fighting Nineteenth—History of the 19th Infantry Battalion A.I.F. 1915–1918*. Loftus, NSW: Australian Military History Publications. p.361.

[2] Carlyon, L. (2006). *The Great War*. Australia: Pan Macmillan. pp.680–681. Matthews, W. and D. Wilson. (2011). *Fighting Nineteenth—History of the 19th Infantry Battalion A.I.F. 1915–1918*. Loftus, NSW: Australian Military History Publications. p.362–363.

Chapter 1

[1] For medieval Christians, water was associated with the plague and spread of other communicable diseases. The breaststroke evolved to keep the swimmer's head above water and arms reaching forward to brush aside foreign matter that might enter the mouth. The European revival was driven by interest in classicism and Romantic poets such as Byron and Shelley, who viewed water as an enervating and erotic force after the rejection of immersion as sinful and aberrant during the Dark Ages. Schmidt, C. (2012). *The Swimsuit: Fashion from Poolside to Catwalk.* London, UK: Berg.

[2] Phillips, M. and Swimming Australia. (2008). *Swimming Australia: One Hundred Years.* Sydney, NSW: UNSW Press. p.3.

[3] Smith, A. (2000). 'Swimming: A Feeling for Water [Transcript].' The Sports Factor, ABC Radio National. Available from: http://www.abc.net.au/radionational/programs/sportsfactor/swimming-a-feeling-for-water/3476374#transcript. [cited Friday 8 December 2015].

[4] Keene, N. 'Kings Cross Activist Juanita Nielsen's 1975 Disappearance Is

Australia's Biggest Murder Mystery.' (2015). *The Daily Telegraph* (Sydney, NSW). Wednesday 1 July, p.18.

[5] 'Death of P.J. Healy.' (1895). *Freeman's Journal* (Sydney, NSW). Saturday 14 September, p.18.

[6] Federal Court of Australia. (1998). *'The Members of the Yorta Yorta Aboriginal Community V the State of Victoria & Ors.* 'Federal Court of Australia. p.6.

[7] The family lived at 92 Elizabeth Bay Road from 1885 to 1889. 'Leyton', at 92 Elizabeth Bay Road, was a two-storey brick and stone terrace with a slate roof valued at £130. Patrick had chambers at Lyndon Chambers, 161 Phillip St in the city, until 1889 when he moved to Denman Chambers at 180 Phillip Street. City of Sydney. (2015).

'Sands Sydney Directory [1889].' John Sands Ltd (Printers and Stationers). Available from: http://www.cityofsydney.nsw.gov.au/learn/search-our-collections/sands-directory/sands-search. [cited 24 June 2015] and City of Sydney Archives. (2015). '92 Elizabeth Bay Road.' Assessment Books 1845–1948. City of Sydney. Available from: http://photosau.com.au/CosRates/scripts/home.asp. [cited 24 June 2015].

[8] On August 29, 1864, at St. Mary's Cathedral in Sydney, Girard (the third son of the late Francois Girard of Branga Park, Walcha) married Annie Louisa, daughter of James Gallott of West Maitland. 'Marriages.' (1864). *The Sydney Morning Herald* (NSW). Wednesday 31 August, p.1.

[9] Francois Girard was born in Normandy in 1793, the year France declared war on Britain. In 1820 while in exile in England, he was convicted of stealing 2 gold watches and sentenced to seven years transportation on what may have been trumped-up charges to remove all potential French revolutionaries from British shores. In 1844, after gaining his freedom and leaving the social scene of Sydney, he became a pastoralist on the Clarence River at *Branga Park* near Walcha. The willow trees he planted along the Cobrabald River are said to come from seedlings imported from St. Helena, where Napoleon died in exile. Francis Girard died on November 16, 1859, in Armidale. Clarke, H. (2013). 'Francois Girard, Dancing Master, Convict.' Australian Colonial Dance. Available from: http://www.colonialdance

.com.au/francois-girard-dancing-master-convict-1608.html. [cited 18 June 2015].

[10] An angry notice from Henry Johnson Brown of Lismore in the Grafton papers 'hereby caution(ed) all parties not to pay any money on my account to Mr. Alphonse B. Girard, Grafton, solicitor.' 'Notice.' (1866). *Clarence and Richmond Examiner and New England Advertiser* (Grafton, NSW). Tuesday 4 December, p.5.

[11] 'District News.' (1867). *The Maitland Mercury and Hunter River General Advertiser* (NSW). Saturday 27 April, p.5.

'Singleton—Police Court—Tuesday 5th November, 1867.' (1867). *The Maitland Mercury and Hunter River General Advertiser* (NSW). Thursday 7 November, p.7.

[12] 'Death of Mr. Alphonse B. Girard.' (1868). *Clarence and Richmond Examiner and New England Advertiser* (Grafton, NSW). Tuesday 9 June, p.2.

[13] 'Marriages.' (1869). *The Sydney Morning Herald* (NSW). Friday 26 February, p.8.

[14] 'Metropolitan District Court. Tuesday'. (1887). *The Sydney Morning Herald* (Sydney, NSW). Wednesday 6 April, p.11.

[15] A snippet on page 6 of the *Evening News* of Saturday 6 September 1890 noted that number 2797, Patrick Joseph Healy, of Roslyn Street, Darlinghurst, barrister-at-law, was under the order of a bankruptcy sequestration, assignee, Mr L.T. Lloyd. 'In Bankruptcy.' (1890). *Evening News* (Sydney, NSW). Saturday 6 September, p.6.

[16] Dyster, B. and D. Meredith. (1990). *Australia in the International Economy: In the Twentieth Century.* New York: Cambridge University Press.

Irving, H. (1999). *The Centenary Companion to Australian Federation.* New York: Cambridge University Press.

[17] Healy, P.J. (1890). *'Bankruptcy File 2797: Debtor's Petition [September 16, 1890].'* State Records NSW: shelf reference 10/22663, series 13655, item 2797, Sydney, NSW. [cited 22 February 2015]. Available from: www.records.nsw.gov.au.

[18] When Patrick's father, Nicholas Healy Snr, died in 1861, he left his household goods and furniture to his wife, his Maitland hotel to his son Nicholas, or to be divided among his remaining

children should Nicholas die before age 25 without lawful issue. 'Probate Packet: Nicholas Healy (No.13660).' (1861). Sydney, NSW. [cited 6 July 2015]. Available from: http://investigator.records.nsw.gov.au/Entity.aspx?Path=\Item\230482.

[19] 'Insolvency: Gallott, James [September 2, 1847].' (1847). State Records NSW: file number 01673, Sydney, NSW. [cited 18 June 2015]. Available from: http://srwww.records.nsw.gov.au/indexes/searchhits_nocopy.aspx?table=Insolvency%20Index&id=10&frm=1&query=Surname:gallott.

In 1865, Gallot's liabilities amounted to £121 7s. 6d.; his assets were £25. 'Insolvency Court.' (1865). *The Sydney Morning Herald* (NSW). Thursday 14 September, p.2.

[20] The Healy family moved to Roslyn Gardens in 1890 and remained there until Harold Healy's death in 1933. City of Sydney. (2015). 'Sands Sydney Directory [1895].' John Sands Ltd (Printers and Stationers). Available from: http://www.cityofsydney.nsw.gov.au/learn/search-our-collections/sands-di

rectory/sands-search. [cited 24 June 2015].

[21] 'Hay Circuit Court.' (1890). *The Hay Standard and Advertiser for Balranald, Wentowrth, Maude* (Hay, NSW). Saturday 11 October, p.8.

[22] 'Bowral Free Press.' (1894). *Bowral Free Press and Berrima District Intelligencer* (NSW). Saturday 15 December, p.5.

[23] 'Preparatory School for Boys.' (1896). *The Scrutineer and Berrima District Press* (NSW). Saturday 14 March, p.5.

[24] 'Scone.' (1894). *The Maitland Daily Mercury* (NSW). Saturday 3 November, p.2.

[25] Kurkulla opened on Monday July 20, 1891, advertised as a 'high class school for boys'. Pulling was highly recommended as master, with his references coming from, among others, the Head Master of the elite Sydney Grammar School. 'Kurkulla, Bowral.' (1891). *Bowral Free Press* (NSW). Wednesday 1 July, p.2.

[26] 'J. Lee Pulling, Esq.'. (1938). *The Torch Bearer, the Magazine of the Sydney Church of England Grammar School, North Sydney, NSW, Australia*. XLII(3): pp.160–228.

[27] 'Matinee.' (1894). *Bowral Free Press and Berrima District Intelligencer* (NSW). Wednesday 19 December, p.5.

[28] The expression was taken from his own published book of Latin verses, *Barbitos: Experiments in verse translation* (1939) [London: Milford].

See also '75 Years, 1889–1964.'. (1964). *The Torch Bearer, the Magazine of the Sydney Church of England Grammar School, North Sydney, NSW, Australia.* LXXIV(1): pp.1–242.

[29] Pulling, J.L. (1909). 'Sport in Relation to School Life.' *Australian Journal of Education.* 7(5): p.12.

[30] 'Swimming.' (1894). *Evening News* (Sydney, NSW). Friday 30 November, p.2.

[31] 'Classified Advertising.' (1895). *Sunday Times* (Sydney, NSW). Sunday 8 September, p.1.

[32] 'Death of P.J. Healy.' (1895). *Freeman's Journal* (Sydney, NSW). Saturday 14 September, p.18.

[33] Schwarz, A., et al. (2000). 'The Outcome of Acute Interstitial Nephritis: Risk Factors for the Transition from Acute to Chronic Interstitial Nephritis.' *Clinical Nephrology.* 54(3): pp.179–90.

Chapter 2

[1] 'The Natatorium.' (1895). *The Cumberland Free Press* (Parramatta, NSW). Saturday 12 October, p.8.

[2] February 23, 1895: 13-year-old Cecil Healy made his first appearance at a club carnival at the Natatorium, swimming off 20 seconds in a 66-yard club handicap and 18 seconds in the 60-yard All Schools' Handicap. 'Swimming: East Sydney Swimming Club.' (1895). *The Sydney Morning Herald* (NSW). Saturday 23 February, p.12.

[3] Hogue, J.A. (1910). *Report Upon the Physical Condition of Children Attending Public Schools in New South Wales, Based Upon Observations Made in Connection with the Medical Inspection of Public School Children 1908–1909, with Anthropometric Tables and Diagrams*. Sydney, NSW: Department of Public Instruction.

[4] Walsh, G.P. (1983). 'Lane, Frederick Claude Vivian (1879–1969).' Australian Dictionary of Biography, National Centre of Biography, Australian National University. Available from: http://adb.anu.edu.au/biography/lane-frederick-claude-vivian-7023. [cited 5 July 2015].

[5] Corry, M. (2000). *Waverley Cemetery: Who's Who Sporting Lives*. Bondi Junction, NSW: Waverley Library. p.45.

[6] 'The Cavill Family (Aus).' (2015). International Swimming Hall of Fame. Available from: http://www.ishof.org/the-cavill-family--%28aus%29.html. [cited 2 July 2015].

[7] Osmond, G. (2012). 'Clipped Histories: Representing the Cavill Family of Swimmers in Historical Feature Articles.' *Journal of Australian Studies*. 36(3): pp.363–376.

[8] City of Sydney Archives. (2015). 'Letter: 5 February 1894: The Manager of the Grand Natatorium Hotel and Baths in Pitt Street Complains About the Very High Cost for the Supply of Salt Water [Ref. 26/271/199].' Letters Received 21 Jan 1843–28 Dec 1899. City of Sydney. Available from: http://archives.cityofsydney.nsw.gov.au/Entity.aspx?Path=\Item\524337. [cited 4 July 2015].

[9] Mould, D.D.C.P. (1953). *Ireland of the Saints*. London, UK: Batsford. p.136.

Leviton, R. (2005). *Encyclopedia of Earth Myths: An Insider's A–Z Guide to Mythic People, Places, Objects and Events Central to the*

Earth's Visionary Geography. Charlottesville, VA: Hampton Roads Publishing. p.280.

[10] Yeats, W. and R. Welch. (1993). *Writings on Irish Folklore, Legend and Myth*. London, UK: Penguin Books Limited. p.69.

[11] Gregory, D. and A. Pred. (2013). *Violent Geographies: Fear, Terror and Political Violence*. New York: Routledge. p.11.

[12] A tax on agricultural land payable to the Church of Ireland, determined according to the valuation of each civil parish. Prior to the Composition Act of 1823, taxes could be paid in kind. Kain, R.J.P. and H.C. Prince. (2006). *The Tithe Surveys of England and Wales*. New York: Cambridge University Press. p.28.

[13] Whyte, J.H. (2001). The Age of Daniel O'connell: 1800–1847. In: T.W. Moody and F.X. Martin. *'The Course of Irish History'*. Cork, IRE: Mercier Press. pp.204–207.

[14] Biographical Database of Australia. (2015). 'Biographical Report for Nicholas Healy.' Available from: http://www.bda-online.org.au/mybda/search/biographical-report/10014173701?f=nicho

las&l=healy&ol=&i=3&s=&p. [cited 14 April 2015] and State Records of New South Wales. (2015). *'Bound Indents, 1818–19.'* [cited 4/4006 Minerva 1819, Entry no.20]; Available from: http://www.records.nsw.gov.au/state-archives/guides-and-finding-aids/using-the-archives-resources-kit/convict-records/convict-records.

[15] National Archives of Ireland. (2014). 'List of Names and Details of 172 Male Convicts Onboard the Convict Ship 'Minerva', Bound for New South Wales [Cso/Rp/1819/247].' Chief Secretary's Office Registered Papers – Francis J. Crowley Bequest. National Archives of Ireland. Available from: http://csorp.nationalarchives.ie/search/index.php?simpleSearchSbm=true&category=27&subcategory=176&searchDescTxt=CSO/RP/1819/247&simpleSearchSbm=Search. [cited 18 April 2015].

[16] Correspondence dated 24 August from Dr Trevor to William Gregory, Under Secretary, Dublin Castle, concerning his superintendence of embarkation of convicts at Cork reveals that there was an attempted mutiny on board prior to the ship sailing. Free Settler

or Felon? (2015). 'Convict Ship Minerva 1819.' Available from: http://www.jenwilletts.com/convict_ship_minerva_1819.htm. [cited 7 April 2015].

[17] The 1819 Bigges Report found that the average length of 44 direct voyages made between 1810 and 1820 was 127 days, with a mortality rate of 0.9%, while voyages via Rio de Janiero averaged 156 days (2.0%) and those via the Cape of Good Hope 146 days (0.5%). The 'economy of lives', reduction in onshore temptations such as purchase of contraband by the crew to sell in the colony and reduced subsistence cost of the direct voyage were all advantages identified in the report. Bigge, J.T. (1822). *Report of the Commissioner of Inquiry into the State of the Colony of New South Wales [19 June, 1822].* The House of Commons, London, UK. Available from: http://gutenberg.net.au/ebooks13/1300181h.html. [cited 5 June 2015].

[18] Ten convicts died aboard the *Three Bees* in 1814 after they had to remain in dock in Dublin for six weeks awaiting suitable winds and received neither clothing nor bedding for the

stay or the short journey to Cork. Few were allowed on deck and they spent most of the time in irons in the hold. The sloop was again detained in Cork before the convicts embarked the transport ship and the preceding delays and neglect were blamed for the high mortality therein. Lohan, R. (2015). 'Sources in the National Archives for Research into the Transportation of Irish Convicts to Australia (1791–1853).' National Archives of Ireland. Available from: http://www.nationalarchives.ie/topics/transportation/transp1.html. [cited 20 April 2015].

[19] Bigge, J.T. (1822). *Report of the Commissioner of Inquiry into the State of the Colony of New South Wales [19 June 1822].*' The House of Commons, London, UK. Available from: http://gutenberg.net.au/ebooks13/1300181h.html. [cited 5 June 2015].

[20] From: Extracts Relating to Transportation, Disembarkation & Servitude.

In: Bigge, J.T. (1822). *Report of the Commissioner of Inquiry into the State of the Colony of New South Wales [19 June, 1822].*'

The House of Commons, London, UK. Available from: http://gutenberg.net.au/ebooks13/1300181h.html. [cited 5 June 2015].

[21] Richard Clarke and fellow death-row inmates Donaher and Madden had their sentences commuted to transportation for life. Four of the five attempted escapees were transported together on the *Providence,* departing Ireland on 10 December 1810. James Sargent was also found guilty and given seven years transportation. Convict Records. (2015). 'Richard Clarke.' Available from: http://www.convictrecords.com.au/convicts/clarke/richard/131024. [cited 26 April 2015].

[22] Records related to Catherine Pendergast occur under a number of alternative surnames, including Clark, Pendigrass, Predergast, Prendergrass and Pendergrass. Tardif, P. (1990). *Notorious Strumpets and Dangerous Girls: Convict Women in Van Diemen's Land 1803–1829.* North Ryde, NSW: Collins/Angus & Robertson Publishers Australia.

[23] There is conjecture about the exact birth date of Mary Anne Clarke, given that her birth was registered not in

Van Diemen's Land but in NSW in 1817, despite her birth in Tasmania some years earlier and well before Catherine Pendigrass's marriage to Richard Clarke. This has also led to speculation that Richard Clarke was not the biological father of the child. Hanke, S. (2013). 'Richard Clarke.' The People in the Life and Times of Lachlan and Elizabeth Macquarie. The 1788–1820 Pioneer Association Inc. Available from: http://www.the1788-1820pioneerassociation.org.au/Richard%20Clarke.html. [cited 28 April 2015].

[24] Clarke was charged with receiving and purchasing, knowing the same to have been stolen, 1000lbs of mutton, from three convicts assigned to John Riseley of Pittwater, in exchange for five gallons of rum. The principal evidence was given by an accomplice, Francis Davidson and corroborated by the Magistrate, Mr. Gordon, himself having found a great quantity of salted mutton on the premises of Clarke at Pitt-water. After a trial of nearly two hours, Clarke was found guilty and sentenced to be transported to Newcastle for three years. 'Sydney:

Assize of Bread, the Loaf of Two Pounds, 5 1/2 D.'. (1821). *The Sydney Gazette and New South Wales Advertiser* (NSW). Saturday 28 April, p.3.

[25] Walsh, B. (2015). 'Richard Clarke & Catherine Flannagan.' Paterson Historical Society. Available from: http://www.patersonriver.com.au/people/clarkerich.htm. [cited 26 April 2015].

[26] On 4 May 1844, while a candidate for a seat on the Maitland District Council, Healy published a letter in the *Maitland Mercury and Hunter River General Advertiser* outlining the principles by which his conduct would be guided should he be honoured with election. 'As punctuality is the soul of business, I pledge myself to attend ... punctually all sittings of the Council', he said. 'Believing, as I do, that partial or oppressive taxation is one of the greatest social evils, it shall be my endeavour to equalise taxation as much as possible ... and to lighten the burden of taxation as much as possible, consistent with the public good.' He concluded, 'I have been long resident among you; all my interests are inseparable with yours; and ... I shall

feel proud to serve you to the utmost of my power.' Healy, N. 'To the Electors of the District of Maitland.' (1844). *The Maitland Mercury and Hunter River General Advertiser* (NSW). Saturday 4 May, p.3.

[27] 'Melancholy Occurrence.' (1845). *Morning Chronicle* (Sydney, NSW). Wednesday 5 November, p.3.

[28] 'Governor Bourke Inn, West Maitland.' (1851). *The Maitland Mercury and Hunter River General Advertiser* (NSW). Saturday 28 June, p.1.

[29] 'Notice.' (1856). *The Maitland Mercury and Hunter River General Advertiser* (NSW). Thursday 24 July, p.2.

[30] 'Death of P.J. Healy.' (1895). *Freeman's Journal* (Sydney, NSW). Saturday 14 September, p.18.

Chapter 3

[1] Natator. 'Swimming: The Quarter-Mile Championship.' (1902). *Referee* (Sydney, NSW). Wednesday 24 December, p.4.

[2] Sussman, H.L. (2009). *Victorian Technology: Invention, Innovation and the Rise of the Machine.* Santa Barbara, CA.: Praeger Publishers. p.134.

[3] The Diver. 'Swimming Splashes.' (1902). *The Arrow* (Sydney, NSW). Saturday 15 March, p.3.

[4] Natator. 'Swimming Notes.' (1901). *The Referee* (Sydney, NSW). Wednesday 4 December, pp.4, 7.

[5] Natator. 'Swimming Notes.' (1901). *The Referee* (Sydney, NSW). Wednesday 11 December, p.7.

[6] Phillips, M. and Swimming Australia. (2008). *Swimming Australia: One Hundred Years*. Sydney, NSW: UNSW Press.

[7] Penguin. 'Swimming Notes.' (1904). *Chronicle* (Adelaide, SA). Saturday 20 February, p.21.

[8] Healy, C. 'Tuppa Tup-Pala: Otherwise Known as the Crawl Stroke.' (1913). *Sunday Times* (Sydney, NSW). Sunday 12 January, p.24.

[9] Penguin. 'Swimming Notes.' (1904). *Chronicle* (Adelaide, SA). Saturday 20 February, p.21.

[10] Natator. 'Swimming Notes.' (1901). *The Referee* (Sydney, NSW). Wednesday December 4, pp.4, 7.

[11] Natator. 'Swimming and Swimmers: Some Sensational Performances.' (1905). *The Referee* (Sydney, NSW). Wednesday 15 February, p.4.

[12]   The Diver. 'Swimming Splashes.' (1902). *The Arrow* (Sydney, NSW). Saturday 15 March, p.3.

[13]   'Swimming: The Prospects of the Season.' (1902). *The Sydney Morning Herald* (NSW). Wednesday 1 October, p.12.

[14]   'Echoes of the Week.' (1902). *The Referee* (Sydney, NSW). Wednesday 5 November, p.4.

[15]   Osmond, G. (2006). '"Look at That Kid Crawling": Race, Myth and the "Crawl" Stroke.' *Australian Historical Studies*. 37(127): pp.43–62.

[16]   The Diver. 'Swimming Splashes.' (1902). *The Arrow* (Sydney, NSW). Saturday 15 March, p.3.

[17]   Natator. 'Swimming: The Three Hundred Yards Championship.' (1902). *Referee* (Sydney, NSW). Wednesday 3 December, p.4.

[18]   Now Australia Day, the holiday commemorates the arrival of the First Fleet of British ships at Port Jackson, NSW and the raising of the flag of Great Britain by Governor Arthur Phillip in 1788.

[19] 'East Sydney Club.' (1903). *The Sunday Times* (Sydney, NSW). Sunday 18 January.

[20] Natator. 'Swimming: The New Zealand Championships.' (1903). *The Referee* (Sydney, NSW). Wednesday 21 January, p.4.

[21] The Diver. 'Swimming Splashes.' (1903). *The Arrow* (Sydney, NSW). Saturday 31 January, p.3.

Chapter 4

[1] 'Swimming: Remarkable Performance by Dick Cavill.' (1904). *The Sunday Times* (Sydney, NSW). Sunday 17 January, p.6. Natator. 'Swimming Notes: More Records Toppled Over.' (1904). *The Referee* (Sydney, NSW). Wednesday 20 January, p.4.

[2] 'Swimming: Fort-Street Carnival.' (1904). *The Sunday Times* (Sydney, NSW). Sunday 6 March, p.8.

[3] Natator. 'Swimming Notes: The Australasian Championship Carnival.' (1904). *The Referee* (Sydney, NSW). Wednesday 16 March, p.4.

[4] State Records Authority of New South Wales. (2015). 'Digital Gallery: Bernard

Bede (Barney) Kieran, Swimmer.' NSW State Records. Available from: http://gallery.records.nsw.gov.au/index.php/galleries/people-of-interest/bernard-bede-barney-kieran/. [cited 12 July 2015].

[5] Natator. 'Swimming.' (1904). *The Referee* (Sydney, NSW). Wednesday 6 April, p.6.

[6] Healy, C. 'Tuppa Tup-Pala: Otherwise Known as the Crawl Stroke.' (1913). *The Sunday Times* (Sydney, NSW). Sunday 12 January, p.24.

[7] Healy, C. 'Tuppa Tup-Pala: Otherwise Known as the Crawl Stroke.' (1913). *The Sunday Times* (Sydney, NSW). Sunday 12 January, p.24.

[8] Penguin. 'Swimming Notes.' (1904). *Chronicle* (Adelaide, SA). Saturday 20 February, p.21.

[9] Carlile, F. (1963). *Forbes Carlile on Swimming*. London, UK: Pelham. pp.126–188.

[10] Natator. 'Swimming: Dick Cavill Will Not Swim This Season.' (1904). *The Referee* (Sydney, NSW). Wednesday 9 November, p.4.

[11] Natator. 'Swimming: Dick Cavill Will Not Swim This Season.' (1904). *The Referee* (Sydney, NSW). Wednesday 9 November, p.4.

[12] 'Swimming: Cecil Healy in the Limelight Again.' (1904). *The Referee* (Sydney, NSW). Wednesday 16 November, p.4.

[13] Natator. 'Swimming: The Three Hundred Yards Championship.' (1902). *The Referee* (Sydney, NSW). Wednesday 3 December, p.4.

[14] Natator. 'Swimming: Healy's Remarkable Hundred.' (1904). *The Referee* (Sydney, NSW). Wednesday 30 November, p.4.

[15] The Diver. 'Swimming Splashes.' (1904). *The Arrow* (Sydney, NSW). Saturday 3 December, pp.3, 6.

[16] Natator. 'Swimming.' (1904). *The Referee* (Sydney, NSW). Wednesday 28 December, p.4.

[17] Natator. 'Swimming: The Hundred Championship.' (1905). *The Referee* (Sydney, NSW). Wednesday 18 January, p.3.

[18] 'Swimming: Waverley Club's Carnival.' (1905). *The Sunday Times* (Sydney, NSW). Sunday 22 January, p.8.

[19] State Records Authority of New South Wales. (2015). 'Digital Gallery: Bernard Bede (Barney) Kieran, Swimmer.' NSW State Records. Available from: http://gallery.records.nsw.gov.au/index.php/galle

ries/people-of-interest/bernard-bede-barney-kieran/. [cited 12 July 2015].

[20] Unda. 'Swimming Notes.' (1905). *The Australasian* (Melbourne, Vic.). Saturday 4 February, p.20.

[21] 'Swimming: The Ballarat Carnival.' (1905). *The Register* (Adelaide, SA). Wednesday 1 February, p.7.

Chapter 5

[1] 'Swimming.' (1905). *Newcastle Morning Herald & Miners' Advocate* (NSW). Saturday 18 November, p.9.

[2] 'Swimming.' (1905). *Newcastle Morning Herald & Miners' Advocate* (NSW). Thursday 14 December, p.3.

[3] 'Healys Home Again.' (1905). *Australian Town and Country Journal* (Sydney, NSW). Wednesday 20 December, p.52.

[4] Healy, C. 'Swimming Champions in the Making: What Is to Be Done for Cadets?' (1913). *Saturday Referee and the Arrow* (Sydney, NSW). Saturday 15 March, p.1.

[5] Unda. 'Swimming Notes.' (1905). *The Australasian* (Melbourne, Vic.). Saturday 16 December, p.23.

[6] 'Notes.' (1905). *Sunday Times* (Perth, WA). Sunday 10 December, p.3.

[7] 'Swimming.' (1905). *Newcastle Morning Herald & Miners' Advocate* (NSW). Thursday 14 December, p.3.

[8] Natator. 'Swimming Notes.' (1906). *The Referee* (Sydney, NSW). Wednesday 31 January, p.9.

[9] 'Swimming.' (1906). *Morning Bulletin* (Rockhampton, Qld). Saturday 6 January, p.11.

[10] Ramsland, J. (2007). 'Barney Kieran, the Legendary "Sobraon Boy": From the Mean Streets to "Champion of the World".' *Sport in History.* 27(2): pp.241–259.

[11] Natator. 'Swimming.' (1906). *The Referee* (Sydney, NSW). Wednesday 21 February, p.6.

[12] The Diver. 'Swimming Splashes.' (1906). *The Arrow* (Sydney, NSW). Saturday 27 January, p.3.

[13] Natator. 'Swimming.' (1906). *The Referee* (Sydney, NSW). Wednesday 21 February, p.6.

Chapter 6

[1]   Mallon, B. (2009). *The 1906 Olympic Games: Results for All Competitors in All Events, with Commentary.* Jefferson, NC: McFarland. p.4.

[2]   Swanton, W. 'The Good Sport.' (2008). *The Sun Herald* (Sydney, NSW). Sunday 27 April, p.74.

[3]   'The Olympian Games: Another Representative for New South Wales.' (1906). *The Sydney Morning Herald* (NSW). Saturday 24 February, p.14.

[4]   'Healy Was a Great Sport.' (1999). *Manly Daily* (Manly, NSW). Tuesday 14 September, p.10.

Morcombe, J. 'Champion Swimmer Renowned for Sportsmanship Was Killed on the Battlefield.' (2015). *Manly Daily* (Manly, NSW). Friday 9 January, p.11.

Gordon, H. (2000). 'From the Trenches to the Track and Back.' *Journal of Olympic History.* May 2000: pp.7–10.

[5]   Mallon, B. (2009). *The 1906 Olympic Games: Results for All Competitors in All Events, with Commentary.* Jefferson, NC: McFarland. pp.46, 61.

[6]   Rushall, B.S. (2004). 'On One Aspect of Wave Resistance in Swimming.' Carlile

Coaches' Forum. Available from: http://coachsci.sdsu.edu/swim/ccf/ccf0901.htm. [cited 17 October 2015].

[7] 'Swimming: Departure of Healy for Athens.' (1906). *The Sydney Morning Herald* (NSW). Wednesday 7 March, p.12.

[8] Natator. 'Swimming Notes.' (1906). *The Referee* (Sydney, NSW). Wednesday 14 March, p.6.

[9] Natator. 'Swimming Notes.' (1906). *The Referee* (Sydney, NSW). Wednesday 14 March, p.6.

[10] Gordon, H. (1994). *Australia and the Olympic Games*. St. Lucia, Qld: University of Queensland Press.

[11] Mallon, B. (2009). *The 1906 Olympic Games: Results for All Competitors in All Events, with Commentary*. Jefferson, NC: McFarland. p.6.

[12] 'Bitten by Vermin.' (1948). *Sporting Globe* (Melbourne, Vic.). Saturday 15 May, p.6.

[13] Sullivan, J.E. (1906). *The Olympic Games at Athens*. Spalding's Athletic Library No.273. New York: American Sports Publishing Company. p.11

[14] 'Swimming at Athens: Cecil Healy Defeated.' (1906). *Evening News* (Sydney, NSW). Thursday 26 April, p.4.

[15] 'Swimming: A Remarkable Swim.' (1906). *Evening News* (Sydney, NSW). Friday 9 March, p.2.

[16] Australian Olympic Committee. (2003). *The Compendium: Official Australian Olympic Statistics 1896–2002.* St. Lucia, Qld: University of Queensland Press. p.15.

[17] 'Personal.' (1906). *Freeman's Journal* (Sydney, NSW). Saturday 25 August, pp.14–15.

[18] Natator. 'Swimming: Cecil Healy's Continental Successes.' (1906). *The Referee* (Sydney, NSW). Wednesday 3 October, p.9.

[19] Natator. 'Swimming: Cecil Healy's Continental Successes.' (1906). *The Referee* (Sydney, NSW). Wednesday 3 October, p.9.

[20] "Honoring the Champion Swimmer." (1906). *Bunbury Herald* (WA) Monday November 5, p.2.

[21] Natator. 'Swimming: Home-Coming of Cecil Healy.' (1906). *The Referee* (Sydney, NSW). Wednesday 26 December, p.9.

[22] 'Local & General.' (1907). *The Age* (Queanbeyan, NSW). Tuesday 16 April, p.2.
[23] 'Dubbo.' (1907). *National Advocate* (Bathurst, NSW). Wednesday 30 January, p.4.

Chapter 7

[1] Ford, C. (2006). 'Gazing, Strolling, Falling in Love: Culture and Nature on the Beach in Nineteenth Century Sydney.' *History Australia*. 3(1): pp.8.1–8.14.
[2] Rodwell, G. and J. Ramsland. (2000). 'Cecil Healy: A Soldier of the Surf.' *Sporting Traditions*. 16(2): pp.3–16.
[3] Knibbs, G.H. (1912). *Official Year Book of the Commonwealth of Australia Containing Authoritative Statistics for the Period 1901–1911 and Corrected Statistics for the Period 1788–1900*. No.5: 1912 ed. Melbourne, Vic.: Commonwealth Bureau of Census and Statistics. p.216.
[4] Champion, S. and G. Champion. (2000). *Bathing, Drowning and Life Saving in Manly, Warringah and Pittwater to 1915*. Glebe, NSW: Book House. p.88.
[5] Benns, M. (2007). *100 Years: A Celebration of Surf Life Saving at North*

Steyne [1907–2007]*. Manly, NSW: North Steyne Surf Life Saving Club. p.16.

[6] William Gocher: In: Corry, M. (2000). *Waverley Cemetery: Who's Who Sporting Lives.* Bondi Junction, NSW: Waverley Library. p.48.

[7] Nicholls, R.L. (2015). Personal communication. 'Interviews with *Ray Moran, Ray Petersen and Mark Maddox* (Wednesday 4 February 2015).

[8] Nicholls, R.L. (2015). Personal communication. 'Interviews with *Vivienne Degenhardt and Mike Downman* (Tuesday 3 February 2015).

[9] 'The Bathers' Revolt.' (1907). *Evening News* (Sydney, NSW). Wednesday 16 October, p.2.

[10] Natator. 'Swimming: Visit of English Champions Unlikely.' (1907). *The Referee* (Sydney, NSW). Tuesday 31 December, p.4.

[11] 'All About People—Tittle Tattle.' (1909). *The Catholic Press* (New South Wales). Thursday 21 January, p.18.

[12] Natator. 'The Australasian Swimming Championships.' (1909). *The Referee* (Sydney, NSW). Wednesday 20 January, pp.1, 4.

[13] Substitute. 'Swimming.' (1910). *The Referee* (Sydney, NSW). Wednesday 2 February, p.8.

[14] 'Sporting Notes.' (1918). *The Catholic Press* (Sydney, NSW). Thursday 10 January, p.31.

[15] 'Attacked by Sharks at Manly.' (1890). *Evening News* (Sydney, NSW). Tuesday 28 October, p.6.

'The Dangers of Open Sea Bathing.' (1896). *The Sydney Morning Herald* (NSW). Tuesday 14 January, p.3.

[16] Stories of natives killing sharks bare-handed, dismissed by most as incredulous 'fish yarns', captured Healy's imagination. 'Such a feat', he wrote, 'should it ever be achieved by a white swimmer, would elevate that man beyond even the toreador in the conquest of nature.' Healy observed that while plenty of white men lined up to take on their dark-skinned counterparts in the boxing ring, few had raised a hand to take on a shark. Healy went so far as to advocate that coastal shire councils invest in 'shark killing schools', with natives as tutors and role models. Healy, H. (1919).

Cecil Healy in Memoriam. Sydney, NSW: John Andrew & Co. p.22.

[17] Not afraid of sharks. Cecil Healy's Great Swim. An Ocean Sprint. *Daily Telegraph* (Sydney, NSW). 19 December 1910. In: Healy, H. (1919). *Cecil Healy in Memoriam.* Sydney, NSW: John Andrew & Co. p.32.

[18] Healy, H. (1919). *Cecil Healy in Memoriam.* Sydney, NSW: John Andrew & Co. p.10. 'Surf Rescues: Good Save at Manly.' (1911). *Evening News* (Sydney, NSW). Monday 30 January, p.6.

[19] Champion, S. and G. Champion. (2000). *Bathing, Drowning and Life Saving in Manly, Warringah and Pittwater to 1915.* Glebe, NSW: Book House.

[20] 'Surfing: The Manly Club.' (1911). *The Sydney Morning Herald* (NSW). Tuesday 26 September, p.20. Nicholls, R.L. (2015). Personal communication. 'Interviews with Ray Moran, Ray Petersen and Mark Maddox (Wednesday 4 February 2015).

Chapter 8

[1] Manly compared with the Riviera. By C.H. In: Healy, H. (1919). *Cecil Healy in Memoriam*. Sydney, NSW: John Andrew & Co. p.20.

[2] The Commonwealth Electoral Rolls of 1909 and 1913 for the subdivision of Manly give Healy's address as 60 Darley Road, Manly; despite subsequent changes to local street numbering, this probably coincides with the boarding house at the corner of Darley and Addison Roads. Ancestry.com. (2010). 'Australia, Electoral Rolls, 1903-1980 [Database online].' Ancestry.com Operations, Inc. Available from: search.ancestry.com.au/. [cited 29 June 2015]. Metherell, T. (2008). '*Addison Road 1877–1930*' Manly Library Local Studies/Manly Council, Manly, NSW. Available from: www.manly.nsw.gov.au/DownloadDocument.ashx?DocumentID=7662.

[3] Mills was a writer of poetry and short prose, and lived in Addison Road. Mills, S.A. 'Australian Short Story: The Romance of the Breakers.' (1906). *The Sydney Mail* (NSW). Wednesday 7 March, p.634.

[4] 'Obituary: Mr. Adam Maitland.' (1936). *The Sydney Morning Herald* (NSW). Saturday 8 August, p.23.

[5] NSW Registry of Births Deaths & Marriages. (2015). *'Birth Registration: Maitland, Muriel B (Per Maitland, Adam–Victoria M E) [Reg. No 21104/1887].'* Department of Police & Justice, NSW Government, Sydney, NSW. [cited 1 July 2014]. Available from: https://familyhistory.bdm.nsw.gov.au/.

[6] 'Woman's Column.' (1902). *The Newsletter: an Australian paper for Australian people* (Sydney, NSW). Saturday 5 July, p.14.

[7] Ages and Conjugal Condition of Persons Married. Commonwealth Bureau of Census Statistics. (1947). *Official Year Book of the Commonwealth of Australia, No.11–1918.* Melbourne, Vic.: L.F. Johnston. p.203. Commonwealth Population at 3rd April, 1911, classified according to conjugal condition and age. (i) Never married. (a) Males. Commonwealth Bureau of Census Statistics. (1947). *Official Year Book of the Commonwealth of Australia, No.11–1918.* Melbourne, Vic.: L.F. Johnston. p.161.

Carmichael, G. (1988). 'With This Ring: First Marriage Patterns, Trends and Prospects in Australia. [Australian Family Formation Project Monograph No.11].' Department of Demography, Australian National University and Australian Institute of Family Studies, Canberra, ACT. [cited 6 September 2015]. Available from: https://aifs.gov.au/publications/ring-first-marriage-patterns-trends-and-prospect.

[8] 'Sporting Echoes.' (1936). *The Referee* (Sydney, NSW). Thursday 30 April, p.12.

[9] 'Cecil Healy's Great Swim.' (1911). *The Sydney Morning Herald* (NSW). Saturday 7 January, p.13.

[10] 'Long-Distance Crawl—Cecil Healy's Discovery.' (1911). *The Sydney Morning Herald* (New South Wales). Thursday 12 January, p.9.

[11] 'The Surf Rescuers: Coming Athletic Carnival.' (1911). *The Sydney Morning Herald* (NSW). Wednesday 1 February, p.9.

[12] 'Swimming Championships: Longworth Long-Distance Champion.' (1911). *The Sydney Morning Herald* (NSW). Monday 6 March, p.7.

[13] 'Swimming Champions: Phenomenal Performances by Longworth.' (1911). *The Sydney Morning Herald* (NSW). Monday 13 March, p.9.

Chapter 9

[1] 'Swimming: State Championships: First of the Carnivals.' (1912). *Evening News* (Sydney, NSW). Saturday 6 January, p.9.

[2] 'Olympic Games: Swimming Events: Australian Team Selected.' (1912). *The Sydney Morning Herald* (NSW). Thursday 1 February, p.12.

[3] Longworth was a notable exception, eschewing the surf and ocean swimming. 'Personally I do not think it advisable for a person training for championship honours to be continually in the surf, but I certainly do believe it has a tendency to give one additional stamina if not done to excess.' Healy, C. 'Australian Swimming Champions and Their Form.' (1913). *The Referee* (Sydney, NSW). Wednesday 12 November, pp.10, 16.

[4] Merman. 'Swimmers for Olympia.' (1912). *The Daily News* (Perth, WA). Friday 9 February, p.8.

[5] 'A Crack Swimmer Discusses the Future.' (1912). *The Daily News* (Perth, WA). Tuesday 23 April, p.4.
[6] 'Eat Not and Be Healthy.' (1912). *The Daily News* (Perth, WA). Tuesday 23 April, p.1.
[7] 'Swimming.' (1912). *The Tamworth Daily Observer* (NSW). Thursday 11 April, p.4.
[8] 'To Stockholm: Australia's Olympic Athletes.' (1912). *Evening News* (Sydney, NSW). Monday 20 May, p.8.
[9] Surf Bathing Abroad. Cecil Healy's Experiences. By C.H. In: Healy, H. (1919). *Cecil Healy in Memoriam*. Sydney, NSW: John Andrew & Co. p.28.
[10] Gordon, H. (2000). 'From the Trenches to the Track and Back.' *Journal of Olympic History*. May 2000, pp.7–10.
[11] 'Training Troubles: Intensely Cold Water.' (1912). *The Sydney Morning Herald* (NSW). Thursday 11 July, p.9.
[12] 'An Olympic Swimmer in Many Lands.' (1912). *Saturday Referee and the Arrow* (Sydney, NSW). Saturday 14 December, p.1.
[13] 'Australia at Olympia.' (1912). *The Sydney Stock and Station Journal* (NSW). Friday 19 July, p.18.

[14] Bervall, E. (1913). *The Fifth Olympiad: The Official Report of the Olympic Games of Stockholm 1912.* The Swedish Olympic Committee. Stockholm: Wahlstrom & Widstrand. p.716.

[15] 'A Crack Swimmer Discusses the Future.' (1912). *The Daily News* (Perth, WA). Tuesday 23 April, p.4.

[16] 'The Olympic Games: Returning Australian Athletes.' (1912). *The West Australian* (Perth, WA). Wednesday 18 September, p.8.

[17] Gordon, H. (2000). 'From the Trenches to the Track and Back.' *Journal of Olympic History.* May 2000, pp.7-10.

[18] The peace of Europe. A warning in 1913 of Germany's Aims. Olympiads as a factor in its preservation. England and Germany compared. From an Athlete's Point of View. By Cecil Healy. Originally published in *The Sunday Times* (Sydney, NSW). 3 February 1913. Reprinted in: Healy, H. (1919). *Cecil Healy in Memoriam.* Sydney, NSW: John Andrew & Co. p.24.

[19] Yttergren, L. and H. Bolling. (2012). *The 1912 Stockholm Olympics: Essays on*

the Competitions, the People, the City. Jefferson, NC: McFarland & Company. p.262.

[20] '100 Metres Olympic Race: Healy's Sportsmanship.' (1912). *The Sydney Morning Herald* (NSW). Wednesday 21 August, p.9.

[21] Bergvall, E. (1913). *The Fifth Olympiad: The Official Report of the Olympic Games of Stockholm 1912.* The Swedish Olympic Committee. Stockholm: Wahlstrom & Widstrand. p.718.

[22] 'Swimming: Healy's Late Effort.' (1912). *Sunday Times* (Sydney, NSW). Sunday 24 November, p.11.

[23] 'Swimming: Three World's Records in One Swim: The Popularity of Healy.' (1912). *The Sydney Morning Herald* (New South Wales). Wednesday 28 August, p.9.

[24] Healy, C. 'Kahanamoku, World's Swimmer.' (1914). *The Referee* (Sydney, NSW). Wednesday 9 December, p.1.

[25] 'Swimming: 'Good Old Cecil.' (1912). *Bunbury Herald* (WA). Saturday 27 July, p.3.

[26] Natator. 'Swimming: Return of Longworth.' (1912). *The Referee*

(Sydney, NSW). Wednesday 25 September, p.10.
[27] Natator. 'Swimming: Australians at the Olympic Games.' (1912). *The Referee* (Sydney, NSW). Wednesday 28 August, p.8.
[28] 'Olympic Honours: Diplomas for Australians.' (1912). *The Sydney Morning Herald* (NSW). Wednesday 30 October, p.11.
[29] Gordon, H. (2000). 'From the Trenches to the Track and Back.' *Journal of Olympic History.* May 2000, pp.7-10.

Chapter 10

[1] 'Cecil Healy; or 'Go Ye and Do Likewise!' (1913). *Saturday Referee and the Arrow* (Sydney, NSW). Saturday 1 February, p.4.
[2] 'Swimming: Success of Sydney Men.' (1912). *The Sydney Morning Herald* (NSW). Friday 9 August, p.10.
[3] Surf Bathing Abroad. Cecil Healy's Experiences. By C.H. In: Healy, H. (1919). *Cecil Healy in Memoriam.* Sydney, NSW: John Andrew & Co. p.28.

[4] 'An Olympic Swimmer in Many Lands.' (1912). *Saturday Referee and the Arrow* (Sydney, NSW). Saturday 14 December, p.1.

[5] The peace of Europe. A warning in 1913 of Germany's Aims. Olympiads as a factor in its preservation. England and Germany compared. From an Athlete's Point of View. By Cecil Healy. Originally published in *The Sunday Times* (Sydney, NSW). 2 February 1913. Reprinted in Healy, H. (1919). *Cecil Healy in Memoriam.* Sydney, NSW: John Andrew & Co. p.24.

[6] 'A Warning in 1913 of Germany's Aims.' (1918). *Sunday Times* (Sydney, NSW). Sunday 15 September, p.5.

[7] Healy, C. 'The Peace of Europe.' (1913). *Sunday Times* (Sydney, NSW). Sunday 2 February, p.19.

[8] Healy, C. 'The Need for Surf Reform.' (1913). *Sunday Times* (Sydney, NSW). Sunday 27 April, p.15.

[9] Benns, M. (2007). *100 Years: A Celebration of Surf Life Saving at North Steyne [1907—2007].* Manly, NSW: North Steyne Surf Life Saving Club. p.32.

[10] Boyle, R. and R. Haynes. (2009). *Power Play: Sport, the Media and Popular*

Culture. Edinburgh, UK: Edinburgh University Press. pp.19–26.

[11] Rowe, D. (1992). Modes of Sports Writing. In: P. Dahlgren and C. Sparks. *'Journalism and Popular Culture'*. London: Sage. pp.96–105.

[12] Healy, C. 'The Bluebottle Pest Is the Terror of the Surfer.' (1913). *Saturday Referee and the Arrow* (Sydney, NSW). Saturday 25 January, p.1.

[13] 'Champion Swimmer: Probably Parliamentary Candidate.' (1913). *Daily Telegraph* (Launceston, Tas.). Saturday 13 September, p.6.

[14] Relph, A.W. 'Lieutenant Cecil Healy.' (1918). *The Sydney Morning Herald* (New South Wales). Saturday 30 November, p.7.

[15] Healy, H. (1919). *Cecil Healy in Memoriam.* Sydney, NSW: John Andrew & Co. p.11.

[16] Healy, C. 'Tuppa Tup-Pala: Otherwise Known as the Crawl Stroke.' (1913). *Sunday Times* (Sydney, NSW). Sunday 12 January, p.24.

[17] 'Swimming: East Sydney Club to Disband.' (1912). *The Sydney Morning Herald* (NSW). Thursday 12 December, p.12.

[18] Champion, S. and G. Champion. (2000). *Bathing, Drowning and Life Saving in Manly, Warringah and Pittwater to 1915.* Glebe, NSW: Book House.

[19] 'Swimming: Reappearance of Olympic Swimmers.' (1912). *The Sydney Morning Herald* (NSW). Wednesday 4 December, p.5.

[20] 'Where Rain Never Falls.' (1913). *Tamworth Daily Observer* (NSW). Saturday 28 June, p.3. 'Sundry Mems.' (1913). *The Gundagai Independent and Pastoral, Agricultural and Mining Advocate* (NSW). Wednesday 20 August, p.2.

[21] Healy, C. 'At the Baths This Afternoon: Grand Parade of Champions.' (1913). *Saturday Referee and the Arrow* (Sydney, NSW). Saturday 18 January, p.1.

[22] Healy, C. 'At the Baths This Afternoon: Grand Parade of Champions.' (1913). *Saturday Referee and the Arrow* (Sydney, NSW). Saturday 18 January, p.1.

[23] Healy, C. 'To Train Olympic Swimmers.' (1914). *Sunday Times* (Sydney, NSW). Sunday 15 February, p.10.

[24] 'Swimming: 440 Yards Championship.' (1914). *The Ballarat Star* (Vic.). Thursday 8 January, p.1.

[25] R.D. 'Great 220 Yards Swimming Race.' (1914). *The Referee* (Sydney, NSW). Wednesday 14 January, p.16.

[26] 'Mentor to Swimming Champions.' (1914). *Daily Standard* (Brisbane, Qld). Saturday 25 July, p.4.

[27] 'Social.' (1914). *The Sydney Morning Herald* (NSW). Saturday 27 June, p.9.

Chapter 11

[1] National Archives of Australia. (2015). *'World War 1 Service Record: Healy Nicholas Dillon: Service Number–78 and 1986: Place of Birth–Cootamundra NSW: Place of Enlistment–Townsville Qld: Next of Kin–(Mother) Melville M.A.'* Canberra, ACT. [cited 14 September 2015]. Available from: http://recordsearch.naa.gov.au/SearchNRetrieve/Interface/ViewImage.aspx?B=4749601.

[2] Higgins, D.R. and P. Dennis. (2014). *Mark Iv Vs A7v: Villers-Bretonneux 1918*. London: Osprey Publishing Limited. p.8.

[3] Healy, C. 'Swimming.' (1914). *The Referee* (Sydney, NSW). Wednesday 4 November, p.13.

[4] Healy, C. 'New Zealand Hero of Battlefield.' (1914). *The Referee* (Sydney, NSW). Wednesday 11 November, p.16.

[5] Healy, C. 'From the French Lines.' (1914). *The Referee* (Sydney, NSW). Wednesday 2 December, p.11.

[6] 'Swimming: News from Kahanamoku.' (1912). *The Sydney Morning Herald* (NSW). Wednesday 25 December, p.14.

[7] It is thought that Kahanamoku's birth corresponded with a visit by the Duke of Cumberland to Honolulu and he was christened in honour of that event. Healy, C. 'Duke, the Human Fish.' (1914). *The Referee* (Sydney, NSW). Wednesday 2 December, p.16.

[8] Healy, C. 'The Duke Reaches Sydney.' (1914). The *Referee* (Sydney, NSW). Wednesday 16 December, p.1.

[9] Morcombe, J. 'Celebrating Duke's Historic Visit to Australia 100 Years Ago.' (2014). *Manly Daily* (Manly, NSW). Sunday 7 December.

[10] 'Dee Why Carnival: Kahanamoku and His Surf Board.' (1915). *The Sydney*

Morning Herald (NSW). Monday 8 February, p.13.

[11] Osmond, G. (2011). 'Myth-Making in Australian Sport History: Re-Evaluating Duke Kahanamoku's Contribution to Surfing.' *Australian Historical Studies*. 42(2): pp.260–276.

Benns, M. (2007). *100 Years: A Celebration of Surf Life Saving at North Steyne [1907–2007]*. Manly, NSW: North Steyne Surf Life Saving Club. p.38.

[12] Healy, C. 'Swimming: Notes by Cecil Healy.' (1913). *Saturday Referee and the Arrow* (Sydney, NSW). Saturday 18 January, p.5.

[13] Argus. 'Here, Sir!' Men Who Have Changed Arena for Trench.' (1915). *The Referee* (Sydney, NSW). Wednesday 21 April, p.16.

[14] Argus. 'Here, Sir!' Men Who Have Changed Arena for Trench.' (1915). *The Referee* (Sydney, NSW). Wednesday 21 April, p.16. 'Surfers for the Front.' (1915). *St George Call* (Kogarah, NSW). Saturday 15 May, p.6.

[15] 'What Right Have We to Play Games in War Time?' (1915). *Sunday Times* (Sydney, NSW). Sunday 27 June, p.9.

[16]	'Swimmers to Help Recruiting.' (1915). *Saturday Referee and the Arrow* (Sydney, NSW). Saturday 17 July, p.5.
[17]	Lowe, M.G. 'Cecil Healy and Longworth Explain Why They Are Still Civilians.' (1915). *Sunday Times* (Sydney, NSW). Sunday 8 August, p.8.
[18]	'Athletes Enlisting.' (1915). *The Farmer and Settler* (Sydney, NSW). Friday 27 August, p.4.
[19]	'Noted Swimmer Enlists.' (1915). *The Ballarat Star* (Vic.). Thursday 16 September, p.1.

Chapter 12

[1]	Extracts from Cecil Healy's letters. Life on a transport at sea. In: Healy, H. (1919). *Cecil Healy in Memoriam*. Sydney, NSW: John Andrew & Co. p.29.
[2]	'Those Rioters.' (1916). *Sunday Times* (Sydney, NSW). Sunday 2 July, p.9.
[3]	The AIF standards in August 1914 were 19-38 years, height of 5 feet 6 inches and chest measurement of 34 inches. During the first year of the war, approximately 33 per cent of all volunteers were rejected. In June 1915, the age range and minimum height

requirements were changed to 5 feet 2 inches and 18–45 years, with the minimum height being lowered again to 5 feet in April 1917. 'Enlistment Standards.' (2015). Australian War Memorial. Available from: https://www.awm.gov.au/encyclopedia/enlistment/. [cited 4 October 2015].

[4] 'Champion Swimmers Enlist.' (1915). *The Farmer and Settler* (Sydney, NSW). Friday 17 September, p.4.

[5] The Stroller. 'Swimming and Surfing: Beck Joins the Minute Breakers.' (1915). *The Referee* (Sydney, NSW). Wednesday 1 December, p.13.

[6] National Archives of Australia. (2015). 'World War 1 Service Record: Healy Cecil: Service Number–Lieutenant/2: Place of Birth–Sydney NSW: Place of Enlistment–Sydney NSW: Next of Kin–(Brother) Healy H.' Canberra, ACT. [cited 1 February 2015]. Available from: http://recordsearch.naa.gov.au/SearchNRetrieve/Interface/ViewImage.aspx?B=4749469&S=1.

[7] 'Troopship Passenger Lists, 1 October 1915–30 September 1920 [Official Record Series Awm31].' (2015). Australian War Memorial. Available from:

https://www.awm.gov.au/research/infosheets/troopship_ww1/. [cited 1 October 2015].

[8] No.93365: The Last Will and Testament of Cecil Patrick Healy: 29 November, 1915. In: National Archives of Australia. (2015). 'World War 1 Service Record: Healy Cecil: Service Number–Lieutenant/2: Place of Birth–Sydney NSW: Place of Enlistment–Sydney NSW: Next of Kin–(Brother) Healy H.' Canberra, ACT. [cited 1 February 2015]. Available from: http://recordsearch.naa.gov.au/SearchNRetrieve/Interface/ViewImage.aspx?B=4749469&S=1.

[9] 'On a Troopship.' (1916). *Daily Examiner* (Grafton, NSW). Saturday 25 March, p.2.

[10] 'Boys of Bulldog Breed.' (1916). *The Referee* (Sydney, NSW). Wednesday 16 February, p.8.

[11] Carlyon, L. (2006). *The Great War*. Australia: Pan Macmillan. p.140.

[12] Extracts from Cecil Healy's letters. A soldier's life in Egypt. Zeitoun, 20th January, 1916. In: Healy, H. (1919). *Cecil Healy in Memoriam*. Sydney, NSW: John Andrew & Co. p.30.

[13] Bean, C.E.W. 'With the Troops: Life at Mena Camp.' (1915). *The Argus*

(Melbourne, Vic.). Friday 19 February, p.6.

[14] Healy, H. 'Cecil Healy Obituary.' (1918). *Pastoral Review* (Sydney, NSW). Wednesday 16 October, p.947.

[15] 'Enlistment Statistics, First World War.' (2015). Australian War Memorial. Available from: https://www.awm.gov.au/encyclopedia/enlistment/ww1/. [cited 4 October 2015].

[16] From 'The Lone Hand', 1 March 1916. Reprinted in Healy, H. (1919). *Cecil Healy in Memoriam.* Sydney, NSW: John Andrew & Co. pp.7–11.

Chapter 13

[1] Slang for Army Service Corps. Hinckley, P. (2015). 'Battlefield Colloquialisms of the Great War (WWI).' Griffith University. Available from: http://www.ict.griffith.edu.au/~davidt/z_ww1_slang/index_bak.htm. [cited 2 October 2015].

[2] Extracts from Cecil Healy's letters. Getting Ready for Christmas. At Divisional Base Depot, France, December, 1916. In: Healy, H. (1919). *Cecil Healy in Memoriam.* Sydney, NSW: John Andrew & Co. p.33.

[3] While Owen used the term 'shambles' to refer to a slaughterhouse, the modern usage indicates untidiness or disorder. Lewis-Stempel, J. (2010). *Six Weeks: The Short and Gallant Life of the British Officer in the First World War.* London: Hachette UK. p.60.

[4] On 18 October 1916, Billy Longworth informed William Henry while on a leave visit to London that he had heard Healy had been taken ill. 'Cecil Healy Sick.' (1916). *The Referee* (Sydney, NSW). Wednesday 18 October, p.10. Whatever sickness Healy had had, it was not noted in his casualty record, indicating that he had not been evacuated to England or elsewhere for treatment. National Archives of Australia. (2015). 'World War I Service Record: Healy Cecil: Service Number–Lieutenant/2: Place of Birth–Sydney NSW: Place of Enlistment–Sydney NSW: Next of Kin–(Brother) Healy H.' Canberra, ACT. [cited 1 February 2015]. Available from: http://recordsearch.naa.gov.au/SearchNRetrieve/Interface/ViewImage.aspx?B=4749469&S=1.

[5] Palmer, H.G. and J.V. MacLeod. (1961). *After the First Hundred Years.* London: Longmans, Green and Company. p.71.

[6] Getting Ready for the Front. A Prophetic Letter. 5th Training Battalion, Wilts, England, 9 June 1918. In: Healy, H. (1919). *Cecil Healy in Memoriam.* Sydney, NSW: John Andrew & Co. p.34.

[7] Carlyon, L. (2006). *The Great War.* Australia: Pan Macmillan. p.244–268.

[8] 'Ring Pars.' (1917). *Sydney Sportsman* (Surry Hills, NSW). Wednesday 12 September, p.7.

[9] Corbett, W.F. 'Swimming: Australians at Front.' (1918). *The Referee* (Sydney, NSW). Wednesday 4 September, p.12.

[10] 'Not Dead: Report About Cecil Healy.' (1917). *Evening News* (Sydney, NSW). Wednesday 24 October, p.5.

[11] Corbett, W.F. 'Back Stroke Swimmers.' (1918). *The Referee* (Sydney, NSW). Wednesday 26 June, p.11.

[12] Extract from a letter written by a fellow officer, Lieut. Q.S. Spedding: London, 26 June 1918. In: Healy, H. (1919). *Cecil Healy in Memoriam.* Sydney, NSW: John Andrew & Co. p.43.

[13] 'Cecil Healy Adds Boxing to Accomplishments.' (1918). *The Daily News* (Perth, WA). Friday 5 July, p.6.

Chapter 14

[1] Murray Phillips, 'Football. Class and War: the Rugby Codes in New South Wales, 1907-1918': In John Nauright and Timothy JL Chandler, *Making Men: Rugby and Masculine Identity*, Frank Cass, London, 1996. Cited in Rodwell, G. and J. Ramsland. (2000). 'Cecil Healy: A Soldier of the Surf.' *Sporting Traditions*. 16(2): pp.3–16.

[2] Extracts from Cecil Healy's letters. The Story of Sport and War in France. On the Heels of the Germans. In the field, France, 4/7/18. In: Healy, H. (1919). *Cecil Healy in Memoriam*. Sydney, NSW: John Andrew & Co. p.40.

[3] Matthews, W. and D. Wilson. (2011). *Fighting Nineteenth–History of the 19th Infantry Battalion A.I.F. 1915–1918*. Loftus, NSW: Australian Military History Publications.

[4] 'Soldiers Letters.' (1918). *The Wyalong Advocate and Mining, Agricultural and Pastoral Gazette (NSW)*. Tuesday 3 September, p.6.

[5] The Cynic. 'Football: Fighting with the Aussies in France.' (1918). *Referee*

(Sydney, NSW). Wednesday 25 December, p.7.

[6] Gordon, H. (2000). 'From the Trenches to the Track and Back.' *Journal of Olympic History*. May 2000, pp.7-10.

[7] Extracts from a few of the numerous letters of condolence received. In: Healy, H. (1919). *Cecil Healy in Memoriam*. Sydney, NSW: John Andrew & Co. p.47.

[8] 'Australian Corps School.' (1918). *The Sydney Morning Herald* (NSW). Tuesday 29 January, p.7.

[9] Extracts from Cecil Healy's letters. His final letter to a friend. In the field, France, 13 August 1918. In: Healy, H. (1919). *Cecil Healy in Memoriam*. Sydney, NSW: John Andrew & Co. p.42.

[10] Carlyon, L. (2006). *The Great War*. Australia: Pan Macmillan.

[11] Corbett, W.F. 'Swimming: Swimming Association's Solomon Cup.' (1918). *The Referee* (Sydney, NSW). Wednesday 12 February, p.7.

[12] Private Alfred S. Henry, Field Ambulance AIF, 7 September 1918. Corbett, W.F. 'Swimming: More Concerning the Late Cecil Healy.' (1918). *The Referee* (Sydney, NSW). Wednesday 20 November, p.12.

[13] This offensive ranged from the Belgian coast through the battlefields of northern and eastern France, including Ypres, Flanders, Somme and St. Mihiel. The campaign around Peronne came as the second part of the Amiens Offensive, which had begun in July as an Allied campaign against weakening German defensive lines in Picardy (Amiens, Montdidier, Noyon and Albert) and saw 30,000 German prisoners captured. 'Battles of the Somme, 1918.' (2015). greatwar.co.uk. Available from: http://www.greatwar.co.uk/somme/somme-battles.htm. [cited 6 October 2015].

[14] Carlyon, L. (2006). *The Great War.* Australia: Pan Macmillan. pp.680–681.

[15] Armstrong, C. (2015). *Newcastle-Upon-Tyne in the Great War.* Barnsley, South Yorkshire: Pen and Sword. p.48.

[16] The grave was located at the fringe of Sword Wood, three-quarters of a mile north of Biaches and one and three-quarters of a mile west of Péronne. Matthews, W. and D. Wilson. (2011). *Fighting Nineteenth–History of the 19th Infantry Battalion A.I.F. 1915–1918.*

Loftus, NSW: Australian Military History Publications. p.364.

[17] The CO reported that Healy was 'killed outright by Machine Gun fire. When approaching an enemy Machine Gun position. He was shot through the head and killed outright.' Further investigation showed that Healy had been shot twice and took more than an hour to die. National Archives of Australia. (2015). *World War I Service Record: Healy Cecil: Service Number–Lieutenant/2: Place of Birth–Sydney NSW: Place of Enlistment–Sydney NSW: Next of Kin–(Brother) Healy H.* Canberra, ACT. [cited 1 February 2015]. Available from: http://recordsearch.naa.gov.au/SearchNRetrieve/Interface/ViewImage.aspx?B=4749469&S=1.

[18] Relph, A.W. 'Lieutenant Cecil Healy.' (1918). *The Sydney Morning Herald (New South Wales).* Saturday 30 November, p.7.

[19] The mountain and the citadel of Peronne were taken by a combination of a magnificent flank attack and an equally magnificent frontal attack. The direct attack saw a seven-mile advance

through the marshes, river and devastated country under heavy artillery and machine-gun fire, swamps where men sank breast-deep under pitiless fire. Springthorpe, J.W. 'The Spearhead: Australians on the Western Front.' (1919). *The Age* (Melbourne, Vic.). Monday 24 February, p.4.

Chapter 15

[1] Australian Frederick Kelly won gold in the 1908 Olympic Games in rowing but competed under the British flag; he was killed in France in 1916 fighting with British forces. Likewise, Victorian Claude Ross, who ran in the 400 metres in Stockholm in 1912, was also killed in France. Gordon, H. (2000). 'From the Trenches to the Track, and Back.' *Journal of Olympic History*. May 2000, pp.7–10. Relph, A.W. 'Lieutenant Cecil Healy.' (1918). *The Sydney Morning Herald* (New South Wales). Saturday 30 November, p.7.

'Giants of the Swimming World: Australia Has Played Fine Part.' (1935).

The Referee (Sydney, NSW). Thursday 14 November, p.30.

[2] 'Cecil Healy Killed While Crossing Somme.' (1918). *The Argus* (Melbourne, Vic.). Tuesday 10 September, p.5.

'The War: Allies at Verdun.' (1918). *Forbes Advocate* (NSW). Friday 13 September, p.4.

[3] 'Death of Swimming Champion.' (1918). *Australian Worker* (Sydney, NSW). Thursday 12 September, p.14.

'Cecil Healy Killed.' (1918). *The Sydney Morning Herald* (NSW). Tuesday 10 September, p.8.

'Australian Swimmer's Death.' (1918). *The Age* (Melbourne, Vic.). Tuesday 10 September, p.5. All About People: Tittle Tattle.' (1918).

The Catholic Press (New South Wales). Thursday 12 September, p.22.

'Cecil Healy: Famous Australian Swimmer Killed.' (1918). *The Mercury* (Hobart, Tas.). Tuesday 10 September, p.5.

[4] The letter was dated 5 September 1918, but the missive would have taken several weeks to reach Sydney. 'Cecil Healy's Death.' (1918). *The Argus* (Melbourne, Vic.). Tuesday 29 October, p.7.

[5] 'Cecil Healy's Death.' (1918). *The Newcastle Sun* (NSW). Friday 25 October, p.5.

[6] Murdoch, K. 'How Cecil Healy Died.' (1918). *The Newcastle Sun* (NSW). Tuesday 24 September, p.1.

[7] 'The Late Lieutenant Cecil Healy.' (1918). *The Catholic Press* (Sydney, NSW). Thursday 26 September, p.25.

[8] Birdwood was given a copy of the Cecil Healy memorial book, and his condolence letter was dated 9 June 1919. 'Birdwood Praises the Late Cecil Healy.' (1919). *The Mirror* (Sydney, NSW). Sunday 17 August, p.1.

[9] From 'The Referee'. In: Healy, H. (1919). *Cecil Healy in Memoriam*. Sydney, NSW: John Andrew & Co. p.46.

[10] 'Pars About People.' (1918). *The Australian Worker* (Sydney, NSW). Thursday 19 September, p.10.

[11] 'Life-Saving as a Sport.' (1921). *Sydney Mail* (NSW). Wednesday 7 December, pp.10, 41.

[12] 'A Soldier Sportsman.' (1918). *Arrow* (Sydney, NSW). Friday 13 September, p.1.

[13] Adrian returned to work in his father's shoe business on Manly Corso, forgotten or shunned by a public that did not understand the effects of shell shock. Gordon, H. (2000). 'From the

Trenches to the Track, and Back.' *Journal of Olympic History.* May 2000, pp.7–10.

[14] Corbett, W.F. 'Swimming: Swimming Association's Solomon Cup.' (1918). *The Referee* (Sydney, NSW). Wednesday 12 February, p.7.

[15] 'Barnett Fund.' (1918). *The Referee* (Sydney, NSW). Wednesday 25 December, p.7.

Chapter 16

[1] 'Passing of the Pioneers.' (1919). *The Farmer and Settler* (Sydney, NSW). Friday 6 June, p.4.

[2] White, E.W. (1918). 'Observations on Shell Shock and Neurasthenia in the Hospitals in the Western Command.' *British Medical Journal.* 1(2989): pp.421–422.

[3] Annie had savings (£475 18s. 7d.), but a good part came from Cecil's estate. Otherwise, her only real possession of value was an 'old gold ring' (value £1) and some furniture, much of which was simple, old, or damaged (£70). 'The Estate of Annie Louisa Healy.' (1919). Sydney, NSW. [cited 30 April 2015].

Available from: http://srwww.records.nsw.gov.au/indexes/searchhits.aspx?table=Deceased%20Estates&id=15&frm=1&query=Surname:healy;Firstname:annie.

[4] 'Mr. J.H. Healy.' (1926). *The Sydney Morning Herald* (NSW). Thursday 23 December, p.13.

[5] The architects of Karoon were Wright and Apperley. The construction of the 24 brick flats on the corner of Addison and Darley road was approved on 07/09/1940. Metherell, T. *'Darley Road, No 84a, Karoon.'* Manly Library Local Studies; 1]. Accessed: 3 February 2015.

[6] Muriel's estate showed she owned no furniture, jewellery, or motor vehicles, just £189 worth of 'other property'. *'The Estate of Muriel Maitland (No 501016, Series 4).'* (1959). Sydney, NSW. [cited 24 February 2015]. Available.

[7] The Cynic. 'Football: Fighting with the Aussies in France.' (1918). The *Referee* (Sydney, NSW). Wednesday 25 December, p.7.

[8] Healy was buried in plot 2, row F, grave 6. CWGC. (2011). *The Commonwealth War Graves Commission 91st Annual Report 2009–2010.* Maidenhead,

Berkshire, UK: Commonwealth War Graves Commission.

[9] Fareneau, B. and D. Wilson. (2013). 'Second Lieutenant Cecil Patrick Healy.' Available from: http://assevillers.80.free.fr/index_en.php?menu=centenaire&p=healy/preface. [cited 10 October 2015].

[10] 'Double Bay District Honors Its Fallen.' (1919). *Sunday Times* (Sydney, NSW). Sunday 3 August, p.3.

[11] The monument was a gift to the people of Manly from solicitor Mark Mitchell, whose son Alan died at Gallipoli in 1915. Morcombe, J. 'The Local Sons Whose Names Are Inscribed on the Manly Cenotaph.' (2015). *The Daily Telegraph* (Sydney, NSW). Tuesday 28 April, p.13.

[12] Walker, F. 'In Living, in Dying, Two Who Have Served.' (2007). *The Sydney Morning Herald* (NSW). Sunday 22 April, p.18.

Epilogue

[1] Feather, N.T. (2005). 'Social Psychology in Australia: Past and Present.' *International Journal of Psychology*. 40(4): pp.263–276.

[2] Feather, N.T. (2012). 'Tall Poppies, Deservingness and Schadenfreude.' *Psychologist.* 25(6): pp.434–437.

[3] Davey, G. and G. Seal. (1993). *The Oxford Companion to Australian Folklore.* New York: Oxford University Press.

[4] Seal, G. (2004). *Inventing Anzac: The Digger and National Mythology.* Brisbane, Qld: University of Queensland Press.

[5] Rodwell, G. and J. Ramsland. (2000). 'Cecil Healy: A Soldier of the Surf.' *Sporting Traditions.* 16(2): pp.3–16.

[6] Extracts from Cecil Healy's letters. The Story of Sport and War in France. On the Hells of the Germans. In the field, France, 4/7/18. In: Healy, H. (1919). *Cecil Healy in Memoriam.* Sydney, NSW: John Andrew & Co. p.40.

[7] Frith, D. (2001). *Silence of the Heart: Cricket Suicides.* Edinburgh: Mainstream Publishing.

Available now online or at all good bookstores

Narrated in a fresh way, with a wonderful gift for taking the unexpected angle, it does great service to this astonishing event.
—Thomas Keneally

Japanese soldiers are now being captured in New Guinea and interned at the Cowra Prisoner of War Camp. Unlike other POWs, the traditional Japanese Bushido Code and their fanaticism leaves them ill-equipped for surrender and imprisonment. Ashamed, subdued and sullen, one man, Second Lieutenant Maseo Naka is an exception. Obstructing the Australian authorities at every turn, he was the first Japanese soldier to escape from Cowra. This action becomes the precursor for the more than 1000 Japanese prisoners who escape in the bloodiest Breakout of World War II that ultimately saw 234 Japanese and four Australian guards killed. His escape and the defiance, guilt, and shame that motivated it, led to his court-martial.

Naka nevertheless stands-out as very human, another tragic victim of the global inferno that was World War II. Adhering to the Samurai Code of Bushido, he doggedly undertakes actions that he views as necessary for the maintenance of his "honour". Through the insights of those around Naka, together with new research including the personal accounts of Australian interrogators, the author shows how this handsome loner provided the impetus for the dramatic events in the early hours of August 5, 1944 where hundreds of Japanese soldiers stormed the Camp defences for honour, or death!

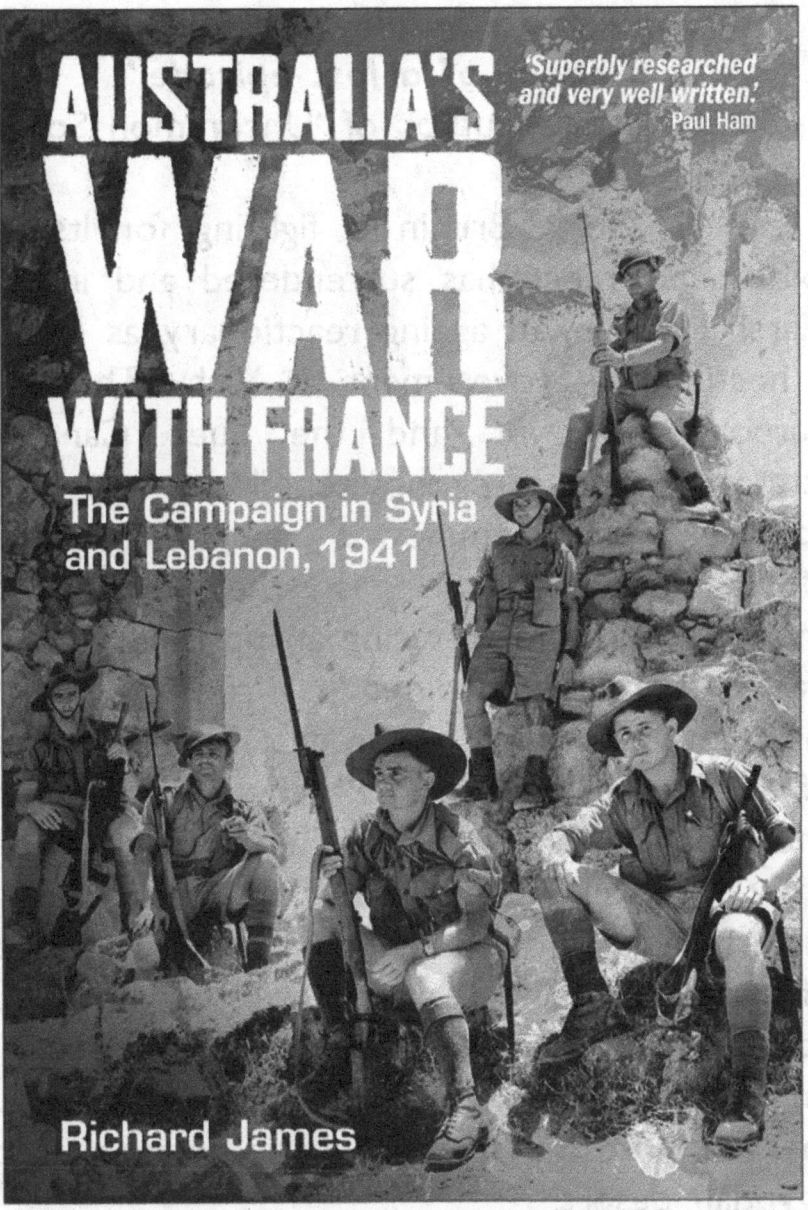

'A superbly researched and very well written history of this little-known conflict ... A story that must be told.'
—Paul Ham, author of 'Kokoda'.

'Thorough and revealing. An accomplished account of a lost episode.'
—Chris Masters, author of 'Uncommon Soldier'.

1941: Great Britain is fighting for its very existence. France has surrendered and installed Marshal Pétain, an ageing reactionary, as head of a hostile new government at Vichy. The Allied outpost in Egypt, and the Suez Canal—its strategic jewel—are threatened on both sizes. To the west, Rommel is rampaging through North Africa. To the east, the Germans are arming rebels and fostering an uprising in British Iraq. Churchill's cabinet is reeling after a disastrous campaign in Greece. There are fears of a German takeover in Vichy-controlled Syria and Lebanon, where a languishing French colonial army may fall in line with the Nazis. Churchill orders a disgruntled General Wavell to take the offensive, assuming that the French will not put up a fight against an Allied show of force. The only troops available are a division of Australians, the 7th: untested recruits, digging ditches in the Egyptian desert.

This is the story of how the 7th Division came to fight against the Army of the Levant—Australia against France—in the rocky hills of Lebanon and the barren wastes of Syria. Contrary to Churchill's expectations, the French resisted viciously. The Australians won the war, but at the price of more than 400 young men, sons of Anzacs who had fought to defend France in the trenches of the western Front. The British were embarrassed, the campaign was forgotten, and the Australians who fought were dubbed 'the silent men.'

No contemporary Australian historian has studied the conflict. British and French accounts exist, but fail to do justice to the Australian contribution. Through interviews with the veterans, archival records, and on-the-ground research, this book seeks to understand a neglected campaign and give it a proper place in Australian history.

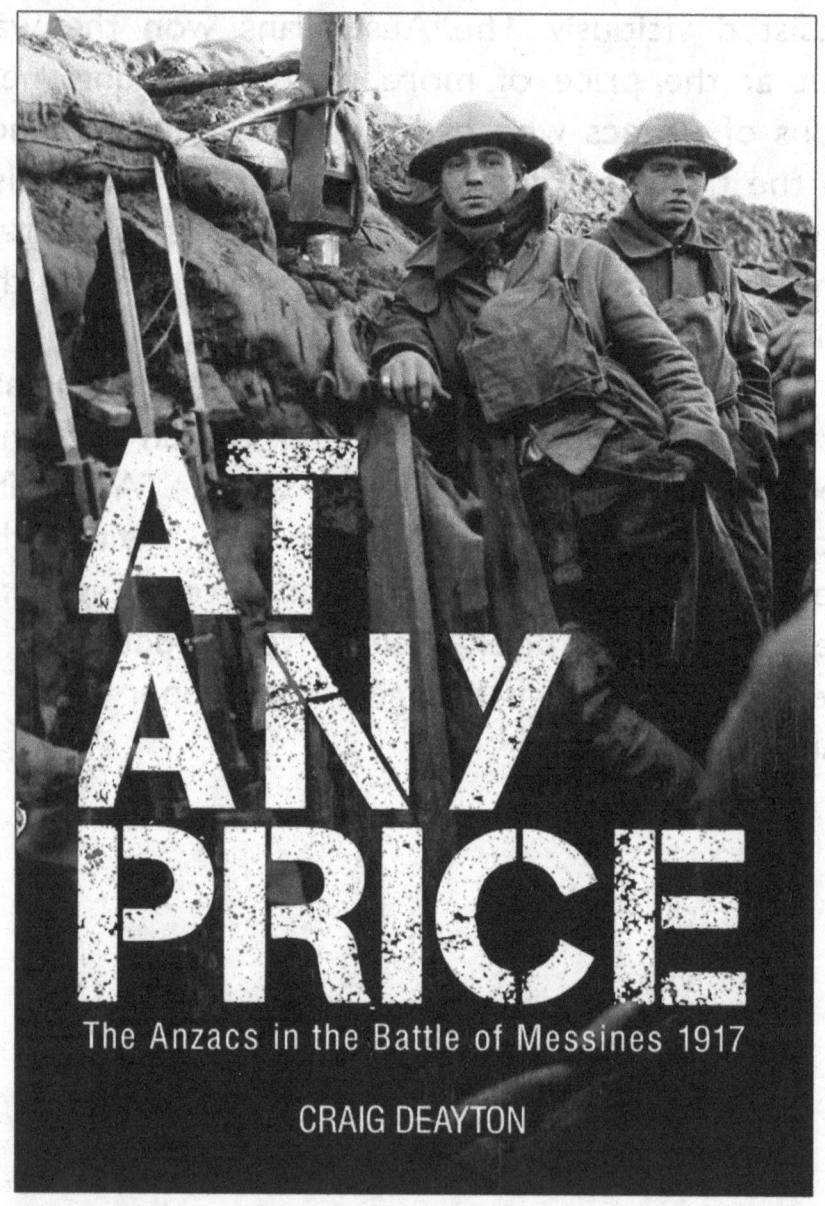

The enemy must not get the Messines Ridge at any price...

So read the orders to German troops defending the vital high ground south of Ypres.

On 7 June 1917, the British Second Army launched its attack with an opening like no other. In the largest secret operation of the First World War, British and Commonwealth mining companies placed over a million pounds of explosive beneath the German front-line positions in 19 giant mines which erupted like a volcano. This was just the beginning. By the end of that brilliant summer's day, one of the strongest positions on the Western Front had fallen in the greatest British victory in three long years of war. For the Anzacs, who comprised one third of the triumphant Second Army, it was their most significant achievement to that point; for the men of the New Zealand Division, it would be their finest hour.

It is difficult to overstate the importance of Messines for the Australians, whose first two years of war had represented an almost unending catalogue of disaster. This was both the first real victory for the AIF and the first test in senior command for Major General John Monash, who commanded the newly formed 3rd Division. Messines was a baptism of fire for the 3rd Division which came into the line alongside the battlescarred 4th Australian Division, badly mauled at Bullecourt just six weeks earlier. The fighting at Messines would descend into unimaginable savagery, a lethal and sometimes hand-to-hand affair of bayonets, clubs, bombs and incessant machine-gun fire, described by one Australian as '72 hours of Hell'. After their string of bloody defeats over 1915 and 1916, Messines would prove the ultimate test for the Australians.

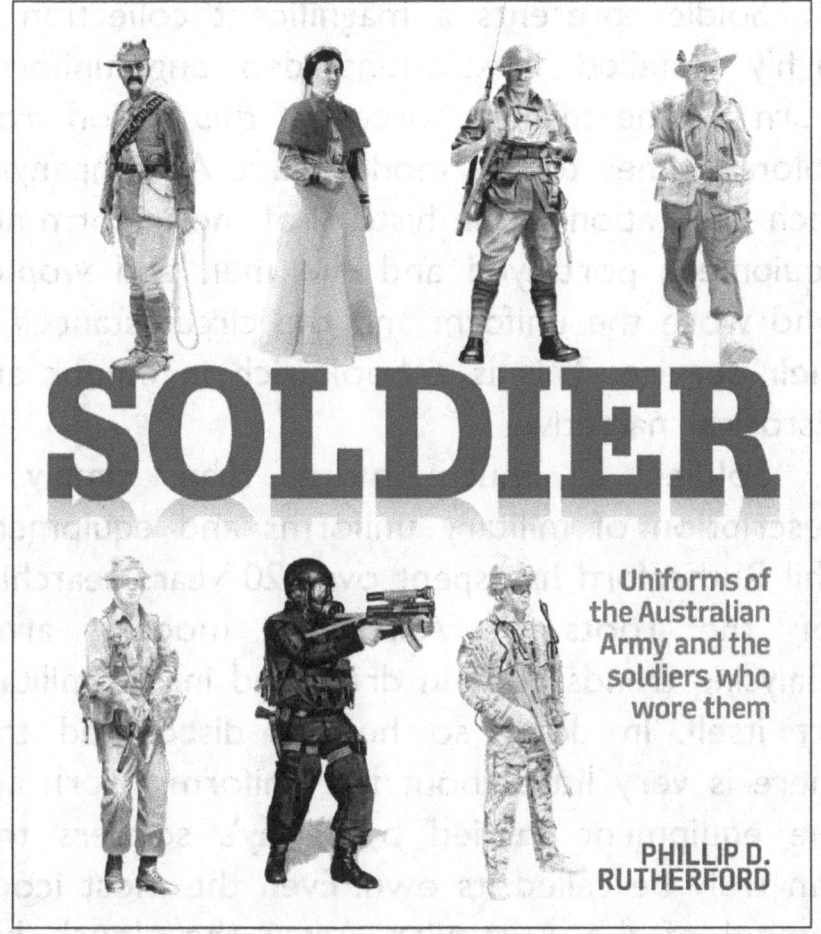

It's a brown slouch hat with the side turned up, and it means the world to me. It's the symbol of our Nation—the land of liberty. And as soldiers they wear it, how proudly they bear it, for all the world to see. Just a brown slouch hat with the side turned up, heading straight for victory.

J. Albert & Son, Sydney, 1942

Soldier presents a magnificent collection of highly detailed illustrations depicting uniforms worn by the military forces of this nation from colonial times to the modern era. Accompanying each illustration is the history of the uniform and equipment portrayed and the men and women who wore the uniform and the circumstances of their service. This is a book rich in colour and historical narrative.

Soldier is much more than simply a description of military uniforms and equipment. Phil Rutherford has spent over 20 years searching for the roots of Australia's modern army, analysing trends both in dress and in the military art itself. In doing so he has discovered that there is very little about the uniforms worn and the equipment carried by today's soldiers that can truly be called its own. Even the most iconic symbol of the Australian Army, the slouch hat, was not invented by a Victorian volunteer as popular rumour suggests, but was worn by troops in seventeenth-century Europe. In fact, there are significant elements of the army's dress and equipment, such as the badges of rank worn by both soldiers and officers, which can be traced to the days of knights in shining armour.

Soldier seeks to map the links between the army's modern dress and its earliest antecedents, describing the formation and history of Australia's army, from the perspective of both the regular and reserve soldiers. This book also reveals the story behind the soldiers themselves—the men and women who wore these uniforms—and the times in which they served since the first volunteers and militias were raised to protect the lives and property of the earliest settlers.

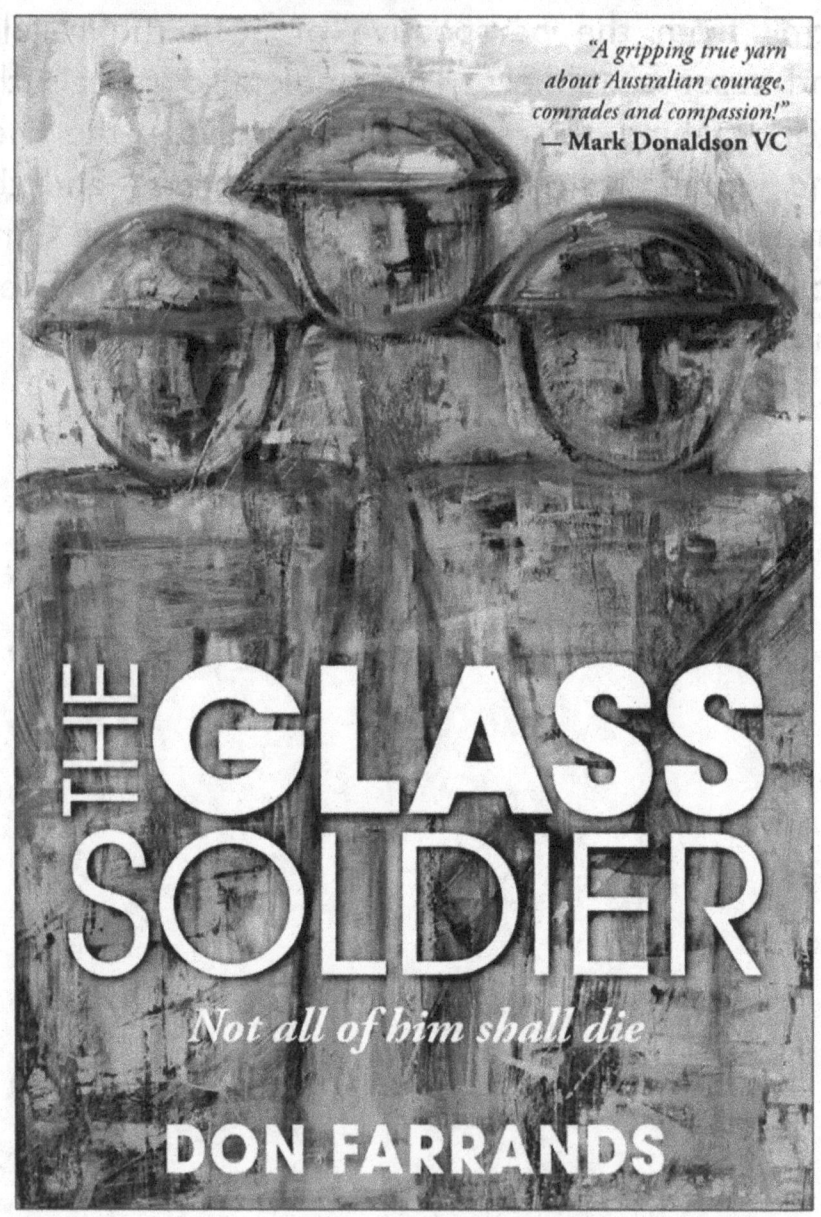

"The Great War changed everything. This true story shows what wonders can be born of such horrors.
And it reminds us that we must never forget."
-Julian Burnside AO, QC

This is the true story of a young Australian soldier whose life of opportunity was cut down by trauma, yet revived by strength and providence.

Nelson Ferguson, from Ballarat, was a stretcher-bearer on the Western Front in France in World War I. He survived the dangers of stretcher-bearing in some of Australia's most horrific battles: the Somme, Bullecourt, Ypres and Villers-Bretonneux. In April 1918, at Villers-Bretonneux, he was severely gassed. His eyes were traumatised, his lungs damaged.

Upon his return home, he met and married Madeline, the love of his life, started a family, and resumed his career teaching art. But eventually the effects of the mustard gas claimed his eyesight, ending his career. Courageously enduring this consequence of war, he continued contributing to society by assisting his son and son-in-law in their stained-glass window business. Advances in medicine finally restored his sight in 1968, allowing him to yet again appreciate the beauty around him, before his death in 1976.

*

View sample pages, reviews and more information on this and other titles at www.bigskypublishing.com.au

BACK COVER MATERIAL

"He was bravery in the extreme – his courage unfaltering. He died the glorious death of a magnificent man..."

The golden boy of Australian swimming and captain of the lifeguards an Manly Beach, Cecil Healy was the poster-boy for all that was decent in Australia before World War I. Powerful, bronzed and daring, his fearlessness made him a leader in the embryonic surf-lifesaving movement, and his unique crawl stroke captured swimming records across the globe. Healy became the darling of the Olympic movement in 1912 when he allowed a disqualified rival to swim and take the 100 metres freestyle title, sacrificing almost certain victory for fair play and honour.

But Cecil Healy's seemingly perfect life was beset by darkness and secrets. His repressed sexuality and inner demons drove him to acts of recklessness which would culminate in his supreme sacrifice on the battlefields of France. As World War I raged, the Olympic champion refused to remain protected behind the lines. His death on the Somme in 1918, charging a German machine-gun post, embodies the tortured self-destructiveness which still drives many male sportsmen to both glory and disaster.

Cecil Healy remains the only Australian Olympic gold medallist to have given his life in the theatre of war. This book chronicles both Healy's glittering sports performances and the torment behind this great, lost Olympian.

www.ingramcontent.com/pod-product-compliance
Lightning Source LLC
Chambersburg PA
CBHW011713290426
44113CB00018B/2655

www.ingramcontent.com/pod-product-compliance
Lightning Source LLC
Chambersburg PA
CBHW011713290426
44113CB00019B/2660